Acknowledgments

Thank you to Kate Garrick.

Thank you to Betsy Gleick.

Thank you to Abby Muller, Stephanie Mendoza, Michael McKenzie, Randall Lotowycz, Travis Smith, Lauren Moseley, David High, Steve Godwin, Chris Stamey, Brunson Hoole, and everyone at Algonquin Books.

Thank you to Rachel Titlebaum Peterson, Kathryn Korfonta, Sam Nelson, Steve Driscoll, John Ralls, Summer Blais, and Jonny Lupsha.

Thank you to John Glynn, Lydia Kiesling, Nick White, and Louis Bayard.

Thank you to the editors of *Anastamos*, in which early versions of several passages first appeared.

Thank you to my family.

Thank you to my friends.

Children's Literature and the
Fin de Siècle

Recent Titles in
Contributions to the Study of World Literature

Children's Literature and the *Fin de Siècle*

EDITED BY RODERICK McGILLIS

Published under the auspices of
the International Research Society for Children's Literature

Contributions to the Study of World Literature, Number 113

Westport, Connecticut
London

Library of Congress Cataloging-in-Publication Data

Children's literature and the fin de siècle / edited by Roderick McGillis.
    p.   cm.—(Contributions to the study of world literature, ISSN 0738–9345; no. 113)
"Prepared under the auspices of the International Research Society for Children's
Literature."
  Includes bibliographical references and index.
  ISBN 0–313–32120–5 (alk. paper)
  1. Children's literature—20th century—History and criticism—Congresses.
I. McGillis, Roderick. II. International Research Society for Children's Literature.
Congress (14th : 1999 : Calgary, Alta.)   III. International Research Society for Children's
Literature.   IV. Children's Literature Association (U.S.). V. Series.
PN1009.A1 C51382 2003
809'.8928—dc21   2001057727

British Library Cataloguing in Publication Data is available.

Library of Congress Catalog Card Number: 2001057727
ISBN: 0–313–32120–5
ISSN: 0738–9345

First published in 2003

Praeger Publishers, 88 Post Road West, Westport, CT 06881
An imprint of Greenwood Publishing Group, Inc.
www.praeger.com

Printed in the United States of America

The paper used in this book complies with the
Permanent Paper Standard issued by the National
Information Standards Organization (Z39.48–1984).

10 9 8 7 6 5 4 3 2 1

Contents

Acknowledgments

I wish to thank all those who participated in the joint IRSCL and ChLA conference held in Calgary, Alberta, Canada, in July 1999. I am also indebted to Sandra Beckett, John Stephens, Ann Lawson Lucas, and Maria Nikolajeva of IRSCL; all four provided necessary assistance in the construction of this volume. I acknowledge the help of Glen Campbell, who not only trips a light fantastic, but who is also engaged in editing a volume of French-language papers from the 1999 conference. David Brown deserves mention for his electronic expertise. For their cheerful help, my thanks to Margaret Hadley, Patricia Gordon, Shaobo Xie, and Michelle Richards. Most importantly, I thank Claude Romney without whose energy, good will, and downright hard work none of this would have happened. Finally, of the many people who helped with the conference and who deserve thanks and recognition, I mention two for reasons I hope are apparent; these two are Kyla McGillis and Frances Batycki. I could not have managed without the two of you.

In the late stages of the preparation of this volume, I received generous and absolutely necessary assistance from people at Queensland University of Technology in Brisbane, Australia. This book would not have come to completion without the help of James Watters, Kerry Mallan, and most especially, Robyn Smith. I cannot express my gratitude strongly enough for the help I have received from these people. Thanks.

Introduction:
Children's Literature and the
Fin de Siècle

Roderick McGillis

The end of a century inevitably brings both retrospection and prognosti-
cation; the time seems to call for taking stock in order for us to see where
we've come from and to prepare for where we are going. And so this book
offers something of a "stock-taking." The various chapters look back over
the past hundred or so years and project forward into the next few years.
As you would expect, not every aspect of children's literature receives
consideration, but the list of topics that the twenty-one writers included
here discuss is impressive: poetry, series books, pacifist fiction, gender
issues, religion and literature, eco-criticism, minority experiences, humor
and the holocaust, fantasy and science fiction, and computer culture. What
allows such disparate topics to cohere is a general interest in ideas encap-
sulated in the curious locution—*fin de siècle*. This volume concerns itself
with the state of children's literature at century's end.

Fin de siècle captures nicely the diversity of thinking evident in this
book's various essays. The phrase reminds us of the end of the nineteenth
century, the end of centuries generally, and the end of our own century
specifically. As Oscar Wilde's use of the phrase in *The Picture of Dorian
Gray* (1891) indicates, *fin de siècle* sounds a millennial ring; more than this,
it has apocalyptic implications. *Fin de siècle; no, fin du globe*. And so how
does children's literature reflect such a portentous moment? The essays
in this volume provide, at least implicitly, some answers. Picture books
that examine the fragile ecosystem remind us that we may be near the
end of things; young adult fictions that interrogate gender identities suggest an end to our traditional binary view of the sexes and their roles; the
mapping of a century's changes in children's poetry, in nonsense verse,

in attitudes to heroism, or in the development of a protest literature tells us how unstable our sense of value and coherence is. Fiction that deals with virtual reality and fiction that finds its place in virtual reality remind us of the uncertainties of the future. Most tellingly, the essays here reflect the elusiveness of our very notions of "child" and "childhood." And so all this talk of uncertainty redounds onto the very notion of ends. *Fin de siècle* communicates uncertainty. An end, even an apocalyptic one, leads to a beginning, even if we cannot know what that beginning may inaugurate.

The end of the twentieth century, like the end of the nineteenth, brought concerns about children and adolescence, sex and sexual identities, end-time anxieties and fears of degeneration, and in the arts a conjunction of visual and print media.[1] Century's end brings out fear and hope, idiosyncrasy and convention, introspection and activism. Just as the turn of the nineteenth century saw an interest in matters of "social engineering" (eugenics and studies of heredity), the turn of the twentieth sees an interest in mapping the genosystem and in cloning. Such activities have both utopian and dystopian implications. And so our children's books reflect such utopian and dystopian visions. Young Adult fiction especially has its dark side. Works such as J. G. Ballard's *Running Wild* (1988), Frances Temple's *Taste of Salt* (1992), Lois Lowry's *The Giver* (1993), Melvin Burgess's *Junk* (1996), Jerry Spinelli's *Wringer* (1997), and Jane Yolen and Bruce Colville's *Armageddon Summer* (1998) deliver bleak visions of the human community even if some of these books offer hard-won victories to their protagonists. And the postmodern fairy tales of writers such as Francesca Lia Block and David Almond present equally troubled visions of contemporary life even as they strive to modernize utopian aspirations.

Representative of *fin de siècle* unease is Philip Pullman's "His Dark Materials" trilogy. In *The Golden Compass* (1995), *The Subtle Knife* (1997), and *The Amber Spyglass* (2000), Pullman posits a myriad of actual worlds just waiting for his characters to find and explore. Opening windows into these worlds is educative and worthwhile, but it is also dangerous and unsettling. Pullman's vision is both utopian and dystopian; it leaves the future open-ended even as it posits an end-game, a war in heaven reminiscent of that played out in Milton's *Paradise Lost* and of course in Milton's source text. Perhaps even more significant is the clouding of categories in "His Dark Materials." Are these children's books? The blurring of distinction between works for children and works for adults is a feature of *fin de siècle* writing marketed ostensibly for the young. I think of picture books by the likes of Scieszka and Smith, Sendak, Van Allsburg, Raschka, and longer fiction by the likes of Pullman, Burgess, Cormier, and a range of contemporary fantasists.

Strange as it may seem, at century's end children's literature and the study of children's literature appear to have a more secure place in both the retail market and the academic market than ever before. The most obvious example of this is the Harry Potter phenomenon. The four books in this series by J. K. Rowling have set publishing records that will be difficult, if not impossible, to match in the future. The fourth book, *Harry Potter and the Goblet of Fire* (2000), is especially noteworthy, for the publishing of this book was preceded by a marketing campaign the like of which we have not seen before. Weeks before the book was to appear—and we knew the exact day the publisher would unleash it—the suspense began to mount. Leaks had informed an eager public that someone—someone important—was going to die in this installment, and speculation as to which character would meet his or her end abounded. The book's title was likewise leaked and had to be changed before publication. As the day approached, expectation became near frenzy, and bookstores planned all-night parties to coincide with the arrival of the book at an auspicous midnight in July. A special train (Hogwart's Express) carried the celebrated author up and down Great Britain for a triumphal reading tour.

Harry Potter seemed to appeal to everyone—except perhaps to the religious right who waged a familiar battle against what it perceived to be the forces of sorcery and witchcraft. Adults and children avidly read the books. Indeed, the first book, sporting a realistic cover photo, appeared in a second edition marketed for adults. The books received praise both for their exciting and innovative plots and for their success in motivating reluctant readers to read. However, some readers—Jack Zipes, for example[2]—noted the conventional and predictable plots, and the connection between the books and market forces. The Harry Potter books, rather than being the liberatory works of literature we might hope for, turned out to be complicit with social forces calling for sameness and conformity. In the Harry Potter phenomenon, we can see the *fin de siècle* tension between optimism and pessimism, the hope for the future of our children and the fear that darkness is without a doubt drawing down.

The essays collected here reflect much of what I have said about *fin de siècle* culture. But they say more. Just as the end of the nineteenth century saw crossfertilization across national borders, so too does the end of the twentieth bring us globalization. The essays here come from writers in the United States, Canada, Great Britain, Finland, Japan, India, the Netherlands, Australia, and Slovenjia. Among the essays, we have a Japanese writer exploring an American classic, an Indian exploring the work of Edward Lear, an American writing about the experience of Vietnamese refugees, and a British person chronicling German pacifist literature. Children's literature does have global connectedness. Indeed, this global connectedness is one of children's literature's greatest gifts to its readers, while it is also an indication of an effort at homogeneity perpetrated by market forces. In short, children's literature manifests *fin de siècle* tensions and paradoxes, and the essays here begin to examine these.

Before closing this introduction, I ought to acknowledge that the essays gathered here were all delivered at the Fourteenth Biennial Congress of the International Research Society for Children's Literature (IRSCL). This congress, however, was unique in that it was a joint meeting of the IRSCL and the Children's Literature Association (ChLA). The two groups met in Calgary, Alberta, Canada, in July 1999. The coming together of these two organizations fit nicely the *fin de siècle* theme of the conference; people came from some twenty-four countries to discuss aspects of children's literature and culture at century's end. What you read in this volume will give you some idea of the scope of the proceedings. The stimulating interaction and conversation of some 250 people in at least two languages, and the dance of ideas as well as persons were truly invigorating.

NOTES

1. For discussions of gender issues, the young, and the connection between visual and literary arts, see among many works: Suzanne R. Stewart, *Male Masochism at the Fin-De-Siècle*. Ithaca & London: Cornell UP, 1998; John Neubauer, *The Fin-de-Siècle Culture of Adolescence*. New Haven & London: Yale UP, 1992; Bram Dijkstra, *Idols of Perversity: Fantasies of Feminine Evil in Fin-De-Siècle Culture*. New York & Oxford: Oxford UP, 1986.

2. Jack Zipes, *Sticks and Stones: The Troublesome Success of Children's Literature From Slovenly Peter to Harry Potter*. New York & London: Routledge, 2001.

REFERENCES

Ballard, J. G. *Running Wild*. 1988. London: Flamingo, 1997.

Burgess, Melvin. *Junk*. 1996. London: Penguin, 1997.

Dijkstra, Bram. *Idols of Perversity: Fantasies of Feminine Evil in Fin-De-Siècle Culture*. New York & Oxford: Oxford UP, 1986.

Lowry, Lois. *The Giver*. New York: Dell, 1993.

Neubauer, John. *The Fin-de-Siècle Culture of Adolescence*. New Haven & London: Yale UP, 1992.

Pullman, Philip. *The Amber Spyglass*. New York: Knopf, 2000.

———. *The Golden Compass*. New York: Knopf, 1995.

———. *The Subtle Knife*. New York: Knopf, 1997.

Rowling, J. K. *Harry Potter and the Goblet of Fire*. London: Bloomsbury, 2000.

Spinelli, Jerry. *Wringer*. New York: Harper Trophy, 1997.

Stewart, Suzanne R. *Male Masochism at the Fin-De-Siècle*. Ithaca & London: Cornell UP, 1998.

Temple, Frances. *Taste of Salt*. 1992. New York: Harper Trophy, 1994.

Wilde, Oscar. *The Picture of Dorian Gray. The Portable Oscar Wilde*, ed. Rich-
     ard Aldington. New York: Viking, 1946, pp. 138–391.
Yolen, Jane and Bruce Coville. *Armageddon Summer*. San Diego, New York,
     London: Harcourt Brace, 1998.
Zipes, Jack. *Sticks and Stones: The Troublesome Success of Children's Literature
     From Slovenly Peter to Harry Potter*. New York & London: Routledge,
     2001.

PART I

Overviews

CHAPTER 1

A Tale of Three Tenses

Sheila A. Egoff

I am told that many of you in this audience are teachers, so in the spirit of the injunction "Do unto others what they often do unto you," I begin with a quiz. Quick now—no thinking carefully about the answer to the question, but just shouting out what comes immediately into your head— shout out the titles of children's books that you remember with great affection.

Well, that was no thunderous shout (maybe a C+), but I thought that I detected responses of *Alice in Wonderland, Winnie the Pooh, The Wind in the Willows, Tom Sawyer,* and *Little Women.* And praise be to the saint of children's literature, I did *not* hear the dreaded sound of *Bobbsey Twins*!

Did your responses have anything in common? Yes, they certainly did: the titles that you have at the top of your head are about, on average, a good hundred years old. (Another thing they have in common is that none of the titles is Canadian, but that is substance for another speech. Shall we say next year, same place, same time?)

But back to the main point: your affection for children's books shows, if you think about it, an unusual—if you compare it with adult literature— a *highly* unusual—attachment to the past. *And that attachment is no accident.* It derives, rather, from certain more or less constant characteristics of books intended for children. To begin with, children's books are not purchased, or, for the most part, selected by the people who actually read them, that is, the children. It is *you*—parents, teachers, librarians, favorite aunts and uncles—who decide which books the children with whom you interact are given the opportunity to read. And you do so mainly on the basis of your *own* values; that is, you perpetuate your own feeling for what is good and bad in books for children as you encountered them a generation ago. So the people who select current children's publications—you and people like you—do so with mindsets and preferences largely determined by the past. The history of children's literature is still very much a part of the present-day character of publishing for children.

Are you beginning now to guess at the meaning of my somewhat cryptic title? It is no great conundrum. I merely thought that, in keeping with children's love of riddles, I would pose one for you at the outset. So now the riddle is solved: what I mean by a "tale of three tenses" is the fact that children's literature, much more than most bodies of writing, exists in three time zones: *past, present*, and *future*. Our children still depend heavily on writings of the past, and the stock of present-day publications will in its turn constitute the corpus from which most of children's future reading will derive. Past, present, and future: three time zones melded into one. So that is my text; the rest is explanation and commentary. Let me now begin my exposition by examining how and why children's literature, in English, began.

Children's literature, and by that term I mean books deliberately written for the young, is the most social of all literatures. It began quite straightforwardly as a simple transmission of knowledge, mores, and manners from one generation to the next. If stone books had been available in the Stone Age, probably one would have reported a cave mother saying to her son: "No, no, Og, you don't hold your bone that way. You hold it like this."

But children's literature soon became more than mere instruction. Somewhere, sometime, someone discovered that if instruction were mixed with narrative, it went down better. The first substantial venture in that direction came from the seventeenth-century English Puritans and their efforts to advance their religious teaching. Theirs was a harsh religion, and they did not add much sugar to make the medicine go down. "The new borne babe," Richard Allestree wrote in 1658, "is full of the stains and pollutions of sin which it inherits from our first parents through their loins." This doctrine of original sin was stridently voiced in Puritan books written for children. The apotheosis of this type of literature is James Janeway's *A Token for Children: Being an Exact Account of the Conversion, Holy and Exemplary Lives, and Joyful Deaths of Several Young Children*, first published in 1672. Although Janeway considered children "brands of hell," they could be saved from going there if they committed themselves to God. So his children, aged from about five to eight, died joyfully because before death claimed them, they repented their sins and exhorted their siblings, friends, parents, and even the nation to do likewise.

Just as our own preferences hark back to earlier patterns of theme and style as I indicated earlier, books in the Puritan-like instructional mode were published in the hundreds in Britain and the United States far beyond the seventeenth century. So, putting aside our snickers about how blatantly they put their views, we do owe the Puritans much. It was they who began a separate stream of writing for children, and they who cast children prominently in those books. Most importantly, they were the first of the confessional writers as opposed to professional writers. The Puritans really believed in what they were saying to children, and they believed that their didactic sermons gave children pleasure. In the Victorian age, several writers, including Charles Kingsley, George MacDonald, and Oscar Wilde, were writing in that same confessional vein. The religious feelings fostered by these later writers were spiritual, not just a set of injunctions; they were immensely more skilled and subtle than their Puritan forebears, as was C. S. Lewis with his *Narnia* books many years later, but they all continued the Puritan confessional tradition.

As a main theme and centerpiece, however, religion has by now almost totally disappeared in books for the young. Today's children's books ignore religion and spirituality. Here I am referring to mainstream publishing, not to Sunday School publications or books emanating from religious publishing houses. Modern writers for children and young adults are existentialists. They may not be so in their personal lives, but professionally they march closely together in their disregard of any religious beliefs. Existentialism is a very courageous philosophy and modern writers certainly give their protagonists the intelligence, the fortitude, and the sensitivity to work their way through their problems—which are considerable. But in essence, they force their characters to "go it alone."

Recently, religion has been rather prodded into a comeback. Several volumes in the Bantam Books "Clearwater Crossing" series feature eight adolescents sporadically contemplating aspects of the Christian faith that could make sense of their lives. Unfortunately, the writing is banal, and the remarks about religion are superficial. If these books are intended to fill a spiritual vacuum, I think we are better off with James Janeway.

Most current books do, of course, mention religion, or at least the Jewish and Catholic versions of religion. But these generally center on festivals, food, and family; in other words, their concerns are more cultural than religious. Let me give you two examples: the short stories of Isaac Bashevits Singer are filled with the humor, drama, and pathos of Jewish *shtetl* life at the turn of the twentieth century. As for Catholicism, I think of such titles as *Runaway* (1996) by Canadian Norma Charles, the story of a lively child in a convent boarding school. And to give the Presbyterians their due, there is a most interesting book, *The Sin Eater*, by the American Gary Schmidt. Yet in all, the lack of a religious content, as opposed to a religious background, can be seen as the greatest division between the literature of the past and that of the present.

Well, if religion as a forceful factor in writing for children is gone, what took its place? The answer is family life, especially unhappy family life.

Although I wonder if this is just the Puritan predilection for misery back in another form, it is probably just an echo of Tolstoy's famous dictum that "All happy families resemble each other, each unhappy family is unhappy in its own way." In other words, happy families do not offer much opportunity for individuality and drama; unhappy families do. This point is particularly apparent in children's literature before the 1960s when families were happy, when the standard family consisted of two parents and several children. But a writer could spice things up if he or she unjustly imprisoned the father, as in Edith Nesbit's *The Railway Children*. Better still, one could kill off both parents and leave the heroine an orphan as in *Anne of Green Gables* and *The Secret Garden*.

However, the family story did change over the years. Typical of the early period is Mrs. Sherwood's *The History of the Fairchild Family*, first published in 1818. Mr. and Mrs. Fairchild belonged to England's upper middle class. Mr. Fairchild is the central figure in the story; his main occupation is the supervision of his children. For a long time indeed, adults were the controlling agents in what became a highly domestic literature. But around the turn of the century, adults began to lose their centrality in the narrative. From Edith Nesbit to Arthur Ransome to Philippa Pearce and Lucy Boston, writers were getting adults off center stage, although a favorite uncle might be allowed some attention or perhaps a grandmother figure such as Lucy Boston's Mrs. Oldknow. In pushing the parents out, such writers aimed to give children room for play and adventure on their own, activities that were seen correctly as preparations for adulthood.

Since the early 1960s, parents seem to be back in full view, but their lot is hardly joyous. Modern writers have opted, first, for what they consider, à la Tolstoy, the more interesting kind of families, the unhappy ones, or better still, the downright dysfunctional ones. This means that adults, especially parents, are once again at the core of the plot, but this time they are most unhelpful. The children, and particularly young adults, face every problem that modern society can hurl at them. Parents divorce, they disappear, or they die. They also become alcoholics, abusive, or at least too busy to give much attention to their progeny. The protagonists (for there are few we could call heroes or heroines) are portrayed as trying to cope with endless problems—in relations with their troubled parents, in dealing with sibling rivalry, difficulties at school with classmates or boyfriends. For example, in Sarah Ellis's *Out of the Blue*, the mother finds the daughter she gave away as a baby, and of course, her legitimate daughter is jealous—that's your family life book of the 1990s. This one is very well written, I hasten to add.

Such books are highly realistic (except for, I would suggest, the resolution of the problem in an incredibly short time span) and plotless, much like life itself. Some writers who use the basic pattern are able to break it or to enrich it, such as Canadian writer Tim Wynne-Jones with *The Maestro*.

It also seems that present day writers, if by some chance they allow happy parents into the household, still ruthlessly require their adherence to certain rules. Some rules have to be obeyed, just as in the past. Thus, the mother must work outside the home; if she does not, she must be a writer or an artist, so that she can have a satisfactory excuse for being at home. The father must be able to do some cooking (at least spaghetti sauce). On the other hand, he must not be portrayed as cleaning the bathroom. No one else does either; presumably the bathroom cleaning is done by extra-terrestrials! Generally, there are just one or two children per family. If only one, the child is generally a girl, one of whose close friends is a neighbor boy whom she dominates. If there are two children, it is a girl and a boy with the girl being the elder (remember the crucial importance of birth order!). Fortunately there are some exceptions to this lockstep scenario. My favorite is The Exiles series by British writer Hilary McKay, which features four young sisters, all bookworms, who, while summering with their grandmother, are deprived of their reading material. The freshness of the children's experiences and the books' crisp style are reminiscent of Edith Nesbit. Tolstoy was wrong: happy families are not all alike.

Time now to consider what has happened from another inheritance from our Puritan progenitors. If their emphasis on religion and the predominance of family is finally gone, what has happened to their other main concern—education? There seems to be general agreement that the young of today are better educated than those of the past. Actually, I think this is debatable if one looks at children's books over the centuries. Some very sound educational theory is evident in the earliest period of children's literature; today, writers tend to confuse, or at least overlay, education with entertainment. In the late eighteenth century, theories of education that entered children's books came to England by way of France through the works of Madame de Genlis and André Berquin. But the greatest impact came from Jean Jacques Rousseau's *Emile* (1762). His idea of a child brought up in isolation with a mentor always present was seized upon by Thomas Day, whose *Sandford and Merton* was published in 1789 and was continuously in print for over 100 years, even in editions of one-syllable words. The mentor system involves to some extent the question-and-answer approach; the curious child answered by the omniscient adult. At that time, it would seem that nobody said to a child, "Find out for yourself," but then, where would a child have gone to do so? Not to the local public library! And if we now object to or laugh at the mentor syndrome, we should remember that we still use it in our universities in "Directed Studies" and in the tutorial system.

Secular education was the prerogative of the middle class; the poor were taught to read chiefly under the auspices of the Sunday School movement and the work of such organizations as the Religious Tract Society and the Society for the Promotion of Christian Knowledge. Their aim was limited:

to teach the poor to read the Bible. However, as we all know, once a person can read, self-education is possible, and those Christian societies certainly produced far more and far different fruit than they ever intended.

The importance of education as a means of rising above one's station in life is well shown by Margery in *The History of Little Goody Two-Shoes* (1765). Margery rises from orphan to Lady of the Manor through teaching herself the alphabet and then through teaching others. (The rest of us teachers should only do so well!) So too in Dorothy Kilner's *The Village School* (ca. 1795), the ability to read well is highly praised. However, there is little doubt that the intellectual quality of nineteenth-century education (and earlier) took a distant second place to its moral quality. Even in the heyday of the boys' public school story, the classics such as Thomas Hughes's *Tom Brown's School Days* (1857) and Frederic Farrar's *Eric, or Little by Little* (1858) were premised on the perceived role of the public schools in developing Manliness and Christianity, which in time gave rise to the term "muscular Christianity."

For girls, the parallel was the boarding school story, which developed a bit later and was perhaps less obvious in its moral emphasis. However I can assure you in the interest of equality that the girls' stories were just as free of any intellectualism as those for the boys. Typically their plots revolved around friendships (or the lack of them), petty jealousies, the infraction of rules, and so on. Indeed, in *The Holiday School*, by Edith Cowper (1927), the girls from an English boarding school are holidaying in France, but they prefer to solve a mystery rather than learn French.

Modern children's books are filled with school scenes and images of classmates and teachers. Here parents play a secondary role. If such books are a true reflection of North American public education, I feel we're in a sorry state. With few exceptions, there is little or no excitement about learning, about discovery, about challenge. If there are elements of the traditional school story in modern realistic fiction, the authors follow the general pattern of the realistic fiction writers in that the young protagonists are never given an opportunity to look outside their own lives; there is no existence for them beyond their immediate concerns. They live very narrow, egotistical lives.

Of course, there are a few books that show some intellectual interest in learning. For example, in Jane Gardam's *Bilgewater* (1976), the young lover of literature is the daughter of a headmaster in an English boys' school. There is also *Make or Break Spring* (1998) by Canadian Janet McNaughton, in which two young teenagers share an intellectual delight in their studies. But most writers who even mention schooling really don't convey any liking for it. The range of antipathy varies. There are the basically light-hearted, child-centerd books such as Florence McNeil's *Miss P. and Me*, in which a child embarrasses her teacher. More pointed are the attacks on education by Daniel Pinkwater with his *The Education of Robert Nifkin*

(1998). In this book, a young junior high school student, weighing 220 pounds, finds himself an outcast in his new public school. One of his teachers rails against the Jews, another against the Communists, and so on. He only begins to get an education at a private summer school where it is a matter of a "hands-on" education: "Go and find out."

Modern writers like to put teachers down. There is the recent and very popular *Frindle* by American Andrew Clements, in which an elementary school child baits his English teacher by instantaneously coining the word "frindle" for a pen. Eventually, however, with the teacher's help, the word makes its way into the dictionary. At any rate, it is safe to say that education, with its joys and tribulations, is not a priority in children's literature, nor has it been since Rousseau and Day.

It is not really surprising that teachers get rather bad press in contemporary children's books. Almost all other adults do too, especially as they are viewed by the children in these books. In an earlier time, children would never have dared to criticize an adult, at least not aloud. Adults could be shown as cruel, as with ships' captains and wicked landlords, for example, but such people simply had to be accepted by the children they bullied.

Gradually, in the nineteenth century, children were allowed to express some feelings about the adult world, although gently. You will remember the children in Kenneth Grahame's *The Golden Age* (1895) who referred to the adults around them as "The Olympians." But these children felt chiefly pity for the adults. "Indeed," says the youthful narrator, "it was one of the most hopeless features in their character (when we troubled ourselves to waste a thought on them: which wasn't often) that, having absolute licence to indulge in the pleasures of life, they could get no good of it. They might dabble in the pond all day, hunt the chickens, climb trees in the most uncompromising Sunday clothes; yet they never did any of these things." By 1905, Sara Crew in Frances Hodgson Burnett's *A Little Princess* was allowed to criticize the formidable Miss Minchin: "You are not kind," she says, "you are not kind, and this house is not a home." However, this kind of criticism was hardly blunt, the reader having been already persuaded that such remarks were well deserved. In any case, in early children's books, opinions by children on adults are few and seldom prominently featured.

Conversely, modern literary children spend an inordinate amount of time observing and commenting on their parents, their teachers, and other adults. Perhaps this is because they spend so much time with them rather than adventuring on their own or with their peers. Some simply voice their opinions to themselves, such as Leonard Neeble in Daniel Pinkwater's *Alan Mendelsohn, the Boy from Mars* (1979). Here is how Leonard muses about his parents: "My parents are sort of dumb—I mean, I love them and all that, but they aren't very interesting. They are only interested in getting things for the house, and barbecuing, and that sort of thing." In *The Exiles* (1991) by Hilary McKay, there is an open exchange between a child and an adult. "Children are beastly when they're tired," remarked Big Grandma. "So're old ladies," commented Phoebe. Phoebe is six years old. If modern realism really reflects life as it is, then adults should beware!

It is ironic that the genre of realistic fiction, which accounts for both the boon and the blight of contemporary children's fiction, flourished alongside another genre-fantasy, which has had a great revival, but this time in a new and not wholly welcome guise.

The subtitle of J.R.R. Tolkien's *The Hobbit* (1939), which is "There and Back Again," epitomizes the tradition of fantasy for children from its beginnings in the middle of the Victorian Age to the 1960s. The protagonists (and so the readers) enter and return from fully created Other Worlds: Lewis Carroll's Wonderland, J. M. Barrie's Never-land, or C. S. Lewis's Narnia. Other fantasies plunged us into make-believe worlds from the first line of the first page and kept us there until the story was over. We live completely in George MacDonald's goblin realm, Tolkien's Middle-Earth, Ursula Le Guin's Earthsea, or Lloyd Alexander's Prydain. Whatever type of unreality these authors contrived, the meaning and purpose of fantasy were the same. Fantasy was used to illuminate (indeed to intensify) reality, not to distort it; to propound a set of universal values, not to preach; to link the natural and the supernatural worlds without degrading either. These aspects of fantasy keep it close to its roots in myth, legend, and folklore.

Since the middle of the 1960s, however, most fantasies have almost reversed these conventions, with writers using the supernatural forces to break into the real world, often bringing with them violence and terror. Frequently the events are caused by the unhappiness or the problems of the chief protagonist, much as in the realistic novel. At any rate, modern writers of fantasy cannot or do not care to create Other Worlds; they are more realists than fantasists. This trend was given great impetus by such writers as New Zealander Margaret Mahy with *The Haunting* (1983) and *The Changeover* (1984) and by Canadian Monica Hughes with *Castle Tourmandyne* (1995). This trend has continued. I think that if a genre does not change it will atrophy. However, it should be pointed out that the new fantasists are not image-makers, nor are they wordsmiths. Who can forget C. S. Lewis's faun carrying an umbrella in *The Lion, the Witch and the Wardrobe* or Pamela Travers's Mary Poppins sliding *up* the bannister? What modern fantasist has matched "Bother! O blow! Hang spring cleaning!"—the first words of Kenneth Grahame's *The Wind in the Willows*? I hope you notice that I have not quoted from Lewis Carroll's *Alice's Adventures in Wonderland*. I do not ask for genius in every children's book, just for a bit of something to linger in the mind.

I come now to the last of the subjects that I want to single out as constituting the most important features of contemporary writing. I refer to the Young Adult novel, an unhappy name for an unhappy body of writing. Emily Neville's *It's Like This, Cat*, which appeared in 1963, set a pattern that has lasted for decades: a teenager alienated from the adult world, a first-person narrative with a simulated confessional tone; rigorously self-centered, limited vocabulary; short in length; and generally set in an urban environment, one big city being much like another. There is no doubt that the novel for teens has improved over the years, but it still remains, to use an old wives' proverb, "neither fish or fowl nor good red herring."

One result of the rise of the Young Adult novel has been the decline of the novel for children, that is, for those aged from about nine to twelve. Some publishers have compounded this problem by labelling any book that has characters eleven years of age and over as "young adult," thus hoping to appeal to two audiences, the pre-adolescent and the young adolescent.

The trouble with most Young Adult novels is that they seem to be written to entice the reluctant reader. By providing settings and themes that are easily recognized, by couching the narrative in language that is linguistically easy, they have gained a world of readers but have lost their own soul. And what profiteth that?

And so now to the last of my three time zones—the future. Some of that future is quite predictable. As always hitherto, children's literature will change as society changes. It will be, as it has always been, a reflection of life—in miniature, of course, but still quite accurate. In its historical role as a barometer of the society in which it exists, children's literature will be no better and no worse than it has always been.

Other trends are a little more difficult to predict. I am pretty certain that the number of titles published each year—15,000 in English—will increase, at least for a while. I think this very growth will work more and more to the detriment of children and their reading. This unhappy fate is already noticeable. In earlier times, with fewer books published and with publishers cherishing a backlist, there was time for a book to make its way into the general consciousness of both children and adults—indeed a world consciousness. Thus are classics born. Already the reading of children is losing its commonality, its shared culture. Each year, many fine books are simply pushed out of the way to make room for a new crop. Libraries and bookstores stock up with the new rather than reordering the possibly half dozen that made an impact the year before. We used to be able to talk of the commonality of childhood reading. Moreover, this commonality was worldwide. As Paul Hazard pointed out in *Books, Children & Men*, "Each country gives and each country receives." We could count on children having read Grimm and Andersen, *Pippi Longstocking*, *Pinocchio, Emil and the Detectives*. I don't know about you, but I haven't read a book in translation for years and years. I am in no way saying that children should read only the classics; they also need the works of their own time and space and concerns. But the proliferation of present-day chaff makes it difficult to find the wheat of the present.

Another safe prediction is that there will be fewer and fewer confessional writers as opposed to professional ones. You will remember the dichotomy that I spoke of earlier: confessional writers feel a personal and psychological need to write a certain book; professional writers are simply practising their profession, that is, exercising their livelihood. Well, I can't really expect all children's books to be the products of inspiration, but professional books do tend to be mediocre in general and, in the specific cases in series such as Goosebumps and The Babysitters Club, they are positively lumpy!

There will probably be a decline in the huge number of books published for reluctant readers. I suspect that the Internet will take up this slack. A good idea too—let the attractive power of new technology persuade reluctant dragons into nibbling at ideas and images.

And another guess: I prophecy that works of fantasy will increase at the expense of the realistic novel, which seems to have run the gamut of emotions from A to D (angst to divorce, disappearing parents, and death). I think that fantasy, with its wider parameters as a genre and its more epic view of life, will attract a new flock of writers. Certainly the phenomenal success of the Harry Potter series by J. K. Rowling demonstrates a yearning on the part of both children and adults for something beyond the ordinary as well as a delight in storytelling.

These fearless forecasts of mine may turn out to be foolish, but I make them quite light-heartedly all the same. After all, the law of averages states that I am bound to guess right some of the time, and anyway, who remembers Nostradamus's many errors?

And so, I end now by leaving to you the fun of checking my last and best guesses of all: that children's literature will continue to exist in three tenses: the earlier books will continue to exert their tidal pulls on succeeding audiences; children's books of the present will find a way of accommodating themselves to the technology of the day; and children's books of the future will meld tradition with change and out of them will appear their own classics. Test me out on these predictions in 2065 when *Alice's Adventures in Wonderland* will be celebrating her 200th birthday. I'll be expecting warm congratulations then—and I'll let you know the place of delivery later!

NOTE

This essay was the closing plenary talk and it appears here as Professor Egoff delivered it.

CHAPTER 2

The Decline and Rise of Literary Nonsense in the Twentieth Century

Michael Heyman

The 1860s and 1870s marked a high point in the popularity of literary nonsense for children. Edward Lear and Lewis Carroll dominated this niche in the children's book market, inspiring many imitators whose names now have mostly been forgotten. After this "golden age," however, it becomes difficult to name many other notable writers of literary nonsense for children until we reach the mid-twentieth century, with Spike Milligan and Dr. Seuss, for example. Filling this gap in time, surprisingly, are mainly nonsense writers for adults. Indeed, under the term "nonsense," the *Dictionary of Literary Terms and Literary Theory* names Lear and Carroll but then continues its broad list with writers such as Joyce and Stein. It seems that children's nonsense all but disappeared for quite some time, while nonsense resurfaced in other, adult forms. The purpose of this chapter is to examine what happened to children's nonsense—very broadly to outline the course of literary nonsense for children since Lear and Carroll, its decline in the beginning of the twentieth century and its resurgence in the second half of the century.

From nonsense alphabets to nonsense botany illustrations, from travel prose to sonnets, from limericks to specific and general parodies, the scope of literary nonsense is as wide and varied as the many forms it inhabits. Consequently, definitions of the genre tend to slip between the fingers: we may begin by classifying "literary nonsense" texts as those based on the models of Lear and Carroll. In such texts there is a type of balance between "sense" and "non-sense." Elizabeth Sewell likens this phenomenon to a game: "The game is a play of the side of order against disorder."[1] This game is interminable, for "it cannot suppress the force towards disorder in the mind, nor defeat it conclusively, for this force is essential to the mind no less than the opposing force of order."[2] Wim Tigges defines nonsense as a genre in which "the seeming presence of one or more sensible meanings is kept in balance by a simultaneous absence of such a meaning."[3] I would add to this the Deleuzean concept of nonsense as the necessary creation of an impossible alternative "sense," a nonentity that nevertheless asserts its impossible existence, trying to disguise itself as a type of sense. As these definitions can get somewhat technical, it is easier to spot nonsense by its themes of defiant individuality, its lack of most emotions, and its common devices, such as the use of infinity, distorted logic, gratuitous or obvious detail, arbitrariness, and *non sequitur*. Particularly in Lear's work, there is often an incongruous relationship between picture and text that heightens the nonsensical effect.

It should not be surprising that nonsense in the twentieth century has been predominantly for adults. The first literary nonsense texts, which *were* for adults, appeared in England in the mid-fifteenth century. After this brief surge, the genre disappeared until John Hoskyns revived it in 1611. After forty years of popularity, however, it soon fell back into obscurity.[4] The nonsense verse of this period was usually highly topical, "intellectual," and exclusively meant for adults. It would be over 150 years before the genre would start anew, but aimed at children, from the pen of Edward Lear. After Lear's and Carroll's "golden age of nonsense," the genre as meant for children fell into decline. Although literary nonsense drastically changed the face of children's literature—as a separate, formal genre for children it seemed to have died away-it returned to its old adult audience in various forms. In the twentieth century, the great, direct inheritors of the nonsense method and style have mostly been "adult" writers such as Edward Gorey and Mervyn Peake, the bulk of whose work steered nonsense down an altogether darker path. There are exceptions, of course, the most obvious being that Lear has never gone out of print.[5] Other writers of nonsense for children have emerged, most recently Michael Rosen,[6] but the genre has never returned to the kind of success and popularity it had with Lear and Carroll.

One of the main causes of the decline of children's nonsense was that "nonsense" writers and imitators around the turn of the century had fundamental misunderstandings as to the genre's mechanics, purposes, and effects. Because of this, they often wrote bad, inane, or plainly *sensical* verse and called it nonsense. Lord Alfred Douglas, for instance, attempted to write nonsense verse for children in the first few years of this century, but his misunderstanding of the genre led him to failure. He writes in his preface to *The Pongo Papers* (1907) that nonsense should be "untainted by the least trace of satire or parody or caricature," and that writing "nonsense rhymes has no effect one way or the other on one's ability or desire to write poetry. It simply has nothing to do with it at all."[7] Douglas's preface betrays his divergence from commonly accepted definitions of the genre. While nonsense cannot *be* satire, parody, or caricature, it can and should include elements of these, which are part of the essential "sense" side of nonsense. The best nonsense usually has an intertextual nature, even though the purpose of the intertextuality is intentionally less clear. His separation of nonsense and poetry also goes against much of the best nonsense poetry, which easily classifies as both. The result of his pronouncements, as seen in his own verse, is nonsense wrung of both its sense-nonsense tension and any vestige of poetic beauty or charm. He claims that his collection of animal verse, *Tails with a Twist*, is perfect nonsense. I quote "The Viper" in full for your judgment:

> The Viper is a sickening snake,
> He comes when you are not awake.
> During the day-time he's all right,
> But then he always comes by night.
> He's quite innocuous by day,
> But that's the time he keeps away.
> He has a very stealthy creep,
> He comes when you are fast asleep.
> Say what you will, do what you like,
> He's ultimately sure to strike.
> His perseverance is immense,
> The pain he causes is intense.[8]

In this lifeless, insipid, entirely sensical verse, Douglas has mistaken inconsequentiality for nonsense, demonstrating all too clearly why "nonsense" for children died away.

Another would-be nonsense imitator, Gordon Brown (A. Nobody) also failed to capture the essence of the genre. In his two volumes, while getting much closer to Lear's nonsense than Douglas does, he nevertheless wrote much "sensical" verse in the guise of nonsense. In the poem "A Little Lamb (and sauce)," for instance, we see the opposite end of sense to Douglas's. This poem is a straight parody of "Mary had a little lamb," describing a man who would rather eat than keep a lamb. Unequivocal parody precludes true nonsense, which cannot have a "point" to it (aside from the point of not having a point). Nevertheless, the poem and its illustration are very Learian and humorous, but it never is anything more than entertaining light verse. Brown also omits one of the most important nonsense devices, the picture/poem discrepancy. Lear's pictorial embellishments usually have a complex and contrary relationship with their accompanying verse, but Brown's merely illustrate, however humorously. By ignoring the key elements of literary nonsense, both Douglas and Brown degrade the genre into light verse at best—and take away its uniqueness. Light verse, parody, fantasy, and other types of writing were labeled "nonsense," while true literary nonsense got left behind and nearly forgotten.

Another reason for the decline of the genre was a change in children's publication trends. Petzold counts 98 works influenced by Carroll alone between the publication of *Alice's Adventures in Wonderland* and the end of the nineteenth century.[9] Carroll himself wrote, in his preface to *Sylvie and Bruno*, "since it [*Alice*] came out, something like a dozen story-books have appeared, on identically the same pattern. The path I timidly explored—believing myself to be 'the first that ever burst into that silent sea'—is now a beaten high-road: all the wayside flowers have long ago been trampled into the dust."[10] Children's book publishers knew what sold, and the market was flooded with "fairy" stories and imitations of nonsense, some better than others, but the end result was a supersaturation. Nonsense went out of fashion. In addition, nonsense no longer had as much against which to rebel. Lear and Carroll, with a Romantic zest, reacted to didactic children's literature from Watts to Sherwood. Lear ridiculed utilitarian educational schemes along with genres like the alphabet and natural history, while Carroll's portrait of Alice broke many of the rules for girls books at the time. But once the market was full of fantasy, rebellion, and topsyturveydom, nonsense may have run out of easy targets.

Carroll's *Sylvie and Bruno* brings us to the last for nonsense's decline. Just as nonsense as a genre is partly rebellion, it also needs the children portrayed in it to be rebels. The characters in Lear's nonsense (though often Old Men, as unruly as children) are wild, breaking all rules of decorum and logic. Alice, likewise, sloughs off the typical roll of submissive, self-sacrificing girl to be an inquisitive, ambitious, and even selfish dreamchild. But Carroll's own work ushered in a new didacticism, stemming from the cult of the child which increasingly portrayed children as delicate angels rather than rough-and-tumble imps. He writes in his Preface to *Sylvie and Bruno*:

If it be needful to apologize to any one for the new departure I have taken in this story—by introducing, along with what will, I hope, prove to be acceptable nonsense for children, some of the graver thoughts of human life—it must be to one who has learned the Art of keeping such thoughts wholly at a distance in hours of mirth and careless ease. To him such a mixture will seem, no doubt, ill-judged and repulsive.[11]

The delicate children who need lessons on mortality had regained control of the nursery and their one-time enemy had crossed to the other side. The mixture of nonsense and didacticism proved to be fatal to the genre. But many attitudes had changed since nonsense first appeared in Lear's 1842 volume. Nonsense needs a certain archness, an element of chaos that faded in the new century. Early twentieth-century children's books were enervated versions of their wilder predecessors: Kate Greenaway and her soft-focus cupids gave way to A. A. Milne, who created suitably gentle worlds for this delicate, innocent image of children.

What happened to the sinister side of nonsense? In the first decades of this century the world had begun to shift, becoming more serious, and more bloody, and nonsense was taken back to the adult world. Its potential for subversion was rediscovered and redirected. The intellectual seriousness of Carroll's nonsense paved the way for more "adult" purposes. Alfred Jarry ushered nonsense into the new century with his *Ubu* cycle; Borges used nonsense devices in his self-reflexive fantasy worlds. Nonsense filtered into surrealism and the absurd, with Ionesco and Beckett's questioning of reality and modern existence. Its tendency toward meaninglessness was exploited by Mervyn Peake and Edward Gorey. Peake, who perhaps comes closest of any writer to Lear, nevertheless creates in his adult works a dark nonsense removed from, yet disturbingly close to, children's literature. Indeed, some critics claimed the same of his children's works. Gorey's "black" nonsense, which also approaches children's literature, drains away all optimism from its Victorian predecessor, leaving only a tainted ennui. In the novel there was Joyce, and in poetry, Wallace Stevens and Gertrude Stein, among others, all exploring the possibilities of nonsense to question the efficacy of language.[12] It even found its way into the Eastern philosophy of Beat-figure Alan Watts. Indeed, nonsense settled back into adult writing with such ease that it makes us wonder if it had ever really left it.

Though the first half of this century saw little nonsense, it had not disappeared entirely. A few capable practitioners kept the new form afloat, even amidst the nonsense failures and general watering-down of popular children's literature. Laura E. Richards, a figure almost completely unknown today, was one of the few successful writers of nonsense at the time, although technically she was mostly a nineteenth-century writer. She began writing nonsense in the 1870s and became popular in the 1880s and 1890s, but dropped into near obscurity until 1932, when by popular demand she published a new compilation, entitled *Tirra Lirra*, of old and some new verse. "The Man and the People," from this volume, demonstrates her debt both to Lear and Carroll, and her success in following their models. She uses such familiar echoes from Carroll and Lear as "frubjub feathers" and the rhyming of "bat" with "what you're at."[13]

Richards echoes the Learian situation of an eccentric individual against a censorious public (not to mention the closeness of "Aunt Katinka" to Lear's "Aunt Jobiska" in "The Pobble Who Has No Toes"), while using Carrollian words like "frubjub"-close to Carroll's "jubjub"-and the reference to the Taylors' "Twinkle Twinkle," as in *Alice*. Richards, however, is really a nineteenth-century writer who had a resurgence in her old age, at the request of a nonsense-starved public. Another nonsense writer on the edge of the century was Kipling, whose *Just So Stories* (1902) included some nonsense, especially in stories like "How the Whale Got His Throat" and "How the Rhinoceros Got His Skin." Carl Sandburg, truly a twentieth-century figure, wrote *Rootabaga Stories* (1922), which has a good deal of nonsense in it, though as a whole most of it would not quite classify as pure literary nonsense. Mervyn Peake's children's book, *Captain Slaughterboard Drops Anchor* (1939) is quite nonsensical, though critics questioned the suitability of both text and illustration for children. These authors provided only a small amount of nonsense in the first half of the century; for the most part, it had receded from public view.

Nonsense did not return to the nursery in earnest until the 1950s, which happened to be soon after Holbrook Jackson published his *Complete Nonsense of Edward Lear* (1947). Spike Milligan's children's rhymes revived the look and feel of nineteenth-century nonsense, especially in his own contradictory, deceptively "naive" illustrations, which work with the verses to increase the nonsense effect. Take "Hipporhinostricow," for instance, from Milligan's *Silly Verse For Kids* (1959): here is a beast that "sleeps all day," "whistles all night," and "wears yellow socks which are too tight."[14]

Besides being related to Lear's Uncle Arly, whose "shoes were far too tight," Milligan's creature also exhibits, in the illustration, some puzzling characteristics. The Hipporhinostricow appears to have a clothesline attached to its horn and tail, from which hangs clothes, but also body parts, including a head (in the hat) and legs (sticking out of the nightshirt). The illustration makes one think twice about laughing at the creature, as, apparently, for *some* reason, people have ended up dismembered, drying out with the laundry. The illustration does not, however, explain how this happens or how the creature is "protected." With equally bizarre, though more polished illustrations, Dr. Seuss also revived nonsense with his picture/poem combinations. Though starting his children's book career in the 1930s, he did not find real popularity until the 1950s with his *The Cat in the Hat* (1957). Although his work cannot be called true literary nonsense, he used many of its devices along with wild, distorted illustration that, like good nonsense, could not be easily separated from the text.

With Milligan and Seuss, nonsense came back into style, but such a resurgence was not an isolated literary trend. As with Victorian nonsense, it arose in a time of rebellion. The Beat generation and rising counterculture lead to the social and political unrest of the 1960s. Schools were knocking down walls, opening classrooms, and introducing *laissez-faire* theories of education, all in response to the more conservative methods used through the 1950s. The "Free To Be You and Me" spirit dominated the classroom, and children's authors rebelled against imposed meaning, gender, and race stereotypes and rigid, "old-fashioned" pedagogy. Children's publishers in the 1960s and 1970s responded to such drastic changes with an unprecedented number of nonsense anthologies. One such anthology, *Oh, What Nonsense,* includes such authors as Shel Silverstein, Spike Milligan, Theodore Roethke, James Reeves, William Jay Smith, and Beatrice Curtis Brown. Interestingly, Lear and Carroll are left out of this volume because, as William Cole claims, they still dominated most nonsense anthologies. Though much nonsense was being published, surprisingly little *new* nonsense was being written for children.

More recently, nonsense has maintained a minor niche in the children's book market. Writers such as Roger McGough, Jack Prelutsky, and Michael Rosen are all creating new, interesting, and technically sound nonsense in the nineteenth-century tradition. But we may ask why nonsense only maintains such a small corner of the market, why it has never regained the status it once had as the most innovative and creative branch of children's literature. One of the causes is that children (and adults) today are significantly different from their Victorian ancestors. Today's children's literature and other media forms such as television have embraced nonsense antecedents fully, from the nonsense words of Dr. Seuss to the outrageous abandonment of the conventional and the intellectual in the *Ren and Stimpy* cartoon. Nonsense, which usually has a parodic basis, simply does not have enough material from which to work. Cartoons like *Tick* and *Tiny Toons* integrate nonsense devices and meta-sense, leaving little room for nonsense as a separate genre. Nonsense needs to rebel from sense, whether against intellectual trends, current pedagogy, children's literature, or almost anything, but nonsense for children seems specifically to feed off children's genres. However, in today's children's market, there is no longer a dominant, serious tradition to fight against, and children's entertainment must continually go further in its pursuit of an audience inundated with novelty, humor, and creativity. Children today are thus far less likely to notice what now seem to be the somewhat tame rhymes and plain illustrations of Lear, Milligan, or even Rosen. What once appeared to be open rebellion in the dull world of children's literature now, to some, appears dull itself.

Yet the picture is perhaps not as bleak as it may appear. Nonsense, both Victorian and late-twentieth-century, obstinately keeps a place, however small and specialized, in the children's market. This may be explainable simply because literary nonsense is only partially a historical construct. Nonsense devices themselves are not bound to anything temporal—they can be applied to any genre with relatively equal effectiveness. We may no longer see all the humor of Lear's botanical drawings, as botanical illustration has gone out of vogue, but such techniques could be applied to superhero comics, Barney, or contemporary political cartoons, for example. It is only once the nonsense devices have been applied that the result is to some extent time-bound. But as long as there are more earnest television shows like *Sesame Street* or *Teletubbies* there will be fuel for the future of literary nonsense.

NOTES

1. Elizabeth Sewell, *The Field of Nonsense*. London: Chatto and Windus, 1952, p. 46.

2. Ibid., p. 47.

3. Wim Tigges, *An Anatomy of Literary Nonsense*. Amsterdam: Rodopi, 1988, p. 255.

4. Noel Malcolm, *The Origins of English Nonsense*. London: Fontana/Harper-Collins, 1997, p. 52.

5. I found the following editions of Lear (or Lear and Carroll) in one bookshop: *The Book of Nonsense and Nonsense Songs* (London: Penguin, 1996); *The Owl and the Pussycat*, illus. Ian Beck (London: Doubleday/Picture Corgi Books, 1995); *Owls and Pussycats: Nonsense Verse* [Lear and Carroll] (Oxford: Oxford UP, 1993); *The Owl and the Pussy Cat* (London: Walker Books, 1991); and *The Jumblies*, illus. Emily Bloom (London: Orchard Books, 1998). The Jackson *Complete Lear* is still in print.

6. Michael Rosen, *Michael Rosen's Book of Nonsense*. Hove, UK: Macdonald Young Books, 1997.

7. Lord Alfred Douglas, *The Duke of Berwick and Other Rhymes*. London: Martin Secker, 1926, p. 15.

8. Ibid., p. 47.

9. Dieter Petzold, *Formen und Funktionen der englischen Nonsense-Dichtung im 19. Jahrhundert*. Nuerenberg: Verlag Hans Carl, 1972, pp. 252–254.

10. Lewis Carroll, *The Complete Works of Lewis Carroll*. London: Nonesuch Press, 1940, pp. 279–280.

11. Ibid., p. 283.

12. See Alison Reike, *The Senses of Nonsense*. Iowa City: University of Iowa P, 1992 for more on modern, adult nonsense.

13. Laura E. Richards, *Tirra Lirra: Rhymes Old and New*. Illus. Marguerite Davis. London: George G. Harrap, 1933, first two stanzas, p. 35.

14. Spike Milligan, *Silly Verse for Kids*. (1959) London: Puffin, 1968, p. 17.

REFERENCES

Brown, Gordon [A. Nobody]. *Nonsense; For Somebody Anybody or Everybody Particularly the Baby-Body*. London: Gardner, Darton & Co. [c. 1895].

Carroll, Lewis. *The Complete Works of Lewis Carroll*. London: Nonesuch Press, 1940.

Cole, William, ed. *Oh, What Nonsense!* Illus. Tomi Ungerer. London: Methuen, 1968.

Cuddon, J. A., ed., revised by C. E. Preston, "Nonsense." In *A Dictionary of Literary Terms and Literary Theory*, 4th edition. Oxford: Blackwell, 1976, 1998.

Deleuze, Gilles. *The Logic of Sense*. Trans. Mark Lester with Charles Stivale, ed. Constantin V. Boundas. London: The Athlone Press (French version, 1969), 1990.

Douglas, Lord Alfred. *The Duke of Berwick and Other Rhymes*. London: Martin Secker, 1926.

Lear, Edward. *The Complete Nonsense of Edward Lear*. Ed. Holbrook Jackson. London: Faber and Faber, 1947.

Malcolm, Noel. *The Origins of English Nonsense*. London: Fontana/Harper Collins, 1997.

Milligan, Spike. *Silly Verse for Kids*. London: Puffin, 1968.

Peake, Mervyn. *Captain Slaughterboard Drops Anchor*. London: Country Life Books, 1939.

Petzold, Dieter. *Formen und Funktionen der englischen Nonsense-Dichtung im 19. Jahrhundert*. Nuerenberg: Verlag Hans Carl, 1972.

Reike, Alison. *The Senses of Nonsense*. Iowa City: U of Iowa P, 1992.

Richards, Laura E. *Tirra Lirra: Rhymes Old and New*. Illus. Marguerite Davis. London: George G. Harrap, 1933.

Rosen, Michael. *Michael Rosen's Book of Nonsense*. Hove, UK: Macdonald Young Books, 1997.

Sewell, Elizabeth. *The Field of Nonsense*. London: Chatto and Windus, 1952.

Tigges, Wim. *An Anatomy of Literary Nonsense*. Amsterdam: Rodopi, 1988.

CHAPTER 3

The Century of the Child: Dutch Children's Poetry in the Twentieth Century

Anne de Vries

My subject is Dutch children's poetry in the twentieth century. Giving a survey of a whole century in 2,000 to 3,000 words may seem a bit reckless. To make things even worse, I must confess that during the past three years I have read all Dutch children's poetry from its beginning in the eighteenth century until the present time, more than 1,500 volumes. As a consequence, I will have to keep most of my material in stock for other publications, starting with a representative anthology of Dutch children's poetry, which appeared in 1999. In this chapter I will broadly survey what I term poetical poems, poems in which a poet expresses his or her views on poetry.

In 1900, Ellen Key proclaimed this century "the century of the child" (*Barnets århundrade*, 1900). I won't go into her pedagogical views: I just want to borrow this title, which is typical of that time. Pedagogues were optimistic about the future: child labor had been abolished, compulsory education had just been adopted, so in the new century children were to enjoy their childhood years in peace. Of course, this was the result of a long process of change in the eighteenth and nineteenth centuries, a gradual extension of childhood, for a growing group of children. This development is reflected in children's poetry and in children's literature in general. Apart from the oral tradition of nursery rhymes, hardly any poetry for children existed before the last quarter of the eighteenth century. At that time, poetry for children had an explicitly moralizing character, only a few poems reflect realistic emotions of children. One could say childhood was not appreciated in itself; rather, it was conceived of as a gateway to adulthood. Needless to say, in stating this view I do not imply a judgment about the poetry of that time.

Our first children's poet, Hieronymus van Alphen, managed to express his moral lessons in a childlike manner, with examples that appeal to children, mostly presented in small, lively scenes; in simple language, he created smooth, rhythmic verses that don't wear off. Let me give one example (I will quote a working translation):[1]

> The little dog
> How grateful is my little dog
>   For bones and some bread!
> He wags his tail, goes round and round,
>   And jumps onto my lap.
>
> They give me meat and bread and wine,
>   And most delicious treats.
> So, looking at my little dog,
>   How grateful should I be!

The nineteenth century exhibits a growing attention to the emotions of children. The majority of children's poets went on in the moralistic tradition for a very long time, but in the work of their more innovative colleagues one can observe a growing attention to children's needs. In other words, the metaphorical discovery of the child, in Europe and in North America, was not accomplished by the end of the eighteenth century; it was a continuing process of gradually changing views on childhood.

At the turn of the twentieth century the typical qualities of the child were emphasized. Later on, one finds different views on this development. In the eyes of some, the emphasis on children's needs was a sign of children's liberation. Finally, childlike qualities were appreciated without reservations, and children had a literature at their own level. For others, the opposite is true: children were banished to an artificial garden of childhood, far from the adult world. Therefore, it is almost impossible to describe this development in objective terms. But one thing is certain: attention to children was at its height and it brought about a flowering in children's literature.

In the first decades of the century, children's poetry concentrated on the everyday experiences of children, their emotions, their play, and their leisure. Besides family life, the arrival of a baby brother or sister, and small children's distresses, playing was an important theme, and especially play that took the form of the imitation of adults, like dolls' tea parties, an infant reading the newspaper, and so on. One also finds many rhymes about pets and other animals.

Nursery rhymes also had a great influence; they were, of course, an important branch of children's poetry. A great number of small collections of these rhymes appeared, often in beautiful editions made by talented artists. The poets of that time were strongly inspired by the old rhymes: in some collections it is hardly possible to draw a line between the oral tradition and new rhymes. Other poets just took over elements from nursery rhymes: they use much alliteration and repetition, and restore genres like play rhymes, riddles, yarns, and topsy-turvies.

Another remarkable phenomenon was the great number of children's poems in books of poetry published for adults. With this rather paradoxical wording I refer to two types of poems: the first is addressed to children explicitly, and form and content of the text are consistent with this; the second is not addressed to a child, but form and content lead to the interpretation that the implied reader is a child. I have collected these poems for my anthology, and I have found almost 100 examples, of which more than fifty percent originate from between 1890 and 1940. Very often they are lullabies, but there are also comical narrative poems and philosophical poems expressing a child's thoughts about the rain, the stars, and so on.

An early example is a series of five "Children's verses," which the poet Albert Verwey published in 1889, when he was 25. In fact, there are just four children's poems, containing nonsensical stories. The series ends with a poetical poem, "A dialogue to conclude with," in which the implied reader is obviously an adult (again I quote a working translation):[2]

> *Critic*
> My friend, your verses are not good.
> > *Poet*
> They aren't? Well, I don't care a bit.
> I did not make them to do well,
> But just for the sake of playing.
>
> If you give a child a handkerchief,
> It will tie a head at one corner;
> Look, now the tails become a dress;
> And the child has a doll to play with.
>
> I say that's fine, though you would like
> A child to make other choices
> And use its hanky as a grown-up would,
> Just to blow its nose, as you think it should.
>
> My little words are my handkerchief,
> And all they can ever teach you
> Is how to make, with a knot and tails,
> A baby in long, long dresses.
>
> If you say: that's not what words are for,
> They are meant to blow your nose in;—
> I'll say: yes, you are grown-up,

So you really can't do without that.
But I'm a little child, and I can't
Be good without a bit of playing.
                    Critic
That may be so, but seriously,
Your verses are not as they should be.

This apology doesn't need a long explanation. The most interesting part is the fact the poet identifies completely with a child. He doesn't play for the sake of his audience, but for his own sake. The poet doesn't have to come down to the level of children, because that's his own level. The world of children is appreciated more than the world of adults.

The great appreciation of the children's world has another side. In realistic poems there is a strong emphasis on the happy side of life, often already indicated by titles like "Sunshine" or "Happy children." And although there are little distresses sometimes, the tears are kissed away very easily.

This changed after the war, most clearly in the work of Annie Schmidt, who is generally recognized as the most versatile and most talented children's book author of the Netherlands. From the beginning her books showed a merrily anarchistic world. In her poems one often finds a rebellion against decorum. The adult world was not avoided anymore; rather it was confronted in a playful way by frank, open-hearted children. In other poems, she showed a topsy-turvy world, in which children are sensible, and grown-up authorities act like unruly children; for instance, the eccentric mayor who paints ducks on the walls of the town hall, but overcomes this habit in the end: "now he paints tigers on the walls."[3]

Just like Albert Verwey, Schmidt dissociates herself from the world of serious, well-adapted adults. A clear example is "For a little girl," first published in 1950, which in spite of the title is a poem for adults.[4]

This is the land, where grown-ups live.
You don't have to go in: it's bad.
There are no fairies over there, but hormones,
and there are problems, problems all the time.

In this land all adventures are alike,
they're all about a woman and a man,
And behind every wall new walls appear,
never a unicorn or bogey man.

And everything has two sides over there
and all teddy-bears are dead.
And angry articles are printed in the papers,
written by angry men, just for their living.

A forest over there is just a lot of trees
and soldiers are no longer made of tin.
This is the land, where grown-ups live.
Don't be afraid: you don't have to go in.
                                        (my translation)

Although this is not an explicitly poetical poem, it may be read that way. It expresses an interesting view on the "garden of childhood": children are not being kept away from the adult world; they just don't have to enter. The real exiles are the adults, locked in their world of seriousness. The idealization of childhood has been replaced by a very critical view of the adult world. That's typical of the work of Annie Schmidt, who has said in more than one interview she "always stayed eight."[5] Her work shows that it is possible to keep the fantasy and the open-mindedness of an eight-year-old, at least until you're 88. In a few of her poems, Schmidt expressed children's emotions in a realistic setting, but mostly they are wrapped in a shining paper of fantasy. That's a general pattern in children's poetry, in which entertainment dominated until the end of the 1960s.

In the 1970s, children's poetry turned to realism. The most important poet who made his debut in this period is Willem Wilmink, who wrote many songs for children's television. In his opinion, an important function of children's literature is that it should comfort children. We can't keep children away from every single problem, because they live in the same world as their parents. Even if they don't have to cope with divorce or loss, children have problems of their own. The emotions and fears of children are among the main themes in his work. Like no other, he manages to immerse himself in the mind of a child who is a slow learner or a bedwetter. With a good mix of seriousness and humor, he manages to avoid even a hint of heaviness.

In the 1980s there was a new step away from the traditional, entertaining children's verse, when a new generation of poets explored new forms and new themes. Some of their poems are rather complex: because of metaphors, symbolism and mental leaps, the implied reader seems to be an educated adult. And sometimes the traditional child's perspective is replaced by childhood memories, either concealed or from an explicitly adult point of view. As a consequence the borders between children's and adults' poetry became less clear.

One could ask why these poems are published in poetry books for children. A possible explanation can be found in a poem by Wiel Kusters, "Catching salamanders," the first poem of a series of five in which the protagonist goes back to the landscape of his childhood years, together with his daughter.[6]

[1]
You and I, we were six.
I a bit earlier than you.
The years I am older than you
are standing in line in the playground

waiting for the second bell.
I hear the church bell striking nine.
The master jingles through the buzzer.
Quickly, I step beside the line.

The number of years that won't walk
in time into the classroom,
and want to stand beside the march,
is thirty, I hope.

Re-count with me. I'm thirty-six
and six you are in first grade.
Thirty years I have skipped school.
[. . .]

Your turn now. You're eleven,
So you also have to lose a bit.
Five years and a few months.
Together we will beat the rap.
                    (my translation)

At first sight, this is not a poetical poem at all. Still, I think it may be read that way in a metaphorical sense. In the first line we find the magic formula of make-believe: "we were six" doesn't refer to a moment in the past. It's the subjunctive mood that children, at least Dutch children, use when they start their play: "you were the father, and I were the mother." This formula is often followed by more detailed instructions for the players. Here it goes on in a similar way: to make sure they go back to the right moment, the protagonist has to do precise calculations, which fill the first poem. In the rest of the series, he and his daughter walk through a landscape that doesn't exist anymore, and catch salamanders that have become extinct.

The poem shows the power of fiction. It expresses the wish of the characters to go back in time, a wish most of us will recognize, and at the same time it is the magic means to fulfill that wish. What is impossible in reality can be done in a poem. These observations also have a poetical dimension. Just like Verwey's poem, Kuster's poem reveals the intentions of the series. Besides, it shows what poetry can do. In that respect, the magic formula in the first line has a key function. And the direct address of the child in this line seems to be an explanation why the poem was published in a book for children.

The paradox of this poem is that the intention to share the past is undermined by the form, which makes it less accessible to children. In my opinion, the personification of the years "standing in line in the playground," which is maintained for more than two stanzas, is too difficult for most children. I must add that the rest of the series, where the childhood years of the protagonist come to life again, is more accessible and appealing to children.

With this poem, the century of the child is completed, both in a literal and a figurative sense. Looking back we see a rather complex change in the views on childhood. The idea that adults and children should live in separate worlds disappeared: the garden of childhood doesn't exist anymore. The pendulum is on its way back after reaching the end of its swing. At the end of the eighteenth century, one tried to prepare children for the adult world as soon as possible; in the beginning of the twentieth century the ideal was to let them enjoy their childhood years by keeping them away from the adult world; and now we want to share more with children, let them participate in our world, without pushing them.

Still, in one respect the idea of a "garden of childhood" still exists. The childhood theme in Kusters' poem, and in the work of other poets, for instance, Ted van Lieshout, shows an appreciation of childhood as a crucial period in life. Throughout the century we find poets who want to preserve or regain something from their childhood years. It may be easier to preserve something than to regain something you have lost; and it is certainly easier to play with children than to share something from a past they have never known. But, although the latter may seem to fail sometimes, it provides fascinating poetry. And the views of Albert Verwey and Annie Schmidt have not disappeared completely. Even most of the poets who write complex poetry also produce verses that are very appealing to children. I predict that, in that respect, the century of the child will continue into the next millennium.

NOTES

1. Hieronymus van Alphen, *Proeve van kleine gedigten voor kinderen*. Utregt: Wed. Jan van Terveen en Zoon, 1778.

2. Albert Verwey, *Verzamelde gedichten*. Amsterdam: W. Versluys, 1889.

3. Annie M. G. Schmidt, *De lapjeskat*. Amsterdam: De Arbeiderspers, 1954.

4. Annie M. G. Schmidt, *Tot hier toe. Gedichten en liedjes voor toneel, radio en televisie; 1938–1985*. Amsterdam: Em. Querido, 1986.

5. For instance: Ischa Meijer, 'Gegroet, ik zit onder de olijf', In: *Haagse Post*, 18 January, 1975; Inge van den Blink, 'Als ik signeer komen er drie generaties voorbij'. In: *Utrechts Nieuwsblad*, 12 October 1990.

6. Wiel Kusters, *Salamanders vangen*. Amsterdam: Em. Querido, 1985.

REFERENCES

Alphen, Hieronymus van. *Proeve van kleine gedigten voor kinderen*. Utregt: Wed. Jan van Terveen en Zoon, 1778.

Blink, Inge van den. "Als ik signeer komen er drie generaties voorbij," *Utrechts Nieuwsblad*, 12 October 1990.

Kusters, Wiel, *Salamanders vangen*. Amsterdam: Em. Querido, 1985.

Meijer, Ischa. "Gegroet, ik zit onder de olijf," *Haagse Post*, 18 January, 1975.

Schmidt, Annie M. G. *De lapjeskat*. Amsterdam: De Arbeiderspers, 1954.

———. *Tot hier toe. Gedichten en liedjes voor toneel, radio en televisie; 1938–1985*. Amsterdam: Em. Querido, 1986.

Verwey, Albert. *Verzamelde gedichten*. Amsterdam: W. Versluys, 1889.

CHAPTER 4

Ending Only to Begin Again: The Child Reader and One Hundred Years of Sequel and Series Writing

Rose Lovell-Smith

A sequel can announce its relationship to an earlier book in many ways. In this discussion I regard as a sequel any book, and as a series any set of books, where the story of main characters is continued. Obviously, books more loosely linked are also often called a series, even in cases where the books could be rearranged in almost any order with minimal revision. But my assumption here is that, to the extent that a number of books continue a story and cannot easily be reordered in sequence, they constitute a series.

While some critical and historical attention has been paid to the commercial series for children,[1] and of course much has been published on individual series authors and their work, little has been done as yet to offer a theory of the genre for children. Lynette Felber, one of the few to write on the series for adults, claims that it is especially well suited to deal with "scope," "vast subjects," "bildung, social change, history, and time."[2] Such material seems more suited to adults than to children, although Peter Hunt, in *Approaching Arthur Ransome*, has also found *bildung* an important theme in one children's series.[3] An obvious assumption to make about children's love of sequels is that children as readers show more tolerance of repetition than adults do and that, like many adults, they prefer their reading to be predictable. But such comments hardly account for the hunger with which children will hunt down all the *Anne of Green Gables* books, all the *Swallows and Amazons* books, all the Narnia books. For many young readers today, to find another book by John Marsden is good, but to find another book in his *Tomorrow, When the War Began* series is more than good. Any attempt to theorize the series must try to account for this acute reading pleasure.[4]

One way to approach the subject is via a kind of writing that only a sequel or a book in a series can produce, writing that derives meaning from reference back to a prior text or texts. A striking instance where recall affects meaning occurs at the opening of the sixth book in Marsden's *Tomorrow* series, *The Night is for Hunting* (1998), where narrator Ellie describes herself and her father at work in the cattle yards on their farm while the local vet pregnancy-tests 150 heifers.[5] A reader new to the series would take this scene as simple fictional reality. The "familiar" reader, though, who has been following the series (which is about the invasion of Australia) would be torn between surmise that the war is already over, and a more solidly based suspicion that the scene is taking place only in Ellie's memory.

Series reading can position different readers very differently, most commonly by recalling events in a prior text, and I will refer to this technique as "recall writing." Adhering to the general view that a falling off in quality between first and subsequent books in a series is all too common, my initial expectations of recall writing were that it might often be frankly commercial, and at best a matter of getting necessary information over to new readers. But what I found was very different. Recall writing, while it has obvious practical functions, is also the source of some of the particular pleasures of sequel reading.

For an example of sheerly practical recall writing, turn to C. S. Lewis's *Prince Caspian: The Return to Narnia* (1951), which begins with a bland summary of the earlier book:

Once there were four children whose names were Peter, Susan, Edmund, and Lucy, and it has been told in another book how they had a remarkable adventure. They had opened the door of a magic wardrobe, and found themselves in a quite different world from ours, and in that different world they had become Kings and Queens in a country called Narnia.[6]

This account seems straightforward enough. But contrast this with an early sequence in the second *Anne* book, *Anne of Avonlea* (1909), where Marilla debates with sixteen-year-old Anne whether she should adopt the six-year-old orphan twins, Davy and Dora. The situation recalls Anne's own adoption by Marilla and Matthew Cuthbert in *Anne of Green Gables* (1908), a likeness that will hardly be missed by the familiar reader. As new readers have to be kept informed, though, Marilla reminds us of this anyway: "It wouldn't be so risky if they were even as old as you were when I took you,"[7] she tells Anne. But Marilla's act of memory provokes the familiar reader not just to remember, but to compare. In the already-mastered prior text, Anne was a strongly androgynous child, successfully substituting for a boy in the adoption arrangement, and manifesting many not-always-ideally-feminine qualities: talkativeness, imagination, bookishness, and academic ambition; love of dominating the scene and "performing" in public and in private. Her fiery temper, her daring feats, her tendency to humorous mishaps and accidents, her gift for leadership and ability to put dreams into practice and even make her friends help act them out are all qualities that might equally fit a boy hero. In fact, many of them had already fitted Tom Sawyer.

But now the twins Davy and Dora arrive to divide the figure of the androgynous child[8] on conventional gender lines. Mischievous talkative Davy resembles the boyish Anne, while Dora gets loaded with the domesticity and obedient feminity that Anne always also exhibited and that become increasingly important (to the detriment of Montgomery's narrative) as Anne grows up. Thus as Anne of Avonlea matures, an image of divided selfhood, boy/girl twins, replaces her in figuring the child and strongly represents to the reader the conventional gender differences that Anne—and girl readers—should accept as a part of growing up. No doubt it is regret for the passing away of the androgynous Anne that is registered in the autumnal scene, with "leafless" woods and "fields sere and brown," which opens the next chapter and is contrasted by Mrs. Rachel Lynde, another rememberer, with the blossoming springtime of Anne's first arrival.[9]

Clearly, Montgomery's writing gains much from recall. An extra dimension of reference backward suggests interpretive possibilities to the reader and also offers guidance forward into the current text. The richness of the passage hinges on remembering, both by characters and by readers. But perhaps the acts of memory required by recall might in themselves be important. For instance, might all this have something to do with growing up? In *Anne of Avonlea* it is clear that adopting two new children at Green Gables will require Anne to cease to be the child of the house. As Marilla sourly points out: "It will mean a good deal of extra work for you. I can't sew a stitch on account of my eyes, so you'll have to see to the making and mending of their clothes. And you don't like sewing."[10] But Anne, longing to mother and busily manipulating Marilla into seeing where her "duty" lies, is growing up-even to the point of "calmly" accepting sewing. Possibly the series is suited to that classic theme of juvenile fiction, growing up, precisely because it is by remembering that the child recognizes its new status, knowing that it is more adult than in the past. Reading a sequel might even exercise the child's memory in a way closely related to this act of self-recognition. Certainly, on the last page of *Anne of Avonlea*, Anne's passage into adulthood is, in fact, registered by an image equating growing up, and reading: "The page of girlhood had been turned, as by an unseen finger, and the page of womanhood was before her with all its charm and mystery."[11] Impending womanhood, and Montgomery's promise of another sequel, coincide.

The richness of recall writing may be similarly illustrated further later in the century in Arthur Ransome's *Swallowdale* (1931), a book I remembered from my own childhood as especially full of recall of its forerunner, *Swallows and Amazons* (1930).

There was the rock where Titty had lain flat on her stomach and seen the dipper bob at her and fly under water. There was the rock she had hidden behind when Nancy and Peggy had come ashore with a lantern in the dark and she had been alone on the island. John, looking at the little waves lapping on the rocks outside, was remembering how Nancy had first shown him how to use the marks.[12]

However, Ransome's recall has the puzzling quality that this writing is not always reminding us of important events in *Swallows and Amazons*. Nobody needs to remember Titty's encounter with the dipper, for instance, to understand the second book—and when John is noticed remembering them, the reader has already heard about the navigation marks by which Swallow is safely got into harbor.[13]

So what is Ransome's recall writing about? A good deal of it is about what much other Ransome writing is about—differentiating the characters. The quoted sentences are reminders, or for new readers, constructions, of Titty as the sensitive observer closely allied to nature, and of John as the captain and navigator. Similarly, the following "recall" sentences are about who Susan and Roger are:

"Wild Cat Island in sight!" cried Roger, the ship's boy, who was keeping a lookout, wedged in before the mast, and finding that a year had made a lot of difference and that there was much less room for him in there . . . than there used to be the year before when he was only seven.

Susan went to look for the old fireplace that she had built last year by the side of the stream, just where it joined the lake. Hardly a trace of it was left.[14]

Possibly Ransome's characters' pauses to remember, like Montgomery's, mainly serve to develop major thematic ideas around the underlying motif of growing up. Among the Walkers, Susan and John are pseudo-parents, Titty and Roger play their children. To adult readers, Ransome may spend a little too much time showing Captain John being steady and responsible in command, First Mate Susan being motherly and sensible and fretting about the food, Able Seaman Titty being imaginative and solitary, and the Ship's Boy, Roger, being childish and irresponsible. But there is no doubt that his sturdy realist techniques of characterization gained Ransome great freedom to mobilize and problematize the boundaries between male and female, child and adult. These boundary shifts occur most notably, but not only, in Nancy Blackett's notorious gender instability and her sudden elevations and demotions between pirate chief and polite niece. The Walkers also have sudden promotions to responsibility (one chapter is called "The Able Seaman in Command") and sudden demotions to childhood, as when John, having wrecked Swallow, reflects miserably, "What would mother say?"[15] While children "take command," and Captain Flint, as an adult, enters temporarily, and playfully, into the child world (ideas already explored in *Swallows and Amazons*) a more serious and instructive variation on this theme is introduced in *Swallowdale* by having the Amazons' terrifying Great Aunt demote Mrs Blackett and Captain Flint to mere children in relation to her.[16] As a good sequel should, *Swallowdale* extends the possibilities of its prior text.

C. S. Lewis's *Prince Caspian* is almost equally resourceful in rendering fuzzy the boundaries that normally separate the categories of "child" and "adult." Fantasy facilitates many imaginative games with maturing and aging, especially with regard to Peter and Edmund, once bearded monarchs of Narnia, and well aware of their previous experience as adults (surely an extraordinary state of mind, when one thinks of it), although now returned to Narnia as the mere schoolboys they remain in England. It is an ambiguous condition to be in vis-à-vis one's own age and supremely useful to Lewis. The gratifying fantasy of Edmund's tournament in Chapter 9 with the dwarf Trumpkin, himself ambiguously a miniature but an adult, and Peter's duel with King Miraz in Chapter 14, would not be possible without this version of time-slip, for thus boys are enabled plausibly to defeat hardened warriors at their own game.

But full enjoyment of Lewis's strategies is dependent, of course, on the reader's recall of the prior book. When in *Prince Caspian* the four children who first visited Narnia in *The Lion, the Witch and the Wardrobe* (1950) are magically transported to the center of a dense woodland—a traditional image of ignorance, of being "lost" or astray—they must orient themselves geographically and also mentally, learning that this is Narnia, that they are on an island, that the island is the site of their own sometime castle, Cair Paravel, and that perhaps a thousand years of Narnian time have passed since their earlier visit. The sequence has been read as "a nonetoo-skillful recapitulation for the benefit of readers who have not read the first volume of the series."[17] Yet the first paragraph of the book, as we have seen, is a remarkably obvious shot at that same goal. Besides, experience of recall writing in earlier sequels should by now warn us that the real effects of recall for the reader probably go well beyond the merely informative. And in fact, a closer examination of the sequence reveals that it is never far from Christian polemic.

Once again, characters pause to remember. This extract is from Chapter 2, where the children rediscover the magical gifts originally given to them by Father Christmas in *The Lion, the Witch, and the Wardrobe*. Susan's gift had been a bow and arrows.

[T]he bow was still in working order. Archery and swimming were the things Susan was good at. In a moment she had bent the bow and then she gave one little pluck to the string. It twanged: a chirruping twang that vibrated through the whole room. And that one small noise brought back the old days to the children's minds more than anything that had happened yet. All the battles and hunts and feasts came rushing into their heads together.[18]

The moment is an evocation (like Proust's) of the reawakening of memory by way of a repeated sensuous experience: it is also a quintessentially Narnian moment, opening a door into a powerful fantasy world that is simultaneously presented as remembering a past world. The effect is analogous to the encounter with Christianity that Lewis, himself busy "[bringing] back the old days to the children's minds," is engineering for the reader: Lewis's idea of faith is very much a matter of recovering a past (and better) state of things. Besides, the intelligence shown by Peter, Susan, Edmund, and Lucy as they experience their own mythical status and rediscover their own past is not only flattering to the familiar child reader, who sees it all before they do, but instructive (in Lewis's terms) as well.

If the legendary figures of the four Pevensies have ceased to be "real" to Narnians in the degenerate modern days of the Telmarines, the child reader, knowing from the previous book exactly how "real" the children are, might make the connection with the thousand-year-old myth of Christianity in England.[19] Recalling the previous book in the series is no workaday task, therefore, but rather presents a powerful introductory allegory or microcosmic prevision of what will happen in *Prince Caspian*: by recovering its own true history Narnia restores a proper relationship with Aslan. And growing up is as central in Narnia as it ever was in Ransome's Lake District or on Montgomery's Prince Edward Island, for Lewis's real subject, Christian faith, does indeed change as the child grows. That is why, in *Prince Caspian*, the children do not at first see Aslan but must pass a test of faith, journeying from the forests of ignorance toward the open mountaintop of knowledge, before being rewarded by his presence. And a final point may be made about Lewis's opening to *Prince Caspian*. As a matter of fact, the reader of *The Lion, the Witch, and the Wardrobe* saw very little of the royal and chivalrous lives of Peter, Susan, Edmund, and Lucy as adult kings and queens of Narnia and equally little of the "battles, hunts and feasts" recalled by Susan's twanging her bow-string. The act of memory here, therefore, hardly belongs to the reader at all, but is, rather, being constructed for the reader. It may be deduced that Lewis's is a "late," and very knowing, exploitation of the possibilities of the series.

My last example from 100 years of series writing for children, John Marsden's *Tomorrow* series, uses by now established conventions of recall in yet another way. This is not because ordinary recall writing is absent from the series: Ellie, the high-school student turned guerilla warrior, often notes changes in herself and companions, and efficiently "remembers" key events of earlier books while setting the narrative ball rolling in each sequel. But there is little emotional weight behind these memories and they evoke only ideas that all readers would already understand to be central to the series—the resilience and resourcefulness teenagers can produce under pressure, and the pain, losses, and distortions of personality inevitable when war enforces early maturity. Yet Marsden's series does not lack emotional weight. Its underlying concerns are better signaled where he shifts the central functions of memory in the series out of fictional time, back to the days before the invasion, a technique I have already mentioned as occurring, with a kind of *trompe l'oeil* effect, in the opening of book six, *The Night is for Hunting*. Ellie's first significant act of memory can therefore occur quite early after the invasion and before the first book, *Tomorrow, When the War Began*, is halfway through:

Passing Mrs Alexander's I stopped for a moment to sniff at the big old roses that grew along her front fence. I loved her garden. She had a party there every year, a Christmas party. It had only been a few weeks since I'd been standing under one of her apple trees, holding a plate of biscuits and telling Steve I didn't want to go with him any more.[20]

Christmas in summer is one of the images by which Australians identify their Australianness. Many more details of day-to-day Australian country life will appear in characters' memories as the series progresses. In *The Dead of the Night* Ellie and companions even take turns at a favorite game called "I remember,"[21] while in *The Night is for Hunting* Marsden has Ellie reflect openly on the role of memory in creating identity.[22] While many young readers doubtless follow this series for its exciting (and flattering) tally of successful acts of war by teenagers, I am inclined to the opinion that the underlying solidity of the series lies in its retrospective vision of a beloved Australia. Strange as this may sound, the impact is comparable to that of Laura Ingalls Wilder's more distinguished vision of a vanished America. Both authors turn their readers' eyes back onto the life they currently enjoy, and teach new ways of assessing its value. The cumulative effect of reading on, and remembering back both into and out of the fictional world, is essential to both.

Sequels and series, as well as having an obvious appeal to the learning reader who seeks repeated and predictable pleasures, also offer much in the collaboration of more adventurous young readers and a creative author. A sequel necessarily provokes acts of memory of what has already happened and thus reproduces through reading the experience of remembering oneself as more childish. It is a form especially well-adjusted to exploring a major theme of children's writing, the passage from childhood to adulthood.

NOTES

1. See, for example, Faye Riter Kensinger, *Children of the Series and How They Grew or A Century of Heroines and Heroes, Romantic, Comic, Moral*. Bowling Green, OH: Bowling Green State U Popular P, 1987; Sherrie A. Inness, ed., *Nancy Drew and Company: Company: Culture, Gender, and Girls' Series*. Bowling Green, OH: Bowling Green State U Popular P, 1996.

2. Lynette Felber, *Gender and Genre in Novels without End: The British Roman-Fleuve*. Gainesville, FL: UP of Florida, 1995, p. 12.

3. See Peter Hunt, *Approaching Arthur Ransome*. London: Jonathan Cape, 1992, p. 164.

4. In the 19 August 1999 *London Review of Books*, Marjorie Garber uses the term "sequelmania." Her review (pp. 3, 5–6) is an excellent introduction to the whole subject of sequels for adults. The book under review is *Part Two: Reflections on the Sequel*, eds. Paul Budra and Betty Schellenberg (Toronto).

5. Sydney: Pan Macmillan, 1999, pp. 1–6.

6. C. S. Lewis, *Prince Capsian: The Return to Narnia*. London: Collins/Lions, 1980, p. 11. Later editions have inserted the name of the forerunner, *The Lion, the Witch, and the Wardrobe*, into the first sentence.

7. L. M. Montgomery, *Anne of Avonlea*. North Ryde, NSW, Australia: Angus & Robertson, 1987, p. 54.

8. Louisa May Alcott's twins Daisy and Demi are clear antecedents of Montgomery's twins. In Alcott's series, the androgynous child is represented by Jo.

9. Montgomery, *Anne of Avonlea*, p. 55.

10. Ibid., p. 55.

11. Ibid., p. 252.

12. Arthur Ransome, *Swallowdale*. London: Random House, 1993, p. 21.

13. Ibid., p. 10, p. 15.

14. Ibid., p. 1, p. 38.

15. Ibid., p. 74.

16. Peter Hunt correctly notes the importance of the incident where the Aunt actually makes Mrs, Blackett cry. See *Approaching Arthur Ransome*, p. 103.

17. Dennis B. Quinn, "The Narnia Books of C. S. Lewis: Fantastic or Wonderful?" *Children's Literature* 12 (1984): 113.

18. C. S. Lewis, *Prince Caspian*, p. 30.

19. Peter J. Schakel is one reader who has made this connection. See his *Reading with the Heart: The Way into Narnia*. Grand Rapids, MI: William B. Eerdmans, 1979, p. 35.

20. John Marsden, *Tomorrow, When the War Began*. Sydney: Pan Macmillan, 1995, p. 77.

21. John Marsden, *The Dead of the Night*. Sydney: Pan Macmillan, 1996, p. 74.

22. See John Marsden, *The Night is for Hunting*. Sydney: Pan Macmillian, 1998, p. 210: "It scared me to realise how shadowy our memories can be. . . . Now I wondered if the opposite to identity was war."

REFERENCES

Alcott, Louisa May. *Little Women*. Oxford: Oxford UP, 1994.

Felber, Lynette. *Gender and Genre in Novels without End: The British Roman-Fleuve*. Gainesville: UP of Florida, 1995.

Garber, Marjorie. [Review of the book *Part Two: Reflections on the Sequel*]. *London Review of Books*, 19 August, 1999: 3, 5–6.

Hunt, Peter. *Approaching Arthur Ransome*. London: Jonathan Cape, 1992.

Innes, Sherrie A., ed. *Nancy Drew and Company: Culture, Gender, and Girls' Series*. Bowling Green, OH: Bowling Green State U Popular P, 1996.

Kensinger, Faye Riter. *Children of the Series and How They Grew or A Century of Heroines and Heroes, Romantic, Comic, Moral*. Bowling Green, OH: Bowling Green State U Popular P, 1987.

Lewis, C. S. *The Lion, the Witch, and the Wardrobe*. London: Collins, 1980.

———. *Prince Caspian: The Return to Narnia*. London: Collins, 1980.

Marsden, John. *Tomorrow, When the War Began*. Sydney: Pan Macmillan, 1995.

———. *The Dead of the Night*. Sydney: Pan Macmillan, 1996.

———. *The Night is for Hunting*. Sydney: Pan Macmillan, 1998.

Montgomery, Lucy Maud. *Anne of Green Gables*. North Ryde, NSW, Australia: Angus & Robertson, 1987.

———. *Anne of Avonlea*. North Ryde, NSW, Australia: Angus & Robertson, 1987.

Quinn, Dennis. "The Narnia Books of C. S. Lewis: Fantastic or Wonderful?" *Children's Literature* 12 (1984): 105–121.

Ransome, Arthur. *Swallows and Amazons*. London: Random House, 1993.

———. *Swallowdale*. London: Random House, 1993.

Schakel, Peter J. *Reading with Heart: The Way into Narnia*. Grand Rapids, MI: William B. Eerdmans, 1979.

CHAPTER 5

Voices of Protest: One Hundred Years of German Pacifist Children's Literature

Susan Tebbutt

The twentieth century has unfortunately not been characterized by its lack of wars. Here I look at 100 years of German-language pacifist children's literature that challenges the dominant ideology that argues for the necessity of war.

SCANNING A CENTURY: A SISYPHEAN TASK

How easy is it to scan a century of children's literature? It is a Sisyphean task. First comes the defining of children's literature: I include works written specifically for a young audience and works read by young people, but also works written *by* young people, the latter remaining a small but significant proportion of the whole. No sooner have I rolled that stone to the summit than it slips down again. I still need to define *German* children's literature. Rather than look at all works available in German, including translations from other languages, I focus specifically on works written originally in German, which may of course include works by non-German nationals. The stone slips down again. What is *pacifist* literature? I define it as work that promotes or contains a pacifist message, which may depict war in general, specific wars and their reverberations, or the absence of war and conflict.

At the end of the twentieth century the English-speaking world remains largely oblivious to the width and depth of the tradition of German pacifist books for young people, despite the fact that many of these works have been successful internationally. Booksellers, librarians, teachers, and literary historians have constructed lists of works that include the themes of war and peace, but these do not take into account the techniques employed or the ideology of the text.

Using Stephens's concept of the interrogative text as outlined in *Language and Ideology in Children's Fiction* (1992), I examine the heterogeneity of German pacifist children's literature and construct a taxonomy that might act as a framework for the study of pacifist literature from other countries.

THE PALETTE OF PACIFIST PROTEST WRITING

Arguably the first work of German pacifist children's literature is *Marthas Tagebuch* (1897), adapted by Hedwig Pötting from Bertha von Suttner's seminal pacifist work *Lay down your arms!* (1897). Unlike many other pacifist diaries published in the twentieth century, the most notable being *The Diary of Anne Frank* (1949) written by a German in exile, but actually first published in Dutch, this work is entirely fictional, since neither Suttner nor her fellow aristocrat Pötting had any firsthand experience of war. By modern standards even the abridged version (reduced to about a third of the length of the original) is long and linguistically and stylistically complex.

The tale is melodramatic, the moral transparent, the role of the female narrator initially that of passive supporter of the husband who does his duty for his country. The scene in which she takes her leave of her husband is indicative of the purple prose:

"Arno, Arno," I cried, holding him tight: "Stay, stay!" I knew that I was demanding the impossible, yet I still cried stubbornly, "Stay, stay!"

"Lieutenant", a voice came from outside, "time is already up." One more kiss—the last—and he dashed out.[1]

Shortly afterward she hears that he has fallen in battle. Her diary entry closes with the words, "I fell in a faint to the ground."[2] The work ends with melancholy thoughts of the joint future that was not to be, the images of the happy ageing couple. *Marthas Tagebuch* is a melodramatic yet highly interrogative work.

The notion of glorious warfare is similarly challenged in Arthur Müller's one-act play *Der Schulinspektor* (*The School Inspector*, 1911), subtitled "Ein Pacifistisches Lehrerstück" ("A pacifist didactic play"). Müller was active in Vienna in the peace movement and wrote a number of didactic works about the importance of peace, including a manual of advice for teachers and educators. The play, written in rhyming couplets, has an all-male cast, the school's inspector, the teacher and four pupils; the setting is the present in a village on the border between Austria and Prussia. There is a binary division between the enlightened pacifist teacher and the traditional inspector, who is horrified at the teacher's rejection of the concept of a glorious death for the fatherland, and fears pupils may be led astray. As in *Marthas Tagebuch* the ideological message is crystal clear. The teacher is the mouthpiece of the author. The pupils are effectively cardboard figures who play a very passive role. One child is actually told: "Der Peter soll denken, was er will./Während der Stunde sei er hübsch still!" ("Peter may indeed think what he will./During the lesson please to be still!").[3]

The teacher's lesson on the seven-year Prussian war is interrupted by a "small-scale war" in the classroom, but in true "time-out" fashion, the play ends with the boys declaring a truce, echoing Suttner's cry to the cause, "Die Waffen nieder!" ("Lay down your arms!").[4]

It might be expected that there would be many pacifist works for children written in the 1920s; the horrors of the First World War had been anticipated in teacher Wilhelm Lamszus's visionary antiwar novel *Das Menschenschlachthaus* (*The human abbatoir*, 1912) and its sequel *Das Irrenhaus* (*The madhouse*, 1919), but it was not until over a decade had passed that World War I itself was thematized.

Instead, a more oblique approach characterizes the writing of the 1920s, most notably in *Die Forschungsreise des Afrikaners Lukanga Mukara ins innerste Deutschland* (*The Journey of Exploration of the African Lukanga Mukara into the Innermost Depths of Germany*, 1921), by Hans Paasche, a committed pacifist, and also a campaigner against alcohol abuse and for vegetarianism and animal rights. In this satirical pseudo-ethnographic travelogue in the form of nine fictitious letters back to King Ruoma of Kitara in Africa, the narrator reverses the colonialist travel writer's revelations about the idiosyncracies of distant parts and the bizarreness of the natives, focusing instead on Paasche's native country, Germany, supposedly through the eyes of the naive outsider, the African. The illogicality and futility of war are highlighted. The narrator links war with commercial interests, writing,

That was why a war came and took all their ships away, killed the people, prevented clothes from being made and reduced the corn crop. Do you now imagine that that brought them to their senses? Not at all! What do they do? They count and write down how many ships sink, how long the war lasts, how many people are killed, how many go mad with fear, how many are wounded, how many of the latter for their part believed in one God and how many in another. They enter this into beautiful books.[5]

The criticism of *Zahlenwahnsinn* (obsession with statistics) extends over several pages. In the seventh letter the narrator looks at the lack of repentance shown by rich people who believe that: "nur sie hätten 'Ehre' und dürften deshalb andere hauen und töten" ("only they had 'honor' and were therefore allowed to clobber and maim others").[6] Paasche skilfully deconstructs myths about other nations, building up a strong case for peaceful coexistence in his many-layered pseudo-travelogue.

In the 1930s the pacifist *novel* gains momentum. Rudolf Frank (1886–1979) served briefly in an artillery regiment on the Eastern Front. In 1936 he emigrated to Vienna and in 1938 the family fled to Switzerland. Set in World War I, *Der Schädel des Negerhäuptlings Makaua* (*The Skull of the Negro Chieftain Makaua*), later reprinted under the title *Der Junge, der seinen Geburtstag vergaß* (*The boy who forgot his birthday*) with the subtitle "Ein Roman gegen den Krieg" ("A novel against war" 1931) has as its central protagonist Jan Kubitzki, a fourteen-year-old Polish boy who refuses to be hailed as a hero. Frank ironises the way in which warmongers depersonalise the language of war to make the act of murder seem less despicable, and consigns the soldiers to the role of antiheroes rather than heroes. The work was banned by the Nazis in 1933 and that same year was consigned to the many works to be publicly burnt on May 10 alongside works by writers as diverse as Thomas Mann, Erich Maria Remarque and Erich Kästner. This work gives a vivid picture of life at the front. Jan is trying to sleep:

There was a new moon and hardly a star in the sky, but on the ground lights were moving round; a fire was burning, there were shadows all around, and endless lines of soldiers were moving along the main roads in grey collars, and wide heavy wheels were creaking in their axles as they turned round.

Dull shadows and painful sounds broke into his dreams' grey coats, grey faces, grey guns, horses were panting, people were snoring. Suddenly someone shouted: "The war is over!"

But he had only dreamed that.[7]

In the chapter titled "Schrapnelwölkchen" ("Little clouds of shrapnel") the scene of the dead and the trenches is characterized by somber tones:

There were people lying there, brown and grey like the rubble and the sods of earth, they lay curled up or stretched out in dust, blood and dirt. Human faces with gaping holes in them. Human rumps sticking out of the ground like tree trunks, human arms and legs were lying like chopped off branches, human hands and fingers were growing out of the earth like plants. . . . That was the seed which had come up from the grenades from their cannons. The whole trench was full of it. It was the antechamber of death which they were looking into.[8]

The antiwar novel is the key genre of the century, with some 200 works in total relating to World War II, and a small number about a war in another country, yet just as after World War I there was a reluctance to thematize its horrors, so the first two decades after the end of World War II were marked by an almost complete absence of works about the atrocities of the Nazi period.

What pacifist work was written in the 1940s? Among the rubble and chaos Erich Kästner (author of *Emil und die Dekektive* [*Emil and the Detectives*]), whose work had been banned by Hitler, was asked by Jella Lepman, founder of the International Children's Library, to write a work to promote international peace. The anthropomorphic parable picture book *Die Konferenz der Tiere* (*The conference of the animals*, 1949) is highly satirical in tone. The central characters, a lion, an elephant, and a giraffe, watch bemused as adults try to bring about peace. The narrator's words have a chilling topicality: "four years after the war the number of refugees has risen to 14 million, predominantly old people and children, and the number is increasing as the months go by."[9] The carnivalesque images of an extremely wide range of creatures, each playfully described and depicted, contrast with the somber images of humans, who are mocked when the animals decide to send in moths to destroy all the uniforms, with the field marshall finally left wearing only his saber.

Whereas *Die Konferenz der Tiere* is subversive, interrogative, carnivalesque, and transgressive in its pacifist message, Austrian author Annelies Umlauf-Lamatsch's *Heimatroman* titled *Hand in Hand ins Friedensland* (*Hand in hand to the land of peace*, 1951) is excessively didactic, and, lest the message is missed, prefaced by a short address from the President of Austria, saying, "This book tells you about war, so that learn to hate it and love peace"; "You really are the hope of the world, you, our young people."[10]

This *Heimatroman* is characterized by its clearly recognizable regional setting, the use of dialect, and a cloying tale. The school group from Vienna are spending the holidays in the Tyrolean Alps, where they learn about how many war-wounded Austria has, about how many mothers mourn their dead sons, and suggest singing cheerful folk songs to the injured survivors. The children decide to give away their guns and tin soldiers and try to stop the production of any war toys, and organize an exhibition on peace and invite all the other classes to see it. All is running smoothly when a fight breaks out within the class (echoes here of Müller's play) and the group is shamed into rethinking how *they* see peace, and they produce a radio program in which they appeal for world peace. The work ends with the words: "We, Austria's children, call on you, the children of the world. Let us close a ring round the earth, forged from the glowing wish; 'Hand in hand to the land of peace'."[11] The characterization is unconvincing, the speeches ring false, the author's attempt to put across a message is too transparent, too heavily preaching in tone.

In contrast, Austrian writer Karl Bruckner's *Sadako will leben* (*Sadako wants to live*, 1961), about the deployment of nuclear bombs over Hiroshima, is highly interrogative and challenging. It won the Austrian Prize for Children's Literature, and the Prize of the City of Vienna, and is postmodern in its range of different narrative perspectives. Bruckner weaves together the reports of the Japanese defence observation post, the tale of an old boat builder, and descriptions of a group of soldiers marching along the side of freshwater lake, a ten-year-old boy on stilts with his four-year-old sister, an American pilot, and a student who had just started working.

Halfway through the novel, the bomb drops: "With the combined force of a hundred hurricanes a wave of air pressure raged towards the dock building. It shook concrete walls, bent metal supports, and outside the ship-building yards swept up iron plates, weighing tons, as if they were made of paper. Splinters of glass, pieces of broken wood, sections of metal hissed like bullets through all the rooms of the ship-building complex."[12] Vivid though this description is, the reader feels the main impact of the bomb in the way it affects each of the people whose lives have been made familiar to the reader in the first part of the novel. Ten years after the explosion, Sadako is suffering from cancer.

Bruckner goes out of his way to detach the responsibility for nuclear bombs from one particular nation and to criticize the invention itself:

The bomb was not just invented by American scientists—people know that now. The English, Italians, Germans, French and academics from other countries also helped. And haven't you heard that the Russians have also been producing nuclear bombs for some time now? And why do you think they are doing that? To be able to boast about it? No. When it comes to a new war, they will drop their nuclear bombs on cities just the same.[13]

Although the threat of a nuclear bomb continues to hang over the world, there have been remarkably few German-language works of children's literature about nuclear war scenarios, notable exceptions being Gudrun Pausewang's awardwinning apocalyptic vision, *Die letzten Kinder von Schewenborn* (*The last children of Schewenborn*, 1983).

Not until the 1970s did large numbers of works about World War II begin to emerge, particularly works with an autobiographical basis. Christine Nöstlinger, arguably Austria's leading writer of contemporary socially critical children's fiction, published *Maikäfer flieg!* (*Fly, ladbird, fly!*), in 1973. For some critics this book does not belong to the category of transgressive works because it stops short of the cataclysmic and does not raise questions of the complicity of the Austrians or Germans in the crimes of the Nazi period, yet I would argue that the novel is a key work in the children's literature pacifist canon of the twentieth century, since the underlying message concerns the friendship between nations, and the breaking down of barriers between traditional foes. Also, the young anti-heroine, the narrator, establishes friendship with a Russian.

Linked to the growth in autobiographical works and authentic documents about World War II during this period is the publication in 1988 of Leo Meter's *Briefe an Barbara* (*Letters to Barbara*) written from the Russian front to his daughter, a work that is literally literature *for* a young person.

Meter, who worked in the 1930s for the left-wing Berlin youth theater *Junge Volksbühne* as a set designer and who also produced and disseminated antifascist posters for the socialist youth movement, was arrested by the Nazis in 1933 and then forbidden to work. He fled to Amsterdam, but once the Nazis occupied Holland he was forced to separate from his wife because she was Jewish. In 1942 he was arrested by the Gestapo and conscripted and sent to the Ukraine; he died in 1944 in Poland.

The letters seem at first to contain little about war, rarely mentioning where he is or what he is encountering; he only once depicts himself in his soldier's uniform. He tells instead of the past, of everyday civilian life and of pleasures he hopes to share with his daughter on his return to Amsterdam, and of his worries that she may forget him. There is no celebration of war, no pride in being a soldier. The futility and unjustifiability of war are highlighted, with moments of peace, of communion with nature, as in a letter dated 4 July 1943: "A few days ago I went by train to other soldiers who live in a wooden house in the middle of the forest. There I picked strawberries, which are growing wild there at the edge of the forest. There is also a large bird living with the soldiers, who is called Jacob. Jacob is very wild and bites and scratches if you try to to stroke him."[14] He writes of the relationship between himself and his daughter and hopes that they will remain close.

The conditional perfect is used frequently to express what might have happened but for war, as in the first letter, written on April 4, 1943: "I would have liked to send you a large cake with candles and toys"; or the conditional, "If the journey to you did not take so long I would of course bring you lots and lots of animals and flowers" (4 July 1943) or the future tense, "When we are together in Cologne I will be able to tell you a whole load of stories" (9 July 1943). These letters are a poignant eulogy to peace, a plea for a world in which fathers need not be separated from daughters.

SEEN BUT NOT HEARD? YOUNG VOICES OF PROTEST

Finally, I move from the 1980s into the last decade of the twentieth century. One of the key developments in German socially critical children's literature is the growing importance of anthologies of writing by young people. Such collections may result from a competition organized around a particular theme, may be the work of a group, a class, a school or a religious or ethnic group. They tend to contain very short prose texts, poems, and imaginative writing, the products of the sound-byte generation, and offer insights into the real preoccupations of young people, young people empowered rather than patronized.

Gewalt: Kinder schreiben über Erlebnisse, Ängste, Auswege (*Violence: Children write about experiences, fears, solutions*, 1993), edited by Regina Rusch, is an anthology of selected entries to a competition held in 1992 on the theme of violence, including writing about war. Rusch aims to "open the minds of the politicians to what the children have to say,"[15] whether it is 12-year-old Björn Mecke Breitenberg from Duderstadt in Lower Saxony, who writes, "The worst form of violence is war. . . . You don't always have to use violence. There are other ways,"[16] or twelve-year-old Antonio Avramides from Wilhelmshaven who writes:

There is no stopping the violence in the Balkans. In the holidays I went to Croatia—and what did I see, experience and hear there. It's madness, or should I say, a nightmare. . . . Houses, schools, churches, Kindergarten, hospitals have been razed to the ground. People are wounded, particularly old people and children, have no legs or hands. They are wandering round under the open sky, are hungry and weak. Their eyes watch me, but their gaze is silent and without any reactions. Animals still lie in the ditches and next to the road, dead and decayed. On your travels you see UN vehicles and soldiers from time to time. But it seems as if these images do not particularly disturb them. I often asked myself: Who can commit such atrocities? Certainly not a normal human being. Only barbarians or monsters can. . . . The world has to put a halt to war! The violence must stop.[17]

CONCLUSION

It is possible to distinguish a number of genres of pacifist writing, from the diary, the drama, travel writing, the antiwar novel, the picture book, the *Heimatroman*, the antinuclear novel, autobiographically based writing, letters, to writing by young people. By far the largest category numerically is the pacifist novel about World War II, whether it be about fighting at the front, evacuation, life in exile, or experiences of the immediate postwar years.

It is indeed a Sisyphean task to scan the German pacifist children's literature of a whole century. In the process the richness and diversity of the palette of colors and techniques used emerges, as do changing writer-reader relationships. In the writing of the 1990s young people themselves are empowered to protest against war. Let us hope that in the twenty-first century people will listen to these voices and that the next century will make pacifist protests redundant.

NOTES

1. Hedwig Pötting, *Marthas Tagebuch*, p. 17. All the translations are my own.
2. Ibid., p. 25.
3. Arthur Müller, *Der Schulinspektor*, p. 28.
4. Ibid., p. 35.
5. Hans Paasche, *Die Forschungsreise des Afrikaners Lukanga Mukara ins Innerste Deutschland*. Bremen: Donat, 1921, pp. 62-63.

6. Ibid., p. 66

7. Rudolf Frank, *Der Junge, der seinen Geburtstag vergaß* (1st published as *Der Schädel des Negerhäuptlings Makaua*, 1931). Ravensburg: Otto Maier, p. 48.

8. Ibid., p. 75

9. Erich Kästner, *Die Konferenz der Tiere*, pp. 9–10.

10. Annelies Umlauf-Lamatsch, *Hand in Hand ins Friedensland*. Vienna: Verlag des Österreichischen Gewerkschaftsbundes, 1951, pp. 3, 5.

11. Ibid., p. 126.

12. Karl Bruckner, *Sadako will leben*. Vienna and Munich: Jugend und Volk, 1961, p. 106.

13. Ibid., p. 167.

14. Leo Meter, *Briefe an Barbara*. Cologne and Zurich: Gertraud Middelhauve, 1988, no page numbers.

15. Regina Rusch, ed., *Gewalt*. Munich: Deutscher Taschenbuch Verlag, 1993, p. 14.

16. Ibid., p. 107.

17. Ibid., pp. 127–128.

REFERENCES

Primary Literature

Bruckner, Karl. *Sadako will leben*. Vienna and Munich: Jugend und Volk, 1961.

Frank, Rudolf. *Der Junge, der seinen Geburtstag vergaß* (1st published as *Der Schädel des Negerhäuptlings Makaua*, 1931). Ravensburg: Otto Maier, 1979.

Kästner, Erich. *Die Konferenz der Tiere*, 1949.

Meter, Leo. *Briefe an Barbara*. Cologne and Zurich: Gertraud Middelhauve, 1988.

Müller, Arthur. *Der Herr Schulinspektor: Pacifistisches Lehrerstück*. 1911.

Nöstlinger, Christine. *Maikäfer flieg!* Weinheim and Basel: Beltz, 1973.

Paasche, Hans. *Die Forschungsreise des Afrikaners Lukanga Mukara ins Innerste Deutschland*. Bremen: Donat, 1921.

Pötting, Hedwig. *Marthas Tagebuch* (Adapted from Bertha von Suttner's *Die Waffen nieder!*), 1897.

Rusch, Regina. *Gewalt: Kinder schreiben über Erlebnisse, Ängste, Auswege*. Munich: Deutscher Taschenbuch Verlag, 1993.

Umlauf-Lamatsch, Annelies. *Hand in Hand ins Friedensland*. Vienna: Verlag des Österreichischen Gewerkschaftsbundes, 1951.

Secondary Literature

Doderer, Klaus. *Zwischen Trümmern und Wohlstand: Literatur der Jugend 1945–1960*. Weinheim and Basel: Beltz, 1988.

Ewers, Hans-Heino, and Ernst Seibert, eds. *Geschichte der österreichischen Kinder- und Jugendliteratur von 1800 bis zur Gegenwart*. Vienna: Buchkultur, 1997.

Freund, Winfried. *Das zeitgenössiche Kinder- und Jugendbuch*. Paderborn, Munich, Vienna, and Zurich: Schöningh, 1982.

Kaminski, Winfrid. *Jugendliteratur und Revolte*. Frankfurt am Main, 1982.

Liebs, Elke. "Das Tabu der Erinnerung: Krieg und Holocaust in der Kinder- und Jugendliteratur." In *Zwischen Bullerbü und Schewenborn*. Ed. Renate Raecke and Ute D. Baumann. Munich: Arbeitskreis für Jugendliteratur e.V., 1995, pp.187–195.

Scharioth, Barbara. *Frieden, Freiheit, Toleranz: Bücher gegen den Krieg*. Munich: Internationale Jugendbibliothek, 1994.

Spaude-Schulze, Edelgard. *Macht das Maul auf!: Kinder- und Jugendliteratur gegen den Krieg in der Weimarer Republik*. Würzburg: Königshausen & Neumann, 1990.

Stephens, John. *Language and Ideology in Children's Fiction*. London and New York: Longman, 1992.

Stier, K., and Ute D. Baumann. *Das Bilderbuch: Eine Auswahl empfehlenswerter Bilderbücher*. Munich: Arbeitskreis für Jugendliteratur e.V., 10th revised ed., 1996.

Tebbutt, Susan. *Gudrun Pausewang in context*, Frankfurt am Main, Berlin, Berne, New York, Paris, and Vienna: Lang, 1994.

———. "New directions in socially critical German Jugendliteratur 1970–1995." In *New Comparison* (Autumn 1995): 106–117.

Whitehead, Winifred. *Old Lies Revisited: Young Readers and the Literature of War and Violence*. London: Pluto, 1991.

Wild, Reiner. *Geschichte der deutschen Kinder- und Jugendliteratur*. Stuttgart: Metzler, 1990.

CHAPTER 6

Walking into the Sky: Englishness, Heroism, and Cultural Identity: A Nineteenth- and Twentieth-Century Perspective

Jean Webb

This chapter demonstrates a pattern of changing attitudes toward Englishness and heroism in nineteenth- and twentieth-century English children's literature, from the seemingly confident and certain position of an imperialist power in the mid-nineteenth century to the uncertainties of a multicultural postmodern society as we stand at the millennium. I construct my argument by briefly noting positions presented in R. M. Ballantyne's two novels *The Coral Island* and *Ungava* both published in 1857, Rudyard Kipling's *Kim* (1901), and Frances Hodgson Burnett's *The Secret Garden* (1911); I'll then turn to Philip Pullman's contemporary work, *Northern Lights* (published as *The Golden Compass* in North America in 1995), which will form the central focus of the discussion.

The construction of "Englishness" in nineteenth-century English children's literature is directly related to Imperialism and the qualities of manliness required to produce both a conquering force, and a body coherent with the requirements of England, the center of the Empire. From the mid-nineteenth century, with the work of Thomas Hughes in *Tom Brown's Schooldays* (1857) and Charles Kingsley in *The Water-Babies* (1863), and later in the Colonial tales of Henty, the requirements of Imperialism militated against individuality, doubt, and a humanist rationalization of the role of the ruler. The certainties of these works were based on an unquestioning nineteenth-century belief that could look to God and the King as absolute centers of truth. However, there were oppositional voices present, surprising undercurrents, for example, in the writing of R. M. Ballantyne, who is usually read as an emblem of colonialism in novels such as *The*

Coral Island (1858). However, in *Ungava* (1858), which was his last book
based on his real experiences before writing his entirely fictional island
adventure, *The Coral Island*, Ballantyne raises doubts about the unques-
tioned position of the conqueror. The text demonstrates an awareness of
the transience of the invading culture despite the will of the colonizer.
Ungava draws on Ballantyne's experiences when he worked for a fur trad-
ing company in northern Canada, and was required to set up a colonizing
outpost. In contrast to *The Coral Island*, where the three shipwrecked lads
successfully take possession of the island in the name of the king, *Ungava*
is a tale of colonial defeat. The adventure tale of *Ungava* leads toward the
expected white domination of all, but this stereotypical outcome is finally
frustrated by the overwhelming task of conquering the inhospitable
landscape.

Ballantyne was not the only writer usually regarded as a confident be-
liever in the imperialist sense of right to express doubts and uncertainties.
Rudyard Kipling also critiqued the English colonial position in *Kim* (1901).
The boy protagonist, Kim, is the child of empire, brought up in India.
Born of an Irish father and working-class mother, he "spoke the vernacular
by preference, and his mother tongue in a clipped uncertain sing-song."[1]
Being both Irish, and in essence "native" in understanding, Kim is already
a displaced subject. He straddles both worlds as he symbolically sits
astride the great gun having unseated a native boy at the opening of the
novel. The task that Kipling sets for Kim is to negotiate the truths of
colonial power and the subject people, that is, the oppositions of imperialism versus Asiatic spirituality. The two narratives of Kim's engagement
with the Great Game of colonial rule, and the spiritual journey with the
lama, intertwine to explore these oppositions. Kim has been chosen to
play a part in the imperial Game, while he has chosen to accompany the
lama as his helper on the journey. The clash between the politics of Imperialism and the spirituality of self-knowledge reaches a climax when
Kim questions his own identity. The lama has fallen sick, and Kim's part
in the Game is temporarily over. Kim is in danger of sliding down, and
disappearing into the crack between two philosophically opposite cultures; he is in grave danger of losing his sense of self.

He tried to think of the lama,—to wonder why he had tumbled into a brook,—
but the bigness of the world, seen between the forecourt gates, swept linked
thought aside.[2]

Kim cannot project himself into the world beyond the gates because he
has lost his place in the imperial system. It now seems too vast and un-
structured to contemplate. Neither is he capable, as yet, of existing without his spiritual mentor, the lama. Kim is in danger of being a lost soul
between universes. The chaos and cacophony of the spheres assaults his
senses and drowns out his capacity to think:

The breezes fanned over him, the parrots shrieked at him, the noises of the populated house behind him—squabbles, orders and reproofs—hit on dead ears.

"I am Kim. I am Kim. And what is Kim?" His soul repeated it again and again.[3]

Kim has not, as yet, had to contemplate the interior truths of how he
situates himself as an independent and coherent subject. He has not had
to confront the construction of his own perceptions between these oppositional systems. One of Kim's strengths to date has been his ability to lie.
He has thus been able to negotiate his own fictional truth to suit the particular situation. Having had the courage to question his very identity and
to realize that this is not a God-given state of imperialist certainty, Kim
finds absolute relief in the tears that release him from the self-destructive
tension that would otherwise tear him apart. He is ready to step once
again onto the Great Road of Life.

Kipling's construction of Kim in 1901 moves away from the stereotypical notions of Englishness that had been the requirements of heroism in
his nineteenth-century counterparts. Kim is more comfortable being native than English; he is a liar and a trickster given to emotional outbursts—
which Kipling attributes, of course, to Kim's Irish heritage. Furthermore,
Kim has to discover and learn his values and beliefs, rather than absorbing
them by cultural osmosis. Heroism, Englishness, and imperialism are under question and undergoing change at the turn of the century.

Frances Hodgson Burnett adds to this ferment of question and revision
in *The Secret Garden* (1911). Brought up in India, Mary Lennox is an orphaned and abandoned child of the empire. Her parents are more interested in their own lives which interrelate with the spoils of colonialism—
the high social life and the power of rule—rather than their own child.
Mary is reared as a potential ruler, issuing orders to the servants, and
behaving in a self-centerd and entirely spoilt manner. The great quest that
Burnett set for her flawed heroine is to discover her natural self beneath
the trappings of imperialism, which imprison the child. In this learning
process and quest of discovery, Mary also frees Colin, the ghost child who
wanes in fear, isolation, and self-centerdness at the diseased heart of the
English country house.

The truths that Mary and Colin discover are in the relationships between self and nature; those truths that move beyond the systems of control and imperialist politics. The site of discovery is in the making of a
new Eden in their secret garden. The acts of heroism and courage are those
that have a humanist perspective, which heal the scars of imperialism and
differentiation. The adventures of the protagonists in *The Secret Garden*
take the aftermath of imperialism and restore the health of the community
through domestic regeneration. Hodgson Burnett's intention is to demonstrate the possibilities of reforming the culture of the imperialist power
in a postimperial situation; in other words, reconsidering the colonial
power in a postcolonial state.

Northern Lights (1995), the first book of Philip Pullman's "His Dark Materials" trilogy and the second book, *The Subtle Knife* (1997), demonstrate the nineteenth and early twentieth-century inheritance sketched above. The challenge for Lyra, the neo-Romantic heroine of *Northern Lights*, is that there are no certainties of knowledge. She is battling with the detritus of the twentieth century in an England that appears to exist in some post-nuclear age. Lyra inhabits a dark world of shades and hostility as she lives the life of an orphaned child in the decaying and once glorious halls of an Oxford College. Lyra has been raised "like a half-wild cat," "a coarse and greedy savage."[4] She is the twenty-first-century construction of the postmodern Romantic child, a female Rousseauesque Emile, the innocent savage, running free without the influence of books-except Lyra's environment is urban and decaying whereas Emile's was the wooded countryside. The University College in Oxford, for example, is devoid of the bustling life of students; the reader is required to construct a world of hallowed knowledge, of philosophers and scholars who protect their way of life against a wild and shadowed environment of social malaise and dark discontent: the tone is one of feudal formality, with college inhabitants holding on to a sense of civilization by observing ritual, the hierarchies of Lord, Master, and servant.

One can read *Northern Lights* as a reconstruction of Imperialist England in a postcolonial, postmodern state. The hierarchical world of Oxbridge academe stands in fragile opposition to the barbaric and dangerous world immediately beyond their walls, where the streets are roamed by Tartars, a people who practise an unpleasant brand of brain surgery akin to scientific scalping, while the kind of play enjoyed by the children is a pastiche of the atmosphere of restrained warfare by which they are surrounded. Lyra is an aggressive heroine suited to survive against such violence, for at this stage in the trilogy, confrontation of violence is necessary. She is equipped with some truths, but the given certainties of education, religious belief, and moral behavior exemplified by adults, are uncertain and untrustworthy. Lyra has to find her own truths.

Like Kipling's Kim, Lyra is also a good liar. She has to be in order to protect herself and also because she must construct other "truths" to replace those that have been given and are inadequate. Again like Kim and Mary Lennox, Lyra lives between cultures. *Northern Lights* is a multicultural text. Lyra's adventures take her into communion and contact with a number of different cultural communities: the Oxford academics, the violent force of the barbaric Tartars; the gyptians-the name being a cross between gypsies and Egyptians, thus giving them a sense of historical nobility while being the traveling people of Europe. She meets Witches, Angels, and Bears who are all presented as cultural groups with their own particualr set of social mores. The Bears, for example, subdivide into two groups, those who align with the savage dictator and those who will fol-

low the codes of chivalry and make a better future. The Witches demonstrate qualities of feminist cooperation. There is even a singular pioneering
American balloonist who hires himself out as a troubleshooter!

Pullman has created a mini-cosmos combining attributes of savagery
versus civilization, and superstition and the fantastic as opposed to scientific knowledge. Lyra stands at the center of the battle for power since
she will lead the next generation onward. She is the inventive, imaginative
figure, and one who holds mystical powers to interpret signs—the ma-
gus—the visionary leader of the future. Lyra's special powers of interpretation are set within a scientific context, for she is able to interpret
intuitively the scientific instrument that has come into her possession, and
it is she who is fundamental in leading the central quest of the novel, the
hunt for the lost children.

The lost children are those who have been transported to the northern
wastelands and have been reduced to soulless, zombie-like creatures because they have been separated from their daemons. Each character has
an individual daemon, that is, a spirit figure in animal form. The common
understanding of the word "daemon" derived from Biblical association is
that of a devilish spirit; the Greek derivation refers to "a genius," a spiritual essence. The animal form of a daemon reflects its owner, but a child's
daemon may change form, reacting in relation to mood and emotion, or
reacting to defend its human partner. Lyra's daemon is seen in the form
of a moth, a mouse, an ermine, and a bird, depending upon her inner
state. When the child reaches adulthood the daemon is fixed as a reflection
of the experienced personality of the owner. For example, Lord Asriel,
Lyra's father, has a daemon that is a snow leopard, haughty and dangerous, yet sleek and fascinatingly beautiful.

At the end of the twentieth century, Pullman created a *fin de siècle* trilogy
(the third book of the trilogy is *The Amber Spyglass*, published in 2000)
employing knowledges that move beyond the constraints of nineteenth-
century certainty. His worlds are post-Darwinist, post-Freudian, postcolonial, and postmodern, yet the central quest of his trilogy, like his
forebears, is to refind Eden. Ballantyne and others searched for their Eden
in the remaking of England in a colonial outpost. Kipling's Kim was to
be forever searching, traveling the Great Road of Life, while Burnett found
a place of solace in the secret garden. At the end of *Northern Lights* Lyra
steps onto a staircase formed from the energy of the Aurora Borealis; she
has with her the scientific instrument that only she can intuitively read.
She also has her daemon Pan, the personification of her soul.

She turned away. Behind them lay pain and death and fear; ahead of them lay
doubt, and danger and fathomless mysteries. But they weren't alone.
So Lyra and her daemon turned away from the world they were born in, and
looked towards the sun, and walked into the sky.[5]

The early nineteenth-century English hero had God, certainty, the power of the knowledge of right, and English Imperialism as unquestionable guides in the great quest. The late twentieth-century child has to be prepared for a very different kind of world where the perfection of Eden cannot exist. Lyra has to be a new colonizer, to explore new worlds, parallel universes where she must be aware of the dividing boundaries between cultures, instead of assuming a seamless hegemony. Instead of the given constructs of Imperialism, she has to believe in and trust herself to walk into the sky.

NOTES

1. Rudyard Kipling, *Kim*. London: Oxford World Classics, 1990, p. 1.
2. Ibid., p. 282.
3. Ibid., p. 282.
4. Philip Pullman, *Northern Lights*. London: Scholastic, 1995, p. 399.
5. Ibid., pp. 398–399.

REFERENCES

Ballantyne, R. M. *The Coral Island*. 1857. Oxford: Oxford Worlds Classics, 1990.
———. *Ungava*. London: Thomas Nelson, 1857.
Burnett, Frances Hodgson. *The Secret Garden*. 1911. New York: Dell, 1973.
Hughes, Thomas. *Tom Brown's Schooldays*. 1857. New York: Airmont, 1968.
Kingsley, Charles. *The Water Babies*. 1863. London: J. M. Dent, 1966.
Kipling, Rudyard. *Kim*. 1901. London: Oxford World's Classics, 1990.
Pullman, Philip. *The Amber Spyglass*. London: Scholastic, 2000.
———. *Northern Lights*. London: Scholastic, 1995.
———. *The Subtle Knife*. London: Scholastic, 1997.

CHAPTER 7

"A Little Child Shall Lead Them": The Child as Redeemer

Margot Hillel

Children's literature, at least since the nineteenth century, has contained a number of recurring representations of children and, although the general setting in which these children are placed changes, the representations themselves can be seen as part of a tradition. One of these representations is of the child as redeemer. While we normally associate the redemptive child with religious themes, this chapter argues that the figure of the redemptive child still exists in late twentieth-century literature, although the strongly religious elements found in earlier books have been usurped by secular ones. This redemptive child works within the framework of her or his family. Of nineteenth-century writers, Maurice Saxby comments that in "their insistence on presenting children with a moral outlook, it was inevitable that children's writers should have exploited the family situation to drive the message home."[1] The same is frequently true with more recent writers, who construct their protagonists as redemptive.

The Evangelical movement of the nineteenth century adopted literature for young readers as an instrument totally suited to their religious ends—to bring about the moral reform of the nation. Having received (and survived) the necessary discipline and training, the ideal Evangelical child was selfless, devoted to a life of goodness and evangelizing. Evangelical children were exhorted by the writers of the tract literature to attend to the saving of their own small souls, but equally importantly to proselytize—to spread the Holy Word and actively seek the redemption of others.

Alice Leigh's Mission is an anonymous book published by the Religious Tract Society. Alice's father is a violent drunkard who was responsible for the fall down the stairs that crippled Alice before the story begins. She lives her life in patient suffering ("she did not mind the pain and weariness of it all if through it her father was good and kind and sober again"[2]), lying on a couch and sometimes wheeled outside by sympathetic friends. Eventually, and inevitably, she reaches the stage of the deathbed scene. And just as inevitably Simon Leigh comes to recognize the damage he has done to his daughter. As Alice lies on her deathbed, she remains committed to reclaiming his soul: Leigh first sings "Abide with me" to her, then takes the Bible she urges him to read after she dies. She extracts the vital promise from him:

"And you'll love Jesus, won't you? And you'll pray to him?
And—and—and oh, father! You won't drink no more?"
"No darling, I'll try to do it all."[3]

Then she acts as comforter: "You mustn't cry . . . I'm very happy—I'm going to Jesus—I'm going to see mother. I must go!—goodbye, father—dear, *dear* father! Love Jesus—come to heaven!"[4] As Gillian Avery says, "what adult could stand up to the eloquent evangelism of [such] children?"[5]

That such literature was read in Australia is evidenced by the copies that can still be found in library collections, often with inscriptions that show them to have been presented as Sunday School prizes.[6] There were Australian writers too who were just as Evangelical. Maud Jean Franc was married to a minister. According to Saxby, her books were "written for young people, to whom the author desired to teach the message of the Gospel" and thus were "favoured by selectors of books for Sunday School libraries and prizes."[7] Her characters are frequently young women, included for the didactic purpose of reminding her audience, older girls, that they too, like their younger sisters, can be redemptive.

Franc also wrote temperance tales, among them *John's Wife* (not dated, the inscription on the fly leaf is 1876). Herbert, a character in this book, is described as "handsome, but utterly marred by the curse of the colony; and the tall well-built form in all the pride of early manhood, trembled like an old man."[8] The narrator is concerned for the physical health and spiritual well-being of both her brother and sister-in-law, a concern that serves two Evangelical purposes: a trial for the narrator and an opportunity for proselytizing:

Dear John! . . . so strong, so good, so kind. And yet he wants the one thing, that to me would make him perfect. He is not a Christian; his heart is in the world-his treasure is there. He does not realise how immensely superior are the joys beyond; or how surpassing sweet is the love of Jesus.[9]

The narrator herself becomes a total abstainer (and is much prettier as a result) and looks after her nephew when John's wife Mabel develops *delirium tremens.* This gives her the opportunity of converting John who comes to fear that Mabel's condition may be a judgment on him because he has loved Mabel too well and forgotten God. His sister brings him to a recognition of the need for God's help in overcoming his earthly problems.[10] As with earlier books, the author is also using the young, religious woman to teach a moral lesson to her readers. And, while the language used has moved closer to twentieth-century sensibilities rather than historian Philip Greven's image of evangelical warfare,[11] the fight against drunkenness, among other things, continues to be waged by children or young women. Furthermore, such books also fit into the tradition of improving books that, as Alan Richardson has claimed for earlier literature of a similar type, taught young readers to conceive of their own lives "in terms of a succession of moral narratives based on those . . . presented in the tales [they] read. . . . The most trivial experience can become a moral tale."[12]

Frances Hodgson Burnett's *Little Lord Fauntleroy* and *The Secret Garden*, which certainly contain religious elements, are nonetheless, largely secular and can be seen as a sort of transition between the purely religious books of a slightly earlier time and twentieth-century books, which become more secular, but which nevertheless contain a redemptive child. Cedric (Little Lord Fauntleroy) is described many times throughout the book as having curly yellow hair, and being handsome, strong, and rosy. Mary, the heroine of *The Secret Garden*, as a child both in need of redemption and as a redeemer, needs the help of the child of nature to become a redemptive child herself. Dickon looks forward to some of the redemptive characters, who will be discussed below, in that he is feminized. His most significant traits are his nurturing nature, his kindliness and gentleness to those (animal and human) weaker than himself. Cedric too, is feminized; although he is described quite often as a manly child, the many redemptive virtues he has are feminine ones, and learned from his mother.

Mary is initially described as a sour little thing, with yellow skin and lank, brown hair. The path of her own redemption is plotted in part by her physical transformation as she becomes prettier and fatter, and with better skin and prettier hair. Better skin here is tantamount to becoming pink and white, more "English." Discourses of racism and redemption intersect here; Mary needs to be deorientalized in order to be good enough to function as a redeemer. In addition, by becoming prettier, Mary becomes a more obvious signifier of femininity—a transformation needed if she is to perform her proper role of redeemer for Colin.

The garden itself functions as a symbol of deorientalizing; Mary learns to appreciate English flora and fauna and to work in a way she never had to do in India, surrounded as she was by servants. The garden also gives her a new sense of purpose and is itself a form of redeemer. Burnett was clearly interested in the power of children to change the lives of those around them, providing they themselves were either innately good or capable of acquiring good. The acquisition came, in Mary's case, not after reading the Bible or tract literature, but by exposure to the wonders of nature and mixing with simple, happy folk which meant "there was no room left for the disagreeable thoughts which affected her liver and her digestion and made her yellow and tired."[13] This statement owes more than a little to Burnett's Christian Scientist beliefs.

Following in the earlier tradition, there developed in Australia a publishing industry of "improving" books for children. The moral gradually came to be taught in a more secular way, but the purpose continued. The importance of self-sacrifice, often as a prelude to an action that brings about the salvation or redemption of another character or characters, continued to be a device used by authors, whose voice is often very intrusive in narratives of this sort. (A sort of patronizing "listen to the good deeds of my characters, child reader, and then you will be inspired to emulate them.")

Saxby describes the work of H. Louisa Bedford: her works "have a feeling of *deja vu* and the tone of a religious tract,"[14] and she too can be seen as following in the tradition of the improving book. Bedford published her books through the Society for Promoting Christian Knowledge and, although English, she set some of her books in Australia. The setting is, however, of little relevance, as the author is much more concerned with the message she is trying to convey. In *A Home in the Bush* (1913), for example, the place becomes significant only because it allows a kind of missionizing on "foreign" soil—apart from the religious missionizing of Prudence, Bruce fights a local boy who speaks disparagingly of the King. The book tells of two English children coming to stay with their cousins in Tasmania. The aptly named Prudence, in her first days with the family, shows them the error of their ways. It is Prudence "who as a matter of fact, folded her hands and said her grace aloud, and Mr. And Mrs. Farrar glanced at each other with a little smile. Saying grace was an old custom that had almost fallen into disuse in the stress of daily life. It was good that the child should remind them of it."[15] Bringing the family back to a daily recognition of God is an important part of Prue's mission, which she completes by bringing comfort and renewed strength to Mrs. Farrar when she discovers the grave of Mrs Farrar's child who has been lost in the bush years before.[16]

Although Ethel Turner's fiction does not generally fit into the model of evangelical literature, on occasion she uses a child as savior or at least conciliator to a family, the child being able to bring together characters in a way adults have been unable to do. In *Little Mother Meg*, which continues the story of the Woolcott family from Misrule, Nell saves the little girl next door from being burned to death, turns the father away from thoughts of suicide, and then is largely instrumental in bringing the estranged parents of the child together again. Like the heroines of earlier books, Nell displays more strength of character than the adults and is described in ways reminiscent of those same books. "Mrs. Saville clung to her as if she, young Nell, had been an elder sister . . . and the leaning made the girl both stronger and more womanly."[17] "Womanly" here connotes nurturing; it suggests sympathetic and domestic virtues; by being a redemptive child, Nell has actually, like many redemptive children in later books, acted as a substitute mother to the adults.

In *Australian Children's Literature: An Exploration of Genre and Theme*, John Foster, Ern Finnis, and Maureen Nimon call Ethel Turner a literary innovator for her parodies of Evangelical literature.[18] This may well be true in the scene of Judy's death in *Seven Little Australians*, but there is something evangelical about the way the picture of Judy hanging in the stairwell at Misrule in *The Family at Misrule* (1896) acts as a daily reminder of the child's sacrifice and her redemptive role in the family. Even more evangelical are Esther's reflections on Judy's death in *Little Mother Meg*:

Oh, Meg . . . the child is best where she is—little Judy I mean; I had a clear vision of that yesterday . . . she would have loved and suffered and lived as one of her nature must have done. And oh the peace, yesterday, on her hill-top . . . and the soft air that seems full of her.

I kissed her grass and smoothed it, and looked up to the shining stars, her eyes and thanked God inasmuch as He had let me see that all had been for the best.[19]

There are discourses of femininity here too. We can discern an underlying fear of female energy and perhaps of female sexuality. It is an extraordinary statement to claim that because a child is lively, and does not conform to notions of obedience and submissive femininity, she is actually better off dead. Notions of that kind of femininity are so naturalized here that there is no suggestion that there should be any kind of societal changes to accommodate different notions of female activity. The whole passage suggests something similar to George Eliot's *The Mill on the Floss*, with Maggie, unable to comply with society's demands for a submissive female child, removed by death. Both she and Judy are caught between conflicting notions; they are brave in ways that are usually inscribed as male but ultimately their bravery is the cause of self-sacrifice, a virtue frequently used as a signifier of femaleness. Judy too, like Maggie, is a wild child, the type of child Puritan notions of childhood cannot condone. They are both in need of taming, and the ultimate way of taming is through death. Liveliness and emergent sexuality, signifiers of loss of childhood innocence, are thus seen as somehow punishable; other female characters who are punished for a similar "crime" are Katy in Susan Coolidge's *What Katy Did* and Eleanor Porter's eponymous Pollyanna, although these girls are punished less spectacularly as they are only "crippled" for a finite period of time, eventually emerging much chastened from being bedridden for months.

The personalization of the story and the direct appeal to the reader to identify with the main character is frequently enhanced by the use of the character's name in the title—*Nellie Doran; A Story of Australian Home and School Life* (1923); *Sue Stanwood* (1927); and *Annette of River Bend* (1941). All the characters are, as is obvious from the titles, female. The feminization of the redeemer is part of the discourse.

Miriam Agatha's *Nellie Doran* brings *fin-de-siècle* values into the twentieth century. Nellie is of Irish parentage, and goes to boarding school with money earned by her brother Pat, who sells horses. She often feels out of place at school, especially as many of the girls are snobbish. She manages to win most of them around, however, and even the most vain girl is eventually humbled by Nellie's actions. Nellie represents humility, and another girl, Millicent, represents pride. Her pride takes a fall when she discovers that the unfashionably dressed Nellie, a real "bush girl," is actually her cousin. (The bush girl here is not someone to be automatically admired as it was in the works of Mary Grant Bruce, for example, nor is the bush seen as a desirable place to live.) Her pride simply will not allow her to acknowledge this relationship, until Nellie is discovered to be a brilliant violinist. Millicent's father is disgusted with her that she now wants to claim kinship with Nellie, after rejecting it for so long. The final mortification for Milcie [sic] comes with the humility of Nellie's speech:

"You do not seem surprised, Nellie, dear," Mother Ita remarked.
"No, Mother. I knew. Pat told me long ago."
"You knew! And you did not tell the girls!" Milcie cried.
    Nellie grew painfully red. "I felt you did not want the girls to know," she said, and Mr. Grogan [Milcie's father] stroked her hair softly, and Mother Ita admired the view from the bay window.[20]

Nellie's reward comes with this discovery that she is a musical genius, although she finally chooses not to go overseas to study, as she prefers to stay home and remain part of her family. The book thus fits with those that, as Kimberley Reynolds argues, flourished after 1880 and had a strong thesis of self-denial and reward.[21] Although Roman Catholic and not Evangelical Protestant, this book can nonetheless be seen as part of the earlier religious discourse that reinforces the domestic realm of the female, as well as part of the discourse that emphasizes the gendering of the redemptive child as female. The book is some-what different from many earlier ones in that it is not just an adult who is redeemed; all the girls in the school, particularly Milcie, benefit from Nellie's piety and humility. The clear didactic purpose of the book is reinforced by the preface, written by the Archbishop of Brisbane, who emphasises the book's "beautiful moral." The Archbishop continues: "We owe Miriam Agatha a debt of gratitude for her excellent work in a field of literature that is but too little cultivated. We feel confident that *Nellie Doran* will be warmly welcomed in school and home."[22]

By the end of the twentieth century, however, the religious dimension had been largely removed—at least in books from mainstream publishers and available from general bookshops. Nonetheless, there are a number of books in which the idea that "a little child shall lead" is retained, books that are the descendants of, or are certainly within the same family as, their nineteenth-century predecessors. Evangelicals believed that the child was the most easily redeemed, after which they became the keepers of true values, just as Patricia Holland has argued children are seen by some people today. Although this arises, she claims, from a "neo-Romantic view of childhood," there are echoes of much of the evangelical tract literature. People who hold this view of childhood claim, she says, that "adults should be learning from children" and children "are owed a better society, but at the same time they are asked to create a better society on our behalf."[23] Many contemporary children's books illustrate this point, with child characters asked to act as *de facto* adults.

The birth of a fourth child, Carl, who is autistic, causes total disruption to the Marriner family in Eleanor Spence's *The October Child* (1976). The second son, Douglas, becomes the "savior" of the family. Although the book is almost entirely secular, some of the tropes can perhaps be described in religious terms. Mrs Marriner, for example, is a sacrificial figure, who refuses to accept the seriousness of Carl's condition and seems to believe that sufficient love and attention from her will overcome it. She also calls on a degree of sacrifice from Douglas, as his singing is almost the only thing to which Carl will respond. As a result, through his sacrifice (giving up his own time, letting his own school-work and music suffer), Douglas becomes the savior of Beth, allowing her to get some much-needed rest by taking charge of Carl on numerous occasions. Douglas, like many of his fictional counterparts of the nineteenth century, is asked to play the role of adult at an unusually (and, by today's standards at least, unsuitably) early age.[24]

Douglas's care for Carl and his mother also allows the rest of the family to abrogate all responsibility, the father particularly becoming an almost totally absentee figure, both to his family and to the reader. There is a strong sense that Spence disapproves of this action, and, although the book is not overtly religious, Spence's ethics seem close to the Puritan. She ultimately supports and indeed lauds the idea of self-sacrifice and she certainly valorizes hard work, duty and altruism.

Again like the sacrifices of many earlier fictional characters, Douglas's sacrifice is for the good of the family. One of the most striking examples is when Douglas has to go to the Music College for an interview to determine whether or not he will be admitted. On the morning of the interview Douglas is called to help the family look for Carl who has run away. When the child is finally found, Douglas is running very late for the interview and has to go alone as his mother is too tired and no one else offers to accompany him, although he is unsure of the way as they have only very recently moved to the city. In addition, he has no clothes ready to wear, as his mother has been too busy with Carl to mend any, so he has to make do with old, torn jeans.[25]

The resolution of this book also contains echoes of nineteenth-century texts that emphasized the value of optimism and the usefulness of experience. The difference here is that the adult voice's call to optimism is somewhat apologetic, although the message is the same as in nineteenth-century texts. One day after he has really had all he can take of Carl, Douglas runs to the house of his music teacher. The woman who is looking after the house is a teacher at the school for autistic children, which Carl attends. She asks Douglas if he has

"ever thought about how much Carl's existence has altered your life—for the better . . . ?"
  Douglas made a valiant effort to marshal his mental processes.
  "I suppose if it hadn't been for him we'd never have left Chapel Rocks. And I wouldn't have gone to the Music College and met all my friends. . . . I could probably find some more."
  "I'm afraid," said Kerry, "that's the best I can do for you right now. The only advice I can give you is to go home . . . and keep on trying as far as Carl's concerned. Does that sound too awful?"
  "It sounds the same as before," admitted Douglas.
  "Not quite," said Kerry "because you know a tiny bit more-about Carl and yourself."[26]

This sounds very much as if Douglas is being urged to continue his role as responsible leader of the family, one who can now, in addition to his other duties, lead the family in what that classically "do-good" character of children's literature, Pollyanna, called "the glad game."[27]

Steven, in Simon French's *Change the Locks* (1992), although not even a teenager is expected to act as parent to his baby half-brother because his mother is seriously depressed following the departure of her abusive boyfriend and, as a result, is largely incapable of fulfilling day-to-day household duties. Steven takes over the nurturing role and by doing so, keeps the family together-in other words, he is its savior. He is the "good mother," the good adult as opposed to the real mother. The feminization of Steven means that he is in a sense desexualized, taking over from his mother, not from the absent *de facto* father. Earlier books most commonly used girls as redeeming figures because, especially in the context of Victorian England, they could most easily be portrayed as pure, domesticated, and able to take over the nurturing role. Attempts to provide gender balance and to show boys in roles less commonly perceived as masculine have meant the appearance of characters like Steven. They fit into the same trope, however, as they are still shown as feminine. They allow a new kind of binary opposition. Earlier we had the good, female child opposed to and ultimately redeeming the bad, male parent. Now the opposition is of good, male child with the bad, female parent. The male child in such books is sanctified and the mother frequently demonized. Discourses and concerns about maternity intersect here with discourses of redemption.

The child has become nurturer to both the baby and the mother; it is largely through Steven's care that his mother eventually regains some normal functioning as a parent. The book's ending has been described as a "dysfunctional resolution,"[28] a description that French himself disputes. Writing in the children's literature journal *Reading Time*, he says: "I intended *Change the Locks* to not only depict [sic] Steven's patience and forbearance in the face of emotional and financial poverty, but to chart his mother's growth as an adult, and her empowerment as parent and protector."[29]

French describes the development of the mother in ways that might more usually be used to discuss the development of a child character. What he says allows for a reading of his work that, as I have argued, sees the child as "savior" of the family, from, for example, possible intervention by government welfare agencies. Perhaps even more importantly, the child is nurturer of and thus savior of his mother, as, by his actions, he allows his mother the time and space to grow as an adult and perhaps develop to the point where she can take over her implied, correct role as mother.

Nadia Wheatley's *Lucy in the Leap Year* (1993) contains a younger redemptive child, this time in the older tradition of female redemptor. Lucy, whose mother is dead, lives in a flat with her father, in a large house that is divided into many similar flats. Wheatley constructs the cast of characters who live in this house with a deft and light touch—Mr Lee, for example, who always dresses in black and white, is described as being gone "in a flicker . . . Like the last moments of an old late-night movie."[30]

In a sense all the other inhabitants of the flats become mothers to Lucy, especially after her father hurts his back and is unable to look after Lucy or go to work (like a classic female heroine languishing on a couch, he is, as Heather Scutter points out, thus feminized and infantilized).[31] The thought that her father is going to be incapacitated for a long time worries Lucy, and she is almost too afraid to allow herself to think he might not get better. The thought of losing another parent is too frightening to be allowed to surface. Lucy looks after her father to the best of her ability, but she, unlike earlier females, is not a sacrificial child and she retains her own life while taking on new responsibilities.

Lucy's father's illness also provides an opportunity for her to get to know all her neighbors in a way she has not before. She shares in their lives in a new way, overcoming her shyness of some and fear of others like Granny Mo. They too become a part of her life, helping her when she has to dress up as a book character for Children's Book Week and coming to school with "a plate" on the last day. It is through knowledge of each of them that Lucy is able to act as a redeemer, leading them all to a new understanding of each other. She is the catalyst that brings them together. On her father's birthday, for example, she plays the song *Lucy in the Sky with Diamonds* and all the neighbors appear at the door, not to complain about the noise, but rather to have what amounts to a family party as "Mr Lee and Wanda came up in their pyjamas, and Moira appeared in her floral brunch coat, and Granny Mac arrived wearing her red wool dressing-gown, and carrying the tin with the kittens on the lid."[32] Granny Mac is doing the equivalent of the Australain tradition of "bringing a plate" (a plate of food brought to a party) as the tin contains a fruit cake that Lucy has previously helped to make. Again, when they all come to the school on the last day, they come as Lucy Townsend's family, "the biggest family that anyone had brought to school that day."[33] They are not just "related" to Lucy, however: through her they have all become family to each other as well.

The absent parent—through illness, death or alcohol—was a theme that recurred in earlier literature. It appears again in contemporary literature, though the absence may be for different reasons. The withdrawal or absence of the parent in all the books discussed allows—indeed necessitates that—the main child character act as the responsible adult. If the parent was functioning normally, the child as adult would obviously be unnecessary and even impossible.

Jill Ireland argues that many award-winning Australian books from about 1970–1985 "are superior in characterisation, style, narrative range and world view than books shortlisted since that time." She also regards the portrayal of adults in these earlier books as superior. Adults in the later books, she claims, "tend to be evil or totally useless." She also claims that, in contemporary futuristic fantasies, "plot takes precedence over character. We hear more about what people do than who they are."[34]

Ireland implies something new has occured in the development of children's literature. I argue for the continuation of a tradition that goes well beyond the time frame she mentions. In much of the literature which shows the child as savior or redeemer, the adults are portrayed as absent, either literally or in the sense of not fulfilling their responsibilities, or they are shown as totally inadequate. As for "hearing more about what people do than who they are," this too is a continuing technique of children's authors and again can be seen as part of a tradition that saw children's literature as having a specific didactic purpose. The characters of the evangelical literature, for example, were often simply ciphers denoting goodness, and the goodness was displayed in their actions. The difference is that in today's Australia which generally regards itself as a Christian country but in which the reality is that a minority of people are regular churchgoers, religious literature is no longer regarded as appropriate in the mainstream.

Children's literature contains recurring tropes, and among these is that of the child as savior, a figure that necessarily implies inadequate adults. In this *fin-desiècle*, the danger that threatens the child in children's literature is not the contamination of worldly sins and the moral inadequacy of a parent that requires her to redeem that parent. What threatens the child in literature today are social problems such as living in a dysfunctional family, where the absentee parent (now very often the mother) still figures prominently, but the problem has not been caused by turning away from Jesus. Nonetheless, from the examples I set out above, it is clear that the child has the strength and morality to cope with these problems. Practical support and help, rather than religious exhortation, is now given to the erring adult by the redemptive child. Kimberley Reynolds and Nicola Humble quote a late nineteenth-century critic as saying that, as an ideal of feminine behavior, "self-sacrifice is out of fashion altogether in our modern school of novelists." Reynolds and Humble disagree, arguing that in "girls' fiction, the old ideal of self-sacrifice and service is perpetuated, not eradicated."[35]

NOTES

1. H. Maurice Saxby, *Offered to Children*. Sydney: Scholastic, 1998, pp. 199–200.

2. Anonymous, *Alice Leigh's Mission*. London: Religious Tract Society, n.d., p. 13.

3. Ibid., p. 149.

4. Ibid, p. 149.

5. Gillian Avery, *Nineteenth-Century Children: Heroes and Heroines in English Children's Stories 1780–1900*. London: Hodder and Stoughton, 1965, p. 93.

6. For example, Mrs. Emma Raymond Pitman's 1883 book *Florence Godfrey's Faith* (Copy held by the State Library of Victoria) was given as a Sunday School prize in Australia in 1887. Harvey Darton discusses the way in which publishers in the Victorian era built "up a standard trade in prizes and discovered in series published for that purpose a firm annual turnover." F.J. Harvey Darton, *Children's Books in England: Five Centuries of Social Life*. Cambridge: Cambridge UP, 1982, p. 322. Among the firms engaged in "prize publishing" were S.P.C.K., R.T.S., and Ward Lock. Books from all these publishers were readily available in Australia.

7. Saxby, *Offered to Children*, pp. 199–200.

8. Maud Jean Franc, *John's Wife*. London: Sampson, Low, Marston, Low & Searle, n.d., p. 77.

9. Ibid., p. 94.

10. Ibid., p. 213.

11. Philip Greven, *The Protestant Temperament: Patterns of Child Rearing, Religious Experience and the Self in Early America*. New York: Alfred A. Knopf, 1977, p. 37.

12. Alan Richardson, *Literature, Education and Romanticism: Reading as Social Practice, 1780–1832*. Cambridge: Cambridge UP, 1994, pp. 140–141.

13. Frances Hodgson Burnett, *The Secret Garden*. London: Puffin, 1951, p. 239.

14. Saxby, *Offered to Children*, p. 211.

15. H. Louisa Bedford, *A Home in the Bush*. London: SPCK, 1913, p. 21.

16. Ibid., p. 106.

17. Ethel Turner, *Little Mother Meg*. London: Ward Lock, 1902, p. 230.

18. John Foster, Ern Finnis, and Maureen Nimon, *Australian Children's Literature: An Exploration of Genre and Theme*. Wagga Wagga, Australia: LIS Press, 1995, p. 16.

19. Turner, *Little Mother Meg*, p. 257.

20. Miriam Agatha, *Nellie Doran: A Story of Australian Home and School Life*. Sydney: E.J. Dwyer, 1923, p. 206.

21. Kimberley Reynolds, *Girls Only? Gender and Popular Children's Fiction in Britain, 1880–1910*. Hemel Hempstead, UK: Harvester Wheatsheaf, 1990, p. 131.

22. Agatha, Preface.

23. Patricia Holland, *What Is a Child? Popular Images of Childhood*. London: Virago Press, 1992, p. 93.

24. Eleanor Spence, *The October Child*. Melbourne: Oxford University Press, 1978, Chap. 8.

25. Ibid., pp. 96–97.

26. Ibid., pp. 150–151.

27. Eleanor H. Porter, *Pollyanna*. Harmondsworth, UK: Puffin, 1969, p. 34.

28. Jill Ireland, "Are they the best books of the year?" *Reading Time* 40, no. 2 (May 1996): p. 16.

29. Simon French, "Letter to the Editor," *Reading Time* 40, no. 4 (November, 1996): p. 2.

30. Nadia Wheatley, *Lucy in the Leap Year*. Adelaide: Omnibus Books, 1993, pp. 7–8.

31. Heather Scutter, *Displaced Fictions*. Melbourne: Melbourne UP, 1999, p. 169.

32. Wheatley, p. 147.

33. Ibid., p. 153.

34. Ireland, pp. 18, 19.

35. Kimberley Reynolds and Nicola Humble, *Victorian Heroines*. Hemel Hempstead, UK: Harvester Wheatsheaf, 1993, p. 32.

REFERENCES

Agatha, Miriam. *Nellie Doran: A Story of Australian Home and School Life*. Sydney: E.J. Dwyer, 1923.

Anonymous. *Alice Leigh's Mission*. London: Religious Tract Society, n.d.

Avery, Gillian. *Nineteenth-Century Children: Heroes and Heroines in English Children's Stories 1780–1900*. London: Hodder and Stoughton, 1965.

Bedford, H. Louisa. *A Home in the Bush*. London: SPCK, 1913.

Burnett, Frances Hodgson. *Little Lord Fauntleroy*. New York: Charles Scribner's, 1886.

———. *The Secret Garden*. London: Puffin, 1951.

Darton, F. J. Harvey. *Children's Books in England: Five Centuries of Social Life*. Cambridge: Cambridge UP, 1982.

Foster, John, Ern Finnis, and Maureen Nimon. *Australian Children's Literature: An Exploration of Genre and Theme*. Wagga Wagga, Australia: LIS Press, 1995.

Franc, Maud Jean. *John's Wife*. London: Sampson, Low, Marston, Low & Searle, 1874.

French, Simon. "Letter to the Editor," *Reading Time* 40, no. 4 (November, 1996): 2.

Greven, Philip. *The Protestant Temperament: Patterns of Child-Rearing, Religious Experience and the Self in Early America*. New York: Alfred A. Knopf, 1977.

Holland, Patricia. *What is a Child? Popular Images of Childhood*. London: Virago Press, 1992.

Ireland, Jill. "Are they the best books of the year?" *Reading Time* 40, no. 2 (May 1996): 16.

Pitman, Emma Florence. *Florence Godfrey's Faith*. London: 1883.

Porter, Eleanor H. *Pollyanna*. Harmondsworth: Puffin, 1969.

Reynolds, Kimberley. *Girls Only? Gender and Popular Children's Fiction in Britain, 1880–1910*. Hemel Hempstead, Herts.: Harvester Wheatsheaf, 1990.

Reynolds, Kimberley and Nicola Humble. *Victorian Heroines*. Hemel Hempstead, UK: Harvester Wheatsheaf, 1993.

Richardson, Alan. *Literature, Education and Romanticism. Reading as Social Practice, 1780–1832*. Cambridge: Cambridge UP, 1994.

Saxby, H. Maurice. *A History of Australian Children's Literature: Vol. II 1941–1979*. Sydney: Wentworth Books, 1969.

———. *Offered to Children*. Sydney: Scholastic, 1998.

Scutter, Heather. *Displaced Fictions*. Melbourne: Melbourne UP, 1999.

Spence, Eleanor. *The October Child*. Melbourne: Oxford UP, 1978.

Tarn, Joseph. *General Catalogue of the Publications of the Religious Tract Society*. London: J. Tarn, 1873.

Turner, Ethel. *Little Mother Meg*. London: Ward Lock, 1902.

Wheatley, Nadia. *Lucy in the Leap Year*. Adelaide: Omnibus Books, 1993.

PART II

Nineteenth-Century Instances

CHAPTER 8

Lear's India and the Politics of Nonsense

Sumanyu Satpathy

Nonsense and the Empire are not disparate, unrelated domains—one cultural, the other political, one innocent, the other nocent. The fact that Edward Lear gave art lessons to the young Queen Victoria when she was twenty-seven, and that his visit to India in 1873 was sponsored by his friend, Lord Northbrook, the then Viceroy of India, should make this evident.[1] Furthermore, Lear returned from India in 1875 soon after "it became apparent to Disraeli that he must find a new governor-general for India because, Northbrook, a Liberal, clearly was not working in India for the furtherance of Great Britain's imperial policy."[2] It would be ridiculous to suggest that Lear was either helping or hindering the furtherance of the imperial cause, in the same way the viceroy did. But, as Edward Said has reminded us, Gramsci's very important formulation about how "culture" works in a civil society would at once make us wary about even "nonsense" writing. In fact, Said's, as well as most discourse analysts', work has depended on this formulation.[3]

But, both because of the way nonsense has been defined and its relatively unimportant status as "children's literature" (which latter category has itself been marginalized in mainstream literary studies, until recently, at any rate), nonsense has not been subjected to any of the rigors of discourse analysis. My hypothesis is that nonsense can yield to discourse analysis; and such analysis can add significantly to our knowledge of nonsense's ideological basis. In what follows, I shall try to show how much of Lear's nonsense actually came from his travels to the East, particularly India. Much of the unpleasantness of my task springs from my attempt to see in this genial spirit and his "innocent" pleasure-giving work an orientalist streak. In the West, feminists and other radical critics who have worked on nonsense as children's literature have concentrated on Lewis Carroll's nonsense. From our postcolonial perspective, however, Lear deserves a similar close scrutiny.

By the time Lear received Lord Northbrook's invitation in 1872, suggesting that he should accompany him to India, he had already traveled widely in the Middle and Near East. But his first visit in 1872 was abortive. Next autumn he set out with a commission to paint India, and arrived in Bombay on November 22, 1873, a date with which his meticulously kept Indian journal begins. His entries clearly show how India elicited contrary responses from him, with the very first one setting the tone: "violent and amazing delight at the wonderful varieties of life and dress here! O new palms! O flowers! O creatures! O beasts! . . . colours and costumes and myriadism of impossible picturesqueness. These hours are worth what you will" (22 November 1873).[4] Throughout his visit he was bewildered and exasperated, even as he was ecstatic in between. He displayed irritation, and regretted having come to India at all and nearly packed up to return on many occasions. That Lear had set expectations becomes clear from the entry of December 6: "Assuredly India is a place to see."[5] Again, he says, "O the misty sultry blueness and orangeness of Calcutta mornings!" (3 January 1874).[6]

These ecstatic outbursts occur whenever his Orientalist preconceptions meet the reality of his Indian experience. But this was not often the case, and within five days of his arrival he was disgusted by "Washing natives; birds; bulls; pigs; goats; dead-body burning," a catalogue of the unexpected (27 November 1873).[7] He reverses his earlier judgement, and vows to go back to Bombay and thence to Genoa. But, of course, he had the Viceroy's commission to fulfill! And he stays on, and spends much of the time in Delhi and Calcutta, using them as base camps, ridiculing inconveniences and the lack of facilities. On March 8, 1874, for example, he quotes approvingly one Mrs. Cracroft's opinion that "Delhi was simply a place of ruin, as everybody stopped here and claimed hospitality."[8] Two days later, he writes, "but I am half sick of marbles. O Delhi! the long contemplated! Verily one hour of Benares or Brindaban is worth a month of thy Britishized beauties which, whatever they once were, please this child very little now" (10 March 1874).[9]

Thanks to the alleged unreliability of Indian officials, he would often arrive at destinations without his baggage. The hustle and bustle of the imperial capital and other attendant irritants or irritating attendants prompted him to dub Calcutta "Hustlefussabad."[10] He also commented on the "Apparent sameness of expression throughout Bengal babuism" (2 January 1874),[11] and thought the "dress of people here (Calcutta) very feminine" (21 December 1873).[12] None of this discomfort and nuisance, however, deters him from representing the landscapes in numerous color paintings and sketches. He is able to capture most of the splendor, ruined or intact. During the months of his stay in India he would continue the good work of constructing the Orient for the Orientalists, and pass whatever received wisdom he had of India onto the stereotypical watercolors filling some 500 drawings and 9 sketch books. The Himalayas are represented by a faint outline of "Kinchinjunga" in Darjiling, accentuating the foreground of trees and tea-plucking tribal laborers.

His many sketches of river banks, the mandatory elephants and elephant rides, and the Taj Mahal at Benares show how stereotypically selective Lear was. He found it difficult to recapture the beauty of the Taj and expressed the frustration in his journal. When he finally painted it, the structure itself was reduced to a faint outline, and again the forefront was highlighted: the trees and the natives reclining reposefully. No one, looking at his sketch, would have believed what he said, "Henceforth—let the inhabitants of the world be divided into two classes—them as has seen the Taj Mahal; and them as hasn't" (16 February 1874).[13] The Ganges of Benares was more full of details, temples covering the background, natives with umbrellas, bathing devotees, fishermen casting their nets and finally the bathing buffaloes in an ironic footnote to the purity of the river. All this was for sale, was serious art for the serious minded Orientalists, and needed to capture the exotic beauty of India.

The caricatures of India appear again in his nonsense verse. Even before his trip to India he had made the subject for a limerick an old man from Nepal. "There was an Old Man of Nepaul,/From his horse had a terrible fall;/But, though split quite in two, by some very strong glue,/They mended that Man of Nepaul."[14] After his India trip, however, people from the subcontinent ran into worse luck. For example: "There was an Old Man of Calcutta,/Who perpetually ate bread and butter,/Till a great bit of muffin, on which he was stuffing,/Choked that horrid Old Man of Calcutta."[15] Lear's "innocent" racism is also apparent in: "There was an Old Man of Jamaica,/Who suddenly married a Quaker!/But she cried out—/'O lack! I have married a black!'/Which distressed that Old Man from Jamaica."[16]

Lear's racist entries in his journal are numerous: The August 31, 1874, entry at "Conjeeveram" reads: "The odious curiosity of loafing Brahmins at these places is always a bore, but 'we cannot change the natives,' as has been safely remarked."[17] And later, "These people hereabouts are sharp enough, and alquanto disagreeable. Malabar fool-starers will always be remembered by this child; they stick by you like flies and are impossible to get rid of" (31 October 1874).[18] By and by Lear becomes familiar with Indian food, maybe because of his faithful servant Giorgio who was apt to see the world in terms of his culinary preferences. When the two, at the end of an arduous journey, reached the ruined city of Petra in the far Arabian mountains, Giorgio exclaimed, "O master! We have come into a world where everything is made up of chocolate, ham, curry powder and salmon!"[19] Following his visit to India, Lear must have started seeing the world in terms of chutney. No wonder he wrote about the "old person of Putney,/Whose food was roast spiders and chutney."[20]

Many of Lear's nonsense words were formed out of his curiosity and encounters with the "native" lingo of the places he visited. One of the first things he did on arrival in a new land was to pick up a few words and sentences, as his entry in his diary on his second day in India shows: "First beginning of lingo. Rusta ke hai?" (25 November 1873).[21] Elsewhere in an Arab country, the natives, on finding out that he was drawing a sketch, exclaimed, "Shaitan Scroo! Shaitan Scroo!"[22] They were not referring to Lear's suspected homosexuality; they inferred that he was the devil himself because he could draw. From "Scroo" he derived his favorite nonsense epithet "scroobious." As applied to "the old man from Cashmere," this might mean that he was both lugubrious and inscrutable, as the accompanying illustration suggests.

Lear's preoccupation with and incomprehensison of Indian/Oriental names and languages receives extended treatment in "The Cummerbund: An Indian Poem," which was published in *The Times of India*, Bombay.[23] With this poem, we reach a point somewhat different from the world of the limericks. Here Lear uses the nonsense device known as the macaronic, a "literary construction that is written in more than one language."[24] "The Cummerbund" has as many as thirteen Indian words, which are notable for their misspelling arising out of mispronunciation and deliberate misuse. "Dhobie" becomes "Dobie" in the line, "She sat upon her Dobie." "Punkehs," "Kamsamahs," "kit mit gars," "Tchokis," "Chuprassies," "Ayakahs," "Mussaks," "Nullahs," "Goreewallahs," "Bheekies," "Jumpan," and "Nimmak" acquire all kinds of attributes and become trees, birds, flowers, animals, and fishes.[25]

This is a wonderfully evocative nonsense poem—with an Indian flavor that can only be marred by interpretation. But I am ready to play the spoilsport by pointing out how the title word "Cummerbund," the Indian waist slash, is turned into a trope for the dreaded native. Lear's sketches of Indians invariably highlight this part of the scant clothing they are made to wear. And the monitory line, "The Cummerband is come," resounds through the poem.

The poem is about a certain "she" who lives a highly protected and perhaps pampered life, very much like the memshahib's daughters. But all of a sudden the Cummerbund comes and swallows her. I have always seen the poem in the context of the so called Sepoy "mutiny" of 1857. Recently, Jenny Sharpe has shown how powerful the image of the atrocities became in English literature after the "mutiny." Ania Loomba has summarized Sharpe's findings: "This event inaugurated the transformation of an existing colonial stereotype, that of the 'mild Hindoo', into another, that of the savage rapist of British women."[26] That Lear was affected by the nearly two-decade old event becomes clear by references in his Journal to the "Ghat Massacre" and to "Horrid memories of Nana Sahib massacre" (10 December 1873).[27]

One of the horror stories told of the cutting off of the noses of some English women and the fantastic talk of the supply of artificial noses. While the cutting off of noses could be true, it has been difficult to ascertain the details of the claim. Equally uncertain are the historical details of the role of Nana Sahib in the massacre. The mutiny narratives are as conflicting as they are diverse. But from the British point of view Nana Sahib becomes a metonym for terror. So much so, rumors were rife until the 1880s that Nana Sahib was alive. It might be interesting to find out when exactly "Nana Sahib" becomes a synonym for a "bad man" in which category the man appears in *Roget's Thesaurus* (1972 edition). Some of the other entries are: "rascal, scoundrel, tiger, monster, devil etc. (demon), devil incarnate, demon in human shape."[28]

It is quite possible that Lear was familiar with some of the accounts, journals kept by some Britishers during the "mutiny."[29] One such journal tells of the siege of Lucknow; it was kept by Maria Germon, wife of Richard Charles Germon, an officer in the 13th Bengal Regiment. Mrs. Germon uses a large number of Indian words in her diary,[30] many of which appear in Lear's poem: "Kitmutgars," "punkahwallah," "dhobie," "ayahs," and so on. Lear mentions in his diary how he "got nearly killed by a punkah" (11 December 1873).[31] Perhaps he meant a punkah-walah. "Punkah" too appears in the "Cummerbund." Similarly, he mentions in a diary entry, for 24 September 1874, that there was some "Fuss about a lost waistcoat, which after great accusations of the poor dhobie was found inside a coat."[32] But the dhobie and the waistcoat are both turned metonymically into villains in the monitory "nonsense" poem. As has already been mentioned, the waist-sash is a metaphor for the native, more particularly, for the "sepoy." For what happens soon after the warning is that "She" is pursued by the Cummerbund:

> In vain she fled:—with open jaws
>   The angry monster followed,
> And so, (before assistance came,)
>   That Lady Fair was swallowed.

The following warning is writ in yellow, blue, and green, all bright colors as if to catch the eyes of those for whom the warning is meant:

> Beware, ye Fair! Ye Fair, beware!
>   Nor sit out late at night,—
> Lest horrid Cummerbunds should come,
>   And swallow you outright.[33]

The nonsense method here seems to be the appropriation of the native vocabulary as nonsense words. The words are of course perfectly sensible even to an English person, as is obvious from their diaries. But they are further rendered nonsensical (read "camouflaged") by changing the attributes, cases, spellings, and so on. So, the "dhobie" (a washer man) is represented by the stone on which he beats the clothes ("She sat upon her Dobie").

Apart from Nana Sahib and the sepoys as possible intertexts, Lear's poem must be read along with the following diary entry: "Meanwhile, two persons are there, with whom I converse, apropos of a big, horrid, vulgar, ill-dressed, gross blacky Indian, who having stared at me for twenty minutes, talked in his own lingo" (20 May 1874).[34] The little girls are to grow up fearing the natives: the cummerbunds are the adoring, lusting natives, "fool-starers," as Lear calls them elsewhere.[35]

The other Indian poem he wrote around the same time is "The Akond of Swat." This too is evocative of an approaching menace, an oriental despot. But the interpretation is tantalizingly kept at bay; the deferral persists until the end of the poem: "Is he tall or short, or dark or fair?" "Does he wear a turban, a fez, or a hat?" In every catalogue of alternatives the sign of the native is stereotypically present but not stated. Lear doesn't answer the questions: the whole poem is a set of unanswered questions. But the footnote says, "For the existence of this potentate see Indian newspapers, passim."[36] The "fat, ill dressed blacky Indian" referred to earlier in the diary entry is identified as "the son of Aga Khan, the very great Mussulman potentate!"[37]

Such, then, is the evidence, and Lear's avowal that his nonsense is not subject to "misinterpretation" flies in the face of such evidence. One of Lear's early admirers, Edward Strachey has said that Lear created every kind of nonsense. "Nonsense songs, nonsense stories, nonsense alphabets, nonsense botany. His visit to India supplied him with what I might call Nonsense philology and nonsense politics."[38] What Strachey may have originally meant as a compliment makes somewhat different sense to us than it did to Strachey.

NOTES

1. John Lehmann, *Edward Lear and His World*. New York & London: Thames and Hudson, 1977, pp. 100–101.

2. E. Neill Raymond, *Victorian Viceroy: The Life of Robert, The First Earl of Lytton*. London: Regency Press, 1980, p. 114.

3. Discussed in Edward Said, *Orientalism*. London: Routledge & Kegan Paul, 1978, pp. 6–7. Some of Said's methods and conclusions have been challenged. Homi Bhabha, for example, questions Said's thesis that "power as discourse is possessed entirely by the colonizer." JanMohammed shows how the literary texts contain features that can be subverted and appropriated to the oppositional and anticolonial purposes of contemporary postcolonial writing (see Bill Ashcroft, et

al., eds., *The Postcolonial Reader*. London: Routledge & Kegan Paul, 1995, pp. 8 and 41, respectively).

4. See Edward Lear, *Indian Journal: Water Colors and Extracts from the Diary of Edward Lear, 1873–1875*, ed. Ray Murphy. London: Jarroldes, 1953.

5. Ibid., p 42.

6. Ibid., p. 54.

7. Ibid., p. 38.

8. Ibid., p. 96.

9. Ibid., p. 98.

10. Ibid., p. 53.

11. Ibid., p. 49.

12. Ibid.

13. Ibid., p. 79.

14. See Edward Lear, *Complete Nonsense*. Hertfordshire, UK: Wordsworth, 1994, p. 74. (Originally published 1845)

15. Ibid., p. 95.

16. Ibid., p. 102.

17. Lear, *Indian Journal*, p. 181.

18. Ibid., pp. 208–209.

19. Lehman, *Edward Lear and His World*, p. 32.

20. Lear, *Complete Nonsense*, p. 169.

21. Lear, *Indian Journal*, p. 37.

22. Lehman, p. 75.

23. *The Times of India*, 22 June 1874. Ray Murphy, editor of Lear's Indian Journal, wrongly mentions the publication date as July 1874.

24. Susan Stewart, *Nonsense: Aspects of Intertextuality in Folklore and Literature*. Baltimore and London: John Hopkins UP, 1978, p. 4.

25. Here I use Lear's spellings without correction.

26. See Ania Loomba, *Colonialism and Postcolonialism*. London: Routledge, 1998, p. 79.

27. Lear, *Indian Journal*, p. 43. Nana Sahib (real name: Dhundu Pant; born: 1821) was the adopted son of the last Peshwa (hereditary Prime Minister) of the Maratha. His request (1853) to the British to grant him the Peshwa's title and pension was refused. In the outbreak of the so-called Mutiny at Kawnpore (modern Kanpur) his men allegedly massacred the British garrison and colony. After suppression of the rebellion, he escaped to Nepal, where he probably died.

28. *Roget's Thesaraus of Synonyms and Antonyms*. London: University Books, 1972.

29. For some the so-called mutiny was a rebellion, a concerted effort to throw off imperial rule. This view rejects the official British version that the protagonists were just a bunch of recalcitrant malcontents causing trouble. Indian history books, especially history textbooks, use this version, and call the event "India's first war of Independence."

30. Maria Germon, *Journal of the Seize of Lucknow: an Episode of the Indian Mutiny*. Ed. Michael Edwards.

31. Lear, *Indian Journal*, p. 44.

32. Ibid., p. 193.

33. Lear, *Complete Nonsense*, p. 338.

34. Lear, *Indian Journal*, p. 140.

35. Ibid., p. 181.
36. Lear, *Complete Nonsense*, p. 333.
37. Lear, *Indian Journal*, p. 140.
38. Lear, *Complete Nonsense*, p. 8.

REFERENCES

Ashcroft, Bill et al., eds. *The Postcolonial Reader*. London: Routledge & Kegan Paul, 1995.

Germon, Maria. *Journal of the Seize of Lucknow: An Episode of the Indian Mutiny*. Ed. Michael Edwards (no date or any publication details appear in the book).

Lear, Edward. *Indian Journal: Water Colors and Extracts from the Diary of Edward Lear, 1873–1875*. Ed. Ray Murphy. London: Jarroldes, 1953.

———. *Complete Nonsense*. Hertfordshire, UK: Wordsworth, 1994. (Originally published in 1845)

Lehmann, John. *Edward Lear and His World*. New York & London: Thames and Hudson, 1977.

Loomba, Ania. *Colonialism/Postcolonialism*. London: Routledge & Kegan Paul, 1998.

Raymond, E. Neill. *Victorian Viceroy: The Life of Robert, The First Earl of Lytton*. London: Regency Press, 1980.

Roget's Thesaraus of Synonyms and Antonyms. London: University Books, 1972.

Said, Edward. *Orientalism*. London: Routledge & Kegan Paul, 1978.

Stewart, Susan. *Nonsense: Aspects of Intertextuality in Folklore and Literature*. Baltimore and London: John Hopkins UP, 1978.

CHAPTER 9

Decadence for Kids: Salgari's *Corsaro Nero* in Context

Ann Lawson Lucas

One of the curious things about Children's Literature studies is that children's writers and texts, while commonly compared with each other, are all too frequently treated as if divorced from the rest of the cultural context, as if writers for children do not read newspapers, go to the theater, listen to music, look at art, or read other books. Salgari's separation by critics from the world of adult culture is the reason why his single most famous novel has never, I believe, been fully understood. For a century its larger-than-life protagonist, the swash-buckling Black Corsair, has retained his status as admirable, pitiable, mythicized, tragic, Romantic hero extraordinaire, the symbol of valor, the symbol of honor.

Il Corsaro Nero was published as a book in 1898, with weekly installments appearing between 1898 and 1899.[1] This chapter is, therefore, something of a centenary celebration, though a corrective one. In 1898 Salgari was at his apogee as Italy's first and foremost writer of adventure novels, and the seal of national recognition had been set upon his work by the awarding, in 1897, of the title "Cavaliere della Corona d'Italia" ("Knight of the Italian Crown"), conferred upon him by the King of the young nation: Italy, with its capital in Rome, had only fully come into being in 1871.

In late nineteenth-century Italy, the burgeoning children's literature consciously contributed to the progressive creation of the nation and of a sense of nationhood. It was characterized by educational storytelling grounded in contemporary domestic reality, and by fairy tales and animal fables (though both these were less prominent than in other countries); the two most notable—and most individual—exemplars of these genres were De Amicis' *Cuore* (1886) and Collodi's *Le avventure di Pinocchio* (1883).[2] Finally, with Salgari, adventure was added to the Italian child reader's repertoire.[3]

Emilio Salgari was, for nearly thirty years, the very archetype of the adventure novelist; sometimes the battle with nature or with villainy served his purpose, sometimes colonial struggles. Yet, for him, empire was simply the locus of physical and moral conflict. In all his four-score novels, there is no reference to the African wars being fought by Italy at the time of writing. His topical work, like the historical, employs other people's empires. Moreover, European colonialism is invariably presented as an evil. Quite extraordinarily in the age of empire, and offering a contradiction to Edward Said's theories concerning European cultural imperialism, Salgari was indeed a postcolonial writer *ante litteram*.[4]

Then—again exceptionally—in his work there was no overt cultivation of young Italians or of young Italy. Salgari never set his adventure novels on Italian soil, and even Italian characters are extremely rare. The essential purpose of his narratives is to present scenery, personalities, and events that are Other; they are at the opposite pole to ordinary experience. Clearly, his art was created substantially as a reaction to orthodoxy, and even perhaps as an escape from reality.

There are, however, points of contact between Salgari's writing and some aspects of contemporary writing for adults. His lavish and mood-laden descriptions run counter to *verismo*, the *fin de siècle* realist movement, but his desire to establish authenticity through catalogues of facts betokens a concern with objective reality, while his reliance on extensive dialogue for narrative—and quasi—theatrical purposes—is thoroughly Verghian (Giovanni Verga was the leading practitioner of *verismo*, whose greatest works appeared just before Salgari's earliest).[5] In a wedding of realism and drama, *Il Corsaro Nero* itself begins with the sound of the human voice, that of the pirate-hero, ringing out over the waves in darkness. As in Verga's masterpiece, *I Malavoglia*, it is as if the reader had stepped into the midst of other people's lives and so "hears" the story.

Unlike children's fairy tales, but as in *verismo*, there is never anything magical or supernatural in Salgari; his awe was reserved for the natural beauty and terror of the real world. Nature is generally more important than man and, like Verga, Salgari saw nature as dangerous to the life of man; yet his sensuous descriptions link him with the opposite literary trends, evident in the work of Pascoli and D'Annunzio, whose poetry—like Salgari's prose—experimented with the music and the minutiae of nature.[6] Salgari's animals—unlike both the traditional and the new creatures in other children's tales—are not anthropomorphic but are conceived as a part of the Darwinian abundance of nature.

As to human beings themselves, Salgari again abandoned the conventions of current writers for the young. The family unit barely exists in his novels and certainly there are no mothers. What is most striking is that the child characters who were now *de rigueur* in most children's literature (even *Treasure Island* has a boy at its center) are not present at all.[7] The world of adventure presented for children is a world populated by adult characters.

No fairies, no magic, no anthropomorphic animals, no children, no families: having more affinity with adult culture, Salgari's work was truly anomalous—and innovative—in relation to contemporary writing for the young. The one powerful feature that it really had in common with other children's books and newspapers was its didacticism. This was efficiently disguised by the exciting narrative and the power of the descriptions ("instructing with delight" was the phrase used by the Queen's equerry), for, in reality, each volume contained in abundance two varieties of didactic material.[8] Frist, there was always bountiful information on historical, geographical, and biological matters. Second, his narratives were typically dependant upon a strong moral structure embracing clearly defined good characters and bad characters; there were no ambiguous roles for charming villains. The morality of the stories was often their very *raison d'être*; his early hero, Sandokan, wages wars in order to defeat evil and restore good; elsewhere, quests, treasure hunts, and rescues are all undertaken for moral reasons. It was, in fact, Salgari's characteristic morality that provoked my re-examination of *Il Corsaro Nero*.

If Salgari's writing was an anomaly in relation to the rest of children's literature in Italy, then *Il Corsaro Nero* was itself anomalous in relation to his other novels. Before 1898, Salgari had written only one truly historical novel.[9] Recounting deeds done in 1696, *Il Corsaro Nero* was normal in its exotic geography (the Caribbean and Venezuela), but wholly abnormal in its hero, an Italian, Cavaliere Emilio di Roccanera, lord of Ventimiglia. The use of Salgari's own forename for the hero is extraordinary and is a central clue to the real purpose of the novel: the new Cavaliere Emilio ("Sir Emilio"), Salgari was not simply boasting about his own elevation, but was paying tribute to the Italian monarchy, which had honored him and was thereby expressing his loyalty, for this is a novel about intense loyalty.

The tribute to monarchy through the heroic and principled figure of an Italian nobleman is all the more remarkable since aristocracy is a concept almost wholly absent from Salgari's other works (nearly as absent as Italians), or is at least negated in them. In many different ways—sexual, racial, social—the novels argue for equality. For a king or noble to play an important part, it is necessary for his throne to have been usurped first or his privileged life abandoned for higher things. Sandokan is a dispossessed sultan. It is true that the corsair-knight has left comfort and position behind in order to command a pirate ship in the Caribbean, but the mood and ambience are aristocratic as nowhere else; aboard his galleon, the "Corsaro Nero" wears sumptous (if somber) apparel: "He wore a fine cloak of black silk, adorned with lace of the same colour . . . long riding-boots and on his head a wide-brimmed felt hat, decorated with a long black feather which curved down to his shoulders."[10] He lives in a floating baronial hall, surrounded by gold-embroidered silks, velvet chairs, magnificent silver, and Venetian mirrors—an aesthete's paradise.[11] His own quarters are an "elegantly furnished cabin, which was lit by a little gilded lamp, even though keeping any light shining after nine at night on board a pirate ship was strictly forbidden."[12]

The "Corsaro Nero" is the acme of refinement, elevated sentiment and higher purpose. He is alone, for his world is hierarchical, whereas Salgari's usual romances advocate and demonstrate egalitarian behavior: "The Corsair was silent, half reclining in the bows, his head resting on his arm, but his gaze, as penetrating as an eagle's, was minutely searching the dark horizon."[13] Apparently incidental touches, like the eagle's eyesight, identify the hero's special quality, and indeed disdain for the limitations imposed on ordinary men. This gentleman-pirate has no equal partner or friend, as Sandokan does. His lieutenant, Morgan, is deferential and his two ultra-loyal followers clearly belong to the lower orders; the Cavaliere commands and they do his bidding; he is socially and morally their superior. The crew see him as different and separate from themselves and comment from afar: "He looks like a spectre . . . he's as sombre as the night."[14] Not only does he dress permanently in mourning, but his mood is permanently saturnine; he exists in a tragic gloom.

Much is made of the extraordinary rigor of his moral code. The key concepts throughout are honor, loyalty, duty, determination, and courage. The "Signore" of Ventimiglia acts supposedly for selfless reasons. His brother, the "Red Corsair," had been mercilessly executed by the Dutch colonial governor of Maracaibo, and the Corsaro Nero has the unique ambition to avenge his brother's death. Rescuing the hanged corpse for a worthy sea burial, he swears a solemn oath to exterminate the Governor and all his family. As usual, in a Salgarian colonial context, the colonizers, with might on their side (here principally the Dutch and the Spanish), are in the wrong; they are the villains of the piece, villified for brutality and treachery.

The "Corsaro Nero" abhors the bad faith of the enemy. He is also, of course, a brilliant ship's commander and military tactician, and, when he is in pursuit of his goal of repaying evil with just vengeance, he too is pitiless and merciless. In other words, he is obsessive: he is obsessed with doing harm to others in order to right a wrong. He does not see it as reprehensible (nor does Salgari) that, in horrific conditions, he must sacrifice the lowly in his pay, or that he must savagely slaughter hundreds of innocent settlers in order to achieve his aim: "Maracaibo, you have visited death on me, and I shall visit death on you," he says;[15] so he will leave the city sacked and in flames.

During Salgari's lifetime, some parents and teachers responded to the passionate enthusiasm of their youngsters by voicing anxiety about the level of violence in his novels. In the main, their fears were exaggerated and ill-founded, but of all the volumes it is this, the most famous, which appears to bear them out. The frequency and scale and intensity—the relishing—of the violence are unparalleled; perhaps partly conditioned by a source, Salgari, quite uncharacteristically, engages in an orgy of brutal detail, like the smashed skulls of the enemy spilling their grey matter, and like the piles of bodies—"with their arms hacked off, gashes in their breasts, or their skulls cleft open"—running with "streams of blood which trickled down the bastions and the steps of the blockhouses, forming puddles which emitted an acrid stench."[16]

But there is worse. This is also a tale capable of moral violence. The tormented, driven, implacable hero falls in love, reciprocally, with a young Duchess, Honorata, only to discover that she is his sworn enemy's daughter. It is, of course, a matter of honor to him that he had vowed to kill all the Wan Guld family. Honorata is his prisoner-cum-guest on board ship, so, unable to run her through, this gallant, punctilious aristocrat, who is the very soul of hypocrisy, abandons her in an open boat upon the high seas.

What we have here is a far cry from the wholesome children's novel, *Cuore* ("A boy's heart"), and the invigorating fun of *Pinocchio*. But Italian Decadentism had come into being in the same period as those works of rectitude, restraint, reforming concern for others and innocence. It had been in 1885 that Vittorio Pica had published his first articles on Decadentism and that *Il Convito* had been founded as the first official journal of the movement in Italy. In 1892 Luigi Gualdo published the novel, *Decadenza*, while D'Annunzio's early novels were appearing throughout these years, *Il piacere* ("Pleasure") in 1889, *Il trionfo della morte* ("The triumph of death") in 1894, *Le vergini delle rocce* ("The virgins of the rocks") in 1895, and *Il fuoco* ("Fire") in 1900.[17] Is it, then, really possible to claim that Salgari's *Corsaro Nero*, rather than being an exhilarating adventure, amounts to "decadence for kids" or even "Decadentism for kids"? I think the answer is yes.

This novel departs from Salgari's norm (which, incidentally, was to be immediately restored). In the recent years of his conscientious writing for children, he had abandoned or at least minimized the love themes central to his early novels for adults; in *Il Corsaro Nero* the focal themes are passionate love and violence, death and vendetta, all of them treated with self-indulgent posturing and agonizing. Far from Salgari's usual clear moral parameters, here the hero, who is extolled for tragic self-sacrifice and virtue, is in reality deeply, morally compromised: he is pursuing that most ignoble of ambitions, revenge; he sacrifices others not to achieve a positive good, but, through wholesale killing, to punish. His is scarcely a righteous cause. Moreover, instead of offering the young a reassuring, optimistic resolution, the novel, exceptionally, has a tragic ending.

As to Decadentism, in his recent literary biography of D'Annunzio, the dominant literary figure of Italy for several decades from the 1890s, John Woodhouse acknowledges that *Il piacere* had affinities with the European Decadentist movement, the personality of Sperelli, its hero, having "much in common with that of Huysmans's protagonist, Des Esseintes" in *A rebours*.[18] He goes on to say that "Both have an exquisitely refined aesthetic sense, both are Anglophile, full of an elitist ambition to escape the mediocrity of bourgeois ideals, to shock the establishment."[19] Apart from the absence of Anglophilia, Byronic though the Black Corsair may be, this description would need only slight adaptation to fit the figure of the aristocratic Cavaliere Emilio and the mood of his creator, the humble Cavaliere Emilio. Later, discussing the doctrines of Nietzsche in relation to *Il trionfo della morte*, Woodhouse refers to the concept of the *ubermensch* or Superman, which the central character, Giorgio Aurispa, fails to embody "because sensuality eventually triumphs."[20] By this measure, the Corsaro Nero, in denying himself his love, with however cruel a grand gesture, supposedly in the service of a higher ideal of honor, triumphs over sensuality and attains the heroic nobility of the Superman. D'Annunzio's text, in Woodhouse's words, frequently alludes to "the concept of the hero as a being free of ordinary restraints."[21] We have seen that the Corsaro Nero, who arrogates to himself a godlike role, is just such a hero.

Similar ideas are present in Silvano Garofalo's description of Decadentism in D'Annunzio's novels, where he contends that "Form and content were dictated by the will of an exceptional individual whose ways distinguished him from other men; his refined sensitivity and his physical sophistication and taste set him apart from others."[22] The pirate's perfection and exquisite sensibility are established early in Salgari's novel: he was "a man of elevated social position," with "aristocratic hands," who was "accustomed to command"; moreover, his features "were exquisite: an elegant nose, lips that were small and red as coral, a high forehead furrowed by a fine line which gave the face a hint of melancholy."[23]

But this painting of the Pensive Cavalier had been preceded by an even more significant sculptural rendition: his looks, like his dress, were funereal, "with that pale visage, almost like marble, which shone forth from his black, beribboned collar and his hat's wide brim and was embellished with a beard that was short, black, slightly curly, its style Christ-like."[24] No doubt unconsciously, Salgari has brought together the funerary monument of a Stuart grandee and the Victorian Pre-Raphaelite Jesus, with his sweet melancholy, wearing the sins of the world across his brow.

Garofalo's definition of Decadentism refers to "the individual's sense of solitude and alienation," and to the complementary idea, repeatedly present in D'Annunzio, that "it was the exceptional individual endowed with superior prowess and sensitivity who experienced moments of supreme inspiration and made meaningful discoveries," and achieved the impossible.[25] Extreme achievements are attained by extremes of experience, and these include a oneness with "the ineffable rhythms of nature" and a profound sense of the mystery of the universe.[26] In the closing lines of *Il Corsaro Nero*, as Honorata is borne away upon the waves, which are "shining with phosphorescence and flashes of lightning," the silent crew of the pirate ship observe the little open boat, "now breasting the crests of the waves, now sinking into the abyss, then rising into view as if protected by some mysterious being."[27] As the lady is engulfed by nature, the pathetic fallacy is completed by the torment of the tragic hero high on the captain's bridge, at once victor and vanquished: "Between the howling of the wind and the crashing of the waves, there could be heard, from time to time, a muffled sob."[28]

Unique in the field of Italian children's literature, Salgari was a child of his times after all. *Il Corsaro Nero* seems to me to be a popular work for children that paradoxically mirrors the adult, elite—and even elitist—culture of its period. The extraordinary, refined, obsessed, narcissistic personality of the hero, the self-indulgent excesses of the violence, the moral ambiguities in human relations, the stereotypical heroine (elevated but dispensable), and above all the morbid *leitmotiv* of death, amounting to a death wish on the part of the hero, all reflect the preoccupations of the Decadentist writer of the *fin de siècle*. It seems to me that, beyond the desire to flatter the royal family, *Il Corsaro Nero* was a grandiloquent gesture in the direction of adults in general, a final attempt to win a mass adult readership on a national scale, and perhaps to attract critical acclaim. The perverse trouble was that the young loved the novel in droves, and refused to let their author go, just as adult assessment refused to see him in the wider context.

NOTES

A fuller version of this chapter appears in Italian as the final chapter of my monograph on Salgari, *La ricerca dell'ignoto: i romanzi d'avventura di Emilio Salgari* (Firenze: Olschki, 2000). The English abridgement appears with the kind consent of the publisher.

1. Emilio Salgari, *Il Corsaro Nero*. Genova: Donath, 1898; the title can be translated as "The Black Corsair," rather like J. Fenimore Cooper's *The Red Rover*.

2. Edmondo De Amicis, *Cuore*. Milano: Treves 1886; sometimes translated as "A boy's heart," this realist novel of a contemporary schoolboy's life nevertheless sought to emphasize the importance of feelings as a counterblast to the objectivity of the current literary *verismo*. Carlo Collodi, *Le avventure di Pinocchio*. Firenze: Paggi, 1883; the fantastic escapades of a rebellious boy-like puppet, watched over by the Blue-haired Fairy, are still read, the world over, as a classic of children's literature.

Both these works had, among other things, hidden reforming agendas. Luigi Capuana had recently published a collection of traditional Italian fairy (folk) tales: *Cíera una volta* (1882); a priest, Antonio Stoppani, had praised the beauty and qualities of the new nation in *Il bel paese* (1875); starting with Giannettino (1876), Collodi himself had embarked on a series of amusing but didactic stories featuring young Italians learning about the world. Meanwhile, the most notable animal story was the autobiography of a chick, by a woman writer for the young: *Le memorie di un pulcino* (1875), by Ida Baccini.

3. Emilio Salgari (1862–1911) wrote nearly 80 adventure novels, originally—from 1883—addressing them to adult readers through the pages of local newspapers, in which they were serialized. His first novel to be unequivocally addressed to children was *La Scimitarra di Budda*. Milano: Treves, 1892, first published as a serial in 1891 in the children's newspaper, *Il Giornale dei Fanciulli*.

4. Edward Said assumes that all western European (and even Russian) attitudes to Empire, as evinced in literature and the other arts, followed the same pattern and expressed the desire to possess. While Italy's government pursued an unpopular colonial policy (to compete with the more established nations), all of Salgari's considerable *oeuvre* argues the opposite case, lauding harmony and equality over conflict and subjugation. See, for example, the Introduction in Edward Said, *Orientalism: Western Conceptions of the Orient*. Harmondsworth, UK: Penguin Books, 1991, pp. 1–28.

5. Giovanni Verga (1840–1922) wrote uncompromising short stories of poverty in Sicily, collected in *Vita dei campi* (1880), while his novel of a Sicilian fishing family and their community, *I Malavoglia*, translated as "The House by the Medlar Tree," was published in 1881. Salgari's first printed serial appeared in 1883 and his first book appeared in 1887.

6. Giovanni Pascoli (1855–1912) experimented with language to reproduce the sounds of nature and published his finest nature poetry in the collections *Myricae* (1891) and *Canti di Castevecchio* (1903). Gabriele D'Annunzio (1863–1938) published his first collection of verse, *Primo vere*, in 1879, but his finest was *Alcyone* (1904), in which ancient myth is made present and felt in the sensations of nature.

7. In the vast and encyclopedic array of Salgari's writings, only minor exceptions to these general rules occur. Children (usually only one at a time, and only one of them a girl) appear in very secondary roles in five of his novels. Mothers appear in two novels, but are not the normal nurturing, restraining figures of family fiction. One has a secondary and largely absent role in a story of competing dynasties: she is the mother of the child who will reconcile the families; the other is a woman in male disguise: a Renaissance warrior "knight" in armor. In both cases, motherhood is a device necessitated by the writing of sequels.

8. At the height of his powers, Salgari made a habit of sending copies of his new novels to Queen Margherita, whereupon an equerry would send a letter of thanks.

9. The slightly earlier historical novel was *Il Re della Montagna* (1895), which was set in eighteenth-century Persia.

10. All translations of extracts provided here are my own. A modern but unabridged edition of Salgari's novel has been used for all quotations: "Portava una ricca casacca di seta nera, adorna di pizzi di egual colore . . . alti stivali alla scudiera e sul capo un grande cappello di feltro, adorno díuna lunga piuma nera che gli

scendeva fino alle spalle," E. Salgari, *Il Corsaro Nero*. Milano: Vallardi, 1967, pp. 7–8.

11. Ibid., p. 94.

12. His quarters were a "cabina ammobigliata con molta eleganza ed illuminata da una piccola lampada dorata, quantunque a bordo delle navi filibustiere fosse proibito, dopo le nove di sera, di tenere acceso qualsiasi lume," ibid., p. 9.

13. "Il Corsaro, semi-sdraiato a prora, col capo appoggiato ad un braccio, stava silenzioso, ma il suo sguardo, acuto come quello di uníaquila, percorreva attentamente il fosco orizzonte," ibid., p. 13.

14. "Sembra uno spettro [. . .] È tetro come la notte," ibid., p. 75.

15. "Maracaybo, tu mi sei stata fatale, ed io sarÚ fatale a te!" ibid., p. 10.

16. "Spruzzi di materia cerebrale," ibid., p. 248; "colle braccia tronche, e coi petti squarciati, o col cranio spaccato," ibid., p.247; "getti di sangue che correvano giˇ per gli spalti o per le gradinate delle casematte, formando delle pozze esalanti acri odori," ibid., p. 247.

17. The translations of the titles are my literal versions and are provided to give a sense of the prevailing mood and emphases.

18. J. R. Woodhouse, *Gabriele D'Annunzio: Defiant Archangel*. Oxford: Clarendon Press, 1998, p. 86.

19. Ibid.

20. Ibid., p. 118.

21. Ibid., p. 120.

22. S. Garofalo, "Decadentism." In P. Bondanella and J.C. Bondanella, *Cassell Dictionary of Italian Literature*. London: Cassell, 1996, p. 152.

23. The phrases "un uomo díalta condizione sociale," "mani aristocratiche," "abituato al comando" and the description, "Aveva . . . i lineamenti bellissimi: un naso regolare, due labbra piccole e rosse come il corallo, una fronte ampia solcata da una leggera ruga che dava a quel volto un non so che di malinconico," are taken from E. Salgari, *Il Corsaro Nero*. Milano: Vallardi, 1967, pp. 8–9.

24. The idea of a Pensive Cavalier was prompted by "The Laughing Cavalier" of Frans Hals, painted around 1620. For the sculptural description: "con quel volto pallido, quasi marmoreo, che spiccava stranamente fra le nere trine del colletto e le larghe tese del cappello, adorno díuna barba corta, nera, tagliata alla nazzarena ed un poí arricciata," see op. cit., p. 8.

25. S. Garofalo, op. cit., p. 161.

26. Ibid., p. 162.

27. The description of the sea, "che la fosforescenza ed i lampi rendevano scintillanti," and of the boat, "Ora si alzava sulle creste, ora spariva negli abissi, poi ritornava a mostrarsi come se un essere misterioso la proteggesse," are found in E. Salgari, op. cit., p. 256.

28. "Fra i gemiti del vento ed il fragore delle onde si udivano, ad intervalli, dei sordi singhiozzi," ibid.

REFERENCES

Fortichiari, V. *Invito a conoscere il Decadentismo*. Milano: Mursia, 1987.

Garofalo, S. "Decadentism" In P. Bondanella and J.C. Bondanella, *Cassell Dictionary of Italian Literature*. London: Cassell (1979) 1996.

Said, Edward. *Orientalism: Western Conceptions of the Orient*. Harmonds-
    worth, UK: Penguin Books, 1996.
Salgari, Emilio. *Il Corsaro Nero*. Genova: Donath, 1898.
Valeri, M., and Monaci, E. *Storia della letteratura per i fanciulli*. Bologna:
    Malipiero, 1961.
Woodhouse, J. R. *Gabriele D'Annunzio: Defiant Archangel*. Oxford: Claren-
    don Press, 1998.

CHAPTER 10

"In These Days of Scientific Charity": Orphanages and Social Engineering in *Dear Enemy*

Claudia Nelson

Jean Webster's epistolary novel *Dear Enemy*, the sequel to her better-known *Daddy-Long-Legs*, was published in 1915, but the attitudes and concerns that it expresses were firmly entrenched in sociological thought by the 1890s, the period when, as a student at Vassar, Webster learned practical lessons in welfare work by investigating the suitability of prospective foster parents. Narrated by the neophyte orphanage superintendent Sallie McBride, *Dear Enemy* details Sallie's efforts to place her charges with appropriate families and to reform the John Grier Home so that those who are not "placed out" may nonetheless grow up to be good citizens. The novel's preoccupation with reshaping soulless institutions, countering bad heredity and environment, and curing the unhappiness of lost adults as well as lost children reflects doctrines that shaped the debate on child-saving from the mid-nineteenth century to at least the 1920s. In this respect, Webster's work also offers an interesting illustration of the child-savers' understanding of their function as social engineers out not merely to ameliorate the lot of destitute children (and lonely adults), but also to protect the United States from later depredations by grown-ups whose lots in childhood had not been ameliorated. Like the social attitudes it preserves, *Dear Enemy* positions itself—as a kind of *fin de siècle* novel *après la lettre*—on the border between the unsatisfactory past and the ideal future. And like the opinion makers of the nineteenth century, it suggests that children are the true key to utopia.

It is presumably Sallie's very youth, lack of earnestness, and amateur status that causes her wealthy friends Judy and Jervis to choose her as the ideal person to oversee "the making over of the John Grier Home into a model institution"; clearly she is meant to represent a breath of fresh air, an approach that is at once innovative and fun.[1] The "dear enemy" of the title, orphanage physician Robin MacRae, is another putative modernist as an up-to-date exemplar of the scientific stance. Since the two ultimately marry, Robin educating Sallie in welfare work and Sallie bringing love into Robin's dreary life, readers are encouraged to infer that science and imagination are not enemies but allies, and that the real "enemy" is the ignorance, rigidity, and selfishness of the traditionalist bureaucrats who hamper Sallie's efforts. The problem, we may be pardoned for concluding, is the dead hand of the past.

But in fact, examination of the attitudes of the child-welfare workers of earlier generations indicates that neither Sallie's nor Robin's beliefs represent a departure from tradition. As Wayne Carp notes in his recent book on adoption in the United States, orphanages were originally founded "with utopian expectations, to reform, rehabilitate, and educate paupers," but by the second half of the nineteenth century, they were under savage attack, partly because they represented a burden for taxpayers but also for their "rigid routines, harsh discipline, and failure to produce independent and hard-working children."[2] Adoption, Elizabeth Cole and Kathryn Donley note, gained popularity precisely because of "the emerging dissatisfaction with the congregate care arrangements of many charitable organizations,"[3] a dissatisfaction largely based on assumptions about the harm that an institutional existence would do to a child's developing character. Hence Sallie's heartfelt desire "to develop self-reliance and initiative in these children, two sturdy qualities in which they are conspicuously lacking" (100), mirrors the comments of earlier child-savers.

Take Anne Richardson, who spoke at the 1880 Conference of Charities and Correction of how institutions' "necessary routine . . . suppresses, sometimes crushes out individuality."[4] Or consider the words of Mrs. Bagg, who mourned at another conference four years later that "in institutions, the children['s] . . . individuality is not developed; and they tend to come up characterless, inert, and helpless."[5] Mrs. Glendower Evans, a trustee of Massachusetts' state primary and reform schools, commented in the magazine *Lend a Hand* in 1895 that even good institutions can offer a child "small chance to develop initiative and small recognition of its individuality"; Henry Smith Williams wrote in the *North American Review* in 1897 that "all spontaneity, independence, and individuality are well nigh pressed out of [the institutionalized child]"; Henrietta Wright remarked in the same periodical in 1900 that orphanage children are typically "dulled in faculty, unthinking, and dependent."[6] Such complaints would be voiced again and again, not only at welfare-workers' conferences but also in lay venues such as the *Delineator*, a women's magazine edited by Theodore Dreiser, which from 1907 to 1910 mounted a pro-adoption campaign predicated on the undesirability of institutions, and

in national forums such as the 1909 White House Conference on Dependent Children. Sallie's horror at the "rows and rows of pale, listless, blue-
uniformed children" she confronts on arriving at the John Grier Home
(5), and her fear that an orphanage devoid of "fun and ice-cream and
kisses" will produce only "useless, ignorant, unhappy citizens" (68), are
nothing new.

Nor, for that matter, is Robin's scientific emphasis on eugenics. He is a
disciple of H. H. Goddard, whose 1912 work *The Kallikak Family: A Study
in the Heredity of Feeble-Mindedness* argued for the overwhelming importance of heredity and the need to bar the unfit from reproducing. Goddard's book was to function, Stephen Jay Gould notes, "as a primal myth
of the eugenics movement for several decades";[7] Webster's mention of it
in this 1915 novel is clearly designed to illustrate that Robin, and through
him Sallie, are *au courant* with developments in the field. A firm supporter
of the professionalization of social work, Robin tells Sallie that

A person in [her] position ought to be well read in physiology, biology, psychology,
sociology, and eugenics; she should know the hereditary effects of insanity, idiocy,
and alcohol; should be able to administer the Binet test [another recent artifact,
created between 1905 and 1911]; and should understand the nervous system of a
frog. (77)

At his instigation, she reads about Goddard's Kallikaks, some of whom
are the degenerate descendants of a feeble-minded barmaid, the others
sprung from "a normal woman . . . judges, doctors, farmers, professors,
politicians,—a credit to their country" (92). Apparently bowled over by
the authority of science, Sallie seems to agree that the "feeble-minded"—
who are, predictably, also prone to criminality—should be "segregate[d]
. . . where they can earn their livings in peaceful menial pursuits, and not
have children. Then in a generation or so we might be able to wipe them
all out" (92–93).

The easy ruthlessness of such a solution is certainly conditioned by
futurism, but also by attitudes long engrained in Anglo-American sociology. Darwin's cousin Frances Galton began publishing his findings on
"hereditary genius" as early as 1865, while another eugenist "primal
myth" that Sallie cites, "Margaret, Mother of Criminals," by Dr. Elisha
Harris of the New York Prison Association, was published in 1874. Together Margaret and the five subsequent generations of her family number
709 persons (Sallie misrenders Harris's figure as 12,100 [77]), dispropor-
tionately paupers and criminals. The fecundity and disreputability of
Margaret's family illustrated for Harris's audience the need for professional intervention in the lives of the feckless and the tremendous effect
that benevolent meddling in the life of even one child might have. As
social scientist Mary Carpenter pondered in 1875, "Had 'Margaret' been

reformed when a child and not allowed to go into society until able and willing to gain an honest livelihood, what would have been saved to the country?"[8]

Note, then, that unlike Robin and unlike Goddard, who in 1915 was still a strict hereditarian unwilling to admit that "morons" might be reclaimed, the older generation believed in reform. Carpenter's plaint hinges on the assumption that Margaret was salvageable; Harris writes that despite the degeneracy of the line, "most of the individual members of it could have been rescued and saved from vice and offences by a prompt and reasonable care and training of the children, and a righteous administration of common justice in the treatment of all dependents."[9] And if Sallie herself writes ingenuously to Robin after reading about the Kallikaks, "I'm tempted to ask you to prescribe arsenic for Loretta's cold. . . . Is it right to let her grow up and found a line of 378 feeble-minded people for society to care for? Oh dear! I do hate to poison the child, but what can I do?" (94), she proves later that she is no true disciple of Goddard. Instead of swallowing arsenic, the unprepossessing Loretta, child of an unknown father and an alcoholic mother, is boarded out with a foster family that has been instructed to provide "a great deal of individual attention . . . to pet her and make her happy" (127–128). The Victorian emphasis on emotion and the magic of domesticity trumps twentieth-century science as the preferred means of reform.

But it is important to note that while the novel takes for granted that children will benefit from placement in a loving home, it simultaneously makes clear that adults need orphans as much as orphans need adults. The John Grier Home is a refuge not only for the destitute young, but also for aimless, dispirited, or unlucky adults. For instance, Sallie's college classmates find in it employment that offers scope for their talents for economics or interior design, while her divorced friend Helen Brooks gains not only meaningful work but also a crowd of children to replace her own dead baby and extinct marriage. Such emotionally symbiotic arrangements, the novel indicates, are far superior to the situation prevailing under Sallie's predecessor Mrs. Lippett, whose "only interest in the John Grier Home was to get a living out of it" (167). As for Sallie herself, her slow seduction by child-saving saves her from a disastrous marriage to a self-satisfied politician. Finally, we have Sallie's—and the Home's—reclamation of Robin. We learn that he is a widower whose wife went mad after the birth of their child; that the child is defective and under constant medical care explains Robin's fixation on heredity. More subtly, it suggests that his work with orphans (themselves often of dubious heredity, the narrative emphasizes, but nonetheless redeemable) has been cathartic and healing, a way for him symbolically to fight the malign fate that has destroyed his family. Sallie's "work" with Robin is essentially the salvaging of an orphan, since she must overcome his bad home environment and teach him to see the fun in life. The John Grier Home, which in *Daddy-Long-Legs* served as the means of introducing Judy Abbott to Jervis Pendleton and enabling their subsequent romance, continues in *Dear Enemy* to play Santa-in-disguise to the deserving adults associated with it. The grown-ups need these children for their own emotional well-being.

Of course, we have also the matter of the adults who agree, often reluctantly, to adopt or foster the child inmates. These people, too, get more than they give, harking back to what Cole and Donley identify as adoption's original purpose: "to serve adult interests rather than child interests. If a child benefited it was a secondary gain."[10] To be sure, would-be foster parents who are simply in search of cheap servants—a motive that was widely accepted up to the 1870s or so—get short shrift from Sallie, who despite her belief in the virtues of family life over institution life has "made one invariable rule—every other is flexible. No child is to be placed out unless the proposed family can offer better advantages than we can give. . . . I am very choosey in regard to homes, and I reject three-fourths of those that offer" (61). Such disdain for purely economic "parenting" was obligatory in social-work circles from the 1890s onward. But at the same time, the belief that adoptive parents could expect important intangible rewards was flourishing.

Thus the approved parents in *Dear Enemy* include a variety of adults with different emotional needs. One "blessed woman" asks for "one of the sickest, weakest, neediest babies I could give her" to foster for the summer because "She had just lost her husband, and wanted something hard to do" (139). An obstreperous Italian-Irish five-year-old boy goes to two spinsters who want "to try [motherhood] for a month to see what the sensation felt like" (161). And the Home's most desirable sibling group finds new parents in the Bretlands; Mr. Bretland is a wealthy businessman, his wife "a charming, kindly, cultivated gentlewoman, just out of a sanatorium after a year of nervous prostration. The doctor says that what she needs is some strong interest in life, and advises adopting a child" (201). In each case, the adoptee is a means to an end, a way of rectifying lacks in an adult's life rather than an individual whose needs are paramount. Yet despite her vaunted belief that children must come first, Sallie eagerly bestows her most attractive orphans upon these parents (even the mentally unsound Mrs. Bretland), perhaps in part because of the opportunities such placements offer for social engineering among adults. Presumably healing the bereaved, the unfulfilled, and the neurotic satisfies Sallie's repeatedly expressed desire "to make over society," to "construc[t] the nation" (93, 246).

We see similar situations in adoption narratives presented in the popular press both before and after the publication of *Dear Enemy*. Bereavement, especially, had long been recognized as a suitable reason for taking in a child; for instance, in 1873 Charles Loring Brace, deviser of the "orphan trains" that transported some 100,000 waifs from Eastern cities to foster or adoptive homes in the Midwest, South, and West, identified "mothers seek[ing] children to replace those that are lost" as a major category of would-be foster parent,[11] and of course this motivation has existed for millennia. But by the late nineteenth century, single-parent adoption by women eager to give vent to their maternal instincts (which the Victorians identified as the most potent of all human urges) was also a relatively common phenomenon. We find it celebrated in magazine profiles of hard-bitten maiden ladies with ten or twenty adopted young, even while we also see it condemned by individual rescue agencies such as the Guild of the Infant Savior, one of whose precepts was that "nonproductive members of society [i.e., the unmarried]. . . . are not fit persons to take care of a child."[12] More generally, magazines asserted the social benefits of adoption and fosterage from the adults' point of view. Adopted children "postpone old age," wrote Charles Gilmore Kerley in the *Outlook* in 1916; "Foster-parentage averts the divorce evil," the *Literary Digest* remarked in 1923.[13] Dr. S. Josephine Baker told the readers of *Ladies' Home Journal* in 1924 that "the child will bring far more to the home than the home can give to the child" (36), and *Cosmopolitan* summed up the state of affairs as early as 1910 when contributor Arno Dosch remarked that adoptive parents no longer say, "'See this poor, little thing we have taken in and are trying to make happy.' Now they cry, 'Look at the fine baby we have been allowed to make our heir.'"[14]

Dear Enemy, in short, identifies two opposed sides in the American adoption debate. On the one hand, we have the progressives, here led by Sallie. Educated, young, attractive, enthusiastic, and attuned to children's and adults' emotional needs, Sallie is licensed to manipulate and finagle to her heart's content, since her machinations are for the good of the orphans, the adults who surround them, and ultimately society (every orphan she places in a good home will presumably not grow up to be a second "Margaret, mother of criminals"). On the other hand, opposing her is an army of the sociologically ignorant: the reprehensible Mrs. Lippett, former superintendent of the John Grier; the inefficient and sentimental Miss Snaith, a holdover from the Lippett administration; the chauvinist trustee Cyrus Wykoff, who despises both women and orphans; and the throng of would-be foster parents who want a child as unpaid help or who fail to understand child psychology. But while Webster implies through Sallie's youth and by references to current landmarks in sociological thought that the forces of retrogression are more powerful than the reformist wing, in fact the point of view that Sallie embodies— and her stance accurately distills the precepts of many adoption workers of the day—dominated social work fully decades before the novel's publication.

Arguably, moreover, the ultimate function of the emphasis on Sallie's professionalization, on her touring of real-life model institutions and her reading of the sacred texts of early-twentieth-century sociology, is to cast a legitimizing aura of intellectualism around the still older belief that is at the core of her behavior, namely the mid-Victorian faith in the unconscious, innocent power of childhood. For all Webster's highlighting of her characters' forward-looking actions and of Sallie's successful self-credentialing and maturation into an educated, sincere, dedicated, and effective social planner, the underlying assumption here is that children-uneducated, casual, and powerless in worldly terms-are the true unacknowledged legislators of the world. Transforming Sallie and Robin, gaining the active involvement of the entire community, and healing the woes of all the adults with whom they come into contact, these formerly overregimented and "listless" orphans prove astonishingly potent. It is no accident that it is the orphan in the background, erstwhile Grier Home inmate Judy, who is the ultimate force reshaping both the Home and the formerly frivolous Sallie, not vice versa. Her work behind the scenes underscores Webster's point that the energies of the institutionalized child may well be a powerful force, for good or for ill, within the society of the future.

NOTES

1. Jean Webster [Alice Jane Chandler], *Dear Enemy*. New York: Dell, 1991, p. 1. Subsequent references to this work will appear parenthetically in the text.

2. E. Wayne Carp, *Family Matters: Secrecy and Disclosure in the History of Adoption* Cambridge: Harvard UP, 1998, pp. 7, 8.

3. Elizabeth S. Cole and Kathryn S. Donley, "History, Values, and Placement Policy Issues in Adoption." In *The Psychology of Adoption*. Ed. David M. Brodzinsky and Marshall D. Schechter. New York: Oxford UP, 1990, p. 275.

4. Anne Richardson, "The Massachusetts System of Placing and Visiting Children." In *Proceedings of the Seventh Annual Conference of Charities and Correction*. Ed. F. B. Sanborn. Boston: A. Williams and Company, 1880, p. 189.

5. "Discussion." In *Proceedings of the National Conference of Charities and Correction*. Boston: George H. Ellis, 1885, p. 361.

6. Mrs. Glendower Evans, "Homes for Homeless Children," *Lend a Hand* 14.1 (January 1895): 31; Henry Smith Williams, "What Shall Be Done with Dependent Children?" *North American Review* 164 (1897): 407; Henrietta Christian Wright, "State Care of Dependent Children," *North American Review* 171 (1900): 112.

7. Stephen Jay Gould, *The Mismeasure of Man*. New York: Norton, 1981, p. 168.

8. Mary Carpenter, "What Should Be Done for the Neglected and Criminal Children of the United States." In *Proceedings of the Conference of Charities*. Boston: Tolman and White, 1875, p. 67.

9. "Discussion of Miss Carpenter's Paper." In *Proceedings of the Conference of Charities*. Boston: Tolman and White, 1875, p. 79.

10. Cole and Donley, *The Psychology of Adoption*, 274.

11. Qtd. in Marilyn Irvin Holt, *The Orphan Trains: Placing Out in America*. Lincoln: U of Nebraska P, 1992, p. 55.

12. Ada Patterson, "Giving Babies Away." *Cosmopolitan* 39.4 (August 1905): 410.

13. Charles Gilmore Kerley, "The Adoption of Children." *Outlook* 112 (12 January 1916): 105; "Cradles Instead of Divorces," *Literary Digest* 77.2 (14 April 1923): 35.

14. S. Josephine Baker, "Choosing a Child." *Ladies' Home Journal* 41 (February 1924): 36; Arno Dosch, "Not Enough Babies to Go Around." *Cosmopolitan* 49.4 (September 1910): 432.

REFERENCES

Baker, S. Josephine. "Choosing a Child." *Ladies' Home Journal* 41 (February 1924): 36.

Carp, E. Wayne. *Family Matters: Secrecy and Disclosure in the History of Adoption*. Cambridge: Harvard UP, 1998.

Carpenter, Mary. "What Should Be Done for the Neglected and Criminal Children of the United States." In *Proceedings of the Conference of Charities*. Boston: Tolman and White, 1875, pp. 66–74.

Cole, Elizabeth S., and Kathryn S. Donley. "History, Values, and Placement Policy Issues in Adoption." In *The Psychology of Adoption*. Ed. David M. Brodzinsky and Marshall D. Schechter. New York: Oxford UP, 1990, pp. 273–294.

"Cradles Instead of Divorces." *Literary Digest* 77.2 (14 April 1923): 35–36.

"Discussion." In *Proceedings of the National Conference of Charities and Correction*. Boston: George H. Ellis, 1885, pp. 354–362.

"Discussion of Miss Carpenter's Paper." In *Proceedings of the Conference of Charities*. Boston: Tolman and White, 1875, pp. 78–88.

Dosch, Arno. "Not Enough Babies to Go Around." *Cosmopolitan* 49.4 (September 1910): 431–439.

Evans, Mrs. Glendower. "Homes for Homeless Children." *Lend a Hand* 14.1 (January 1895): 29–33.

Gould, Stephen Jay. *The Mismeasure of Man*. New York: Norton, 1981.

Holt, Marilyn Irvin. *The Orphan Trains: Placing Out in America*. Lincoln: U of Nebraska P, 1992.

Kerley, Charles Gilmore. "The Adoption of Children." *Outlook* 112 (12 January 1916): 104–107.

Patterson, Ada. "Giving Babies Away." *Cosmopolitan* 39.4 (August 1905): 405–412.

Richardson, Anne B. "The Massachusetts System of Placing and Visiting Children." In *Proceedings of the Seventh Annual Conference of Charities* and Correction. Ed. F. B. Sanborn. Boston: A. Williams and Company, 1880, pp. 186–200.

Webster, Jean [Alice Jane Chandler]. Dear Enemy. 1915. New York: Dell, 1991.

Williams, Henry Smith. "What Shall Be Done with Dependent Children?" North American Review 164 (1897): 404–414.

Wright, Henrietta Christian. "State Care of Dependent Children." North American Review 171 (1900): 112–123.

PART III

Modern and Postmodern Instances

CHAPTER 11

Refugee Status: The Displaced Southeast Asian Adolescent in Post-1975 Life and Literature

Alida Allison

At the turn of the century, we are accustomed to seeing the wretched faces of refugees on television, children and teenagers among them, shocked at the ruin of their lives. A very small number become known to us as individuals. The young Kosovar Albanian Adona became familiar to National Public Radio listeners as her email was read over the air. During President Clinton's visit to a refugee camp in Macedonia, for another example, he was grabbed by a young girl who wouldn't stop hugging him. She was later asked why she was so avid about Clinton; "It's not Clinton," she said. "I lost both my parents a month ago and I hoped if I stayed near enough to the President, they'd see me on TV and find me."[1] If this savvy child does find her parents, no doubt we'll be seeing her sometime soon on an early morning TV talk show.

But if I remember back about thirty years, I see across from me in a crowded hospital, in the flesh, the wretched face of a young Vietnamese girl of about my age at the time, 20 or so. I was in Vietnam staying at the Quaker Rehabilitation Center south of Da Nang, and of everything I saw there, I remember her most. Napalm had fused her chin to her chest in a permanent scar. She was unable to move her head. I've often wondered what happened to her. Her life would have been very difficult anywhere, but especially in wartime Vietnam. Many of the wounded and disabled killed themselves. But if she survived, I'm quite sure she was not among the "First Wave" of refugees who left from 1975–1978; these were the English-speaking elite with connections to the West. They escaped with most of their family and possessions intact, and, statistically speaking, they have done well. No, my individual was an upcountry peasant; if she did become a refugee, she fled Vietnam after 1978, in the "Second Wave" of refugees known as the "Boat People." Leaving her highland province, she fled over land and by sea to refugee camp limbo, penniless, anonymous, and packed into warehouses in countries of first asylum like Thailand and Hong Kong. Most likely, for her trouble, she was forcibly repatriated to Vietnam—the last place in the world she would choose to go; sent eventually to make a new life in Finland or British Columbia; or left in the camp. (It's useful here for our purposes to define "refugees" as "typically distinguished from other classes of immigrants as being pushed out of their homelands rather than pulled to a new location like immigrants under easier circumstances."[2] They are escaping the present as opposed to planning the future—with no idea when or where their troubles will end.)

Because I was in Vietnam and Laos, my interest in Southeast Asian refugees has this personal face to it, but there is a more contemporary reason for all of us to be especially interested in these particular people: their children are now our students. And though being at university bespeaks some measure of success, the testimony of these students contradicts the cliché of the genius Vietnamese student who is, say, acing biochemistry at Berkeley or mastering math at MIT. The stories I am told contradict the plots in the optimistic novels currently available; if you want to find what is a much more typical tale, you have to read between the lines. The devil's in the details—or more accurately, in the subplots.

Western involvement in the war in Southeast Asia ended in 1973. But with its end, with the fall of Saigon to the North Vietnamese in 1975, with the incursions of the communist Pathet Lao in the Laotian highlands where our allies the Hmong had lived, and with Vietnam's invasion of Cambodia in 1978—releasing Cambodians from the years of Khmer Rouge rule but creating other tribulations—in all, with the end of the West's war in Southesat Asia began one of the longest refugee migrations of "modern history."[3] And, a quarter century later, the movement of refugees from Southeast Asia to the West is still considerable, changing the demographics of both Southeast Asia and recipient nations, especially Canada and the United States.

In addition to duration, the influx to the West of post-Vietnam War refugees has also been one of the largest in terms of numbers; from 1975 to 1995, "more than 2 million Southeast Asians . . . fled" Vietnam, Cambodia, and Laos. Well over a million have been resettled—note the passive voice—in the United States. For the most part, the others were resettled in Canada, Australia, France, Finland, and Sweden. And yet some million Indochinese are still in refugee camps waiting to go . . . somewhere else.[4]

Not that landing somewhere else is usually a matter of "they lived happily ever after." For my contemporaries, the parents of our students, the defining moment in their lives was getting their families out. In the

States, former architects wash dishes in Vietnamese restaurants, and mothers who would have stayed home work long hours in manicure salons. For the youngsters who came with them, however, the defining moments are taking place in a land their parents may never negotiate well but through which their younger siblings move with utter ease. They must cope concurrently with "two crisis-producing and identity-defining life transitions. [These are] (1) adolescence . . . and (2) acculturation; their parents . . . face only the latter [acculturation]; [while] children . . . born . . . in the United States . . . confront only the former [adolescence]."[5]

The city of San Diego, where I teach, has one of the largest Indochinese populations in the United States. I think most of the college-age refugees enroll in children's literature courses at San Diego State, because I meet a lot of Southeast Asians. Not all of them are acing Children's Literature, much less Biochemistry. They say they are lost, "unable to define themselves in respect to both their society of origin, to which they may never return, and to their adoptive society, which is itself rapidly changing."[6] One Vietnamese student told me she had spent four years in Thai refugee camps. After weeks of longing, one day she wanted a piece of candy so badly that she stole her mother's only pair of sandals and traded them for peppermints. A few months later her mother died, the daughter having been too ashamed ever to confess her theft. The very next month the daughter landed in San Diego as an "unaccompanied child," that is, without known family. She arrived in time to be taken out by social workers on her first Halloween. Mournfully, she told me, "Imagine, all I had to do to get candy in this country was knock on a stranger's door and hold out my hand." The magnitude of hurt at the inexplicable differences in human experience was clear in her expression.

And yet, for these adolescent cases of classic Post-Traumatic Stress Disorder and the characters who represent them in Young Adult novels, there is even more complication; "America has been. . . . a 'moving target' for refugees, requiring not merely adjustments to a new culture but to rapidly changing conditions within the receiving society itself: 'culture shock' thus is compounded by 'future shock.'"[7] It's difficult for them to keep up; refugee students don't have computers at home and they spend a lot of time on the bus.

These are the students right now in my classes in California, and, judging from the many Southeast Asian faces I saw on a recent trip to Vancouver, I imagine in several Canadian classes too. Talking to them about their experiences has reminded me of how difficult their young lives have already been. To varying degrees, they remember their homelands, and to varying degrees they remember the journey from there to here. They can tell you a lot about the failure of bilingual education and a lot about loneliness. One adolescent survivor of the Killing Fields said that living in the United States was the most difficult thing she had ever done.[8] Their testimonies in recent books like the 1995 *Teenage Refugees from Vietnam Speak Out*[9] highlight their particular displacement. From *Pearls of Great Price: Southeast Asian Writings* (1986), a self-described "small book of biographical incidents by immigrants from Southeast Asia . . . who had the war violently thrust upon them" (back of dustjacket),[10] here are just three sentences:

> The golden years of childhood; what is a lovely age for some is awful for others. However that may be, no one forgets what happened then. Neither do I.[11]

Adolescents such as the young Laotian quoted above are called the "1.5" generation, refugee "(c)hildren who were born abroad but who are being educated and come of age in [in his case] the United States."[12] They're represented, but my experience says not typified, by the most widely known Southeast Asian teenager in refugee fiction, the Cambodian Sundara in Linda Crew's 1989 *Children of the River*.[13]

Sundara lives in Oregon with her aunt and uncle, cosmopolitan Cambodians. My students' parents, from places like the Plain of Jars and the Mekong Delta, find themselves on overload in a strange country, "often amid conditions of poverty, prejudice, minority status, pervasive uncertainty, and 'culture shock.'"[14] Many Cambodian and Hmong refugee families are headed by overwhelmed widows who are the illiterate and traumatized parents of these students. A complicated role reversal called "status inconsistency"[15] frequently occurs, in which the 1.5 adolescent, more adaptable to language and culture, functions as the cultural interpreter and head of the household, navigating, for example, through doctors' appointments, government forms, and bus schedules. Although members of Sundara's extended family in Crew's novel span three generations, like actual adult refugees they are all to varying degrees and in different ways traumatized and culture-shocked. Her aunt Soka, for example, panics volubly every time she misreads an official document, and Sundara's grandmother won't even go out of the house.

Many factors are involved in adjustment, among them the educational and linguistic level of the parents and, of course, how much money they have. Another is the circumstance of the refugees' departure from their homeland. Psychiatric interviews with 46 Cambodian high school students in Oregon showed that the six of them who—like Sundara—had fled Cambodia before the Khmer Rouge had come to power "suffered no major traumas." The remaining forty of these teenagers had spent years in Pol Pot's camps and "(p)sychiatric disorders were very common."[16]

A young Cambodian came to my office last year for academic advising. I could hardly understand what he was saying, but I finally figured out he wanted to change his major to English. I couldn't see how he could possibly pass a single English class. When I recognized his name as Cambodian and asked a couple of questions, he told me that he had not escaped the Khmer Rouge. He and his parents and the other villagers had been marched to Phnom Pehn. Years of starvation later, he and his parents escaped to the jungle, slowly making their way to a refugee holding station in Thailand. He was then about 18 years old and had eaten a lot of crickets. By the time they were resettled in the States, he said, his parents did nothing but stare at the walls, existing on California welfare and incapable of providing anything for their son. They were illiterate and spoke no English. Their company in a studio apartment constituted his home and social life. Students like him are caught in a time warp, too young when they became refugees and too old when they got wherever they wound up to feel at home anywhere. In *Dan Thuy's New Life in America* (1992), the thirteen-year-old Dan Thuy says, "I have many fears. . . . I am afraid people will not understand what I say when I write or speak."[17] This is true, even though Dan Thuy is one of the more fortunate refugees, having been sponsored by her established family of First Wave refugees. Yet she shares with the two students of mine I've mentioned a basic apprehension, even identifying it as the language barrier.

This barrier is no doubt largely the reason that most of the twenty some-odd books I read were written by Westerns. Some of the books are very good, and they serve the purpose of recording much that will be lost by the time those who actually experienced the events use English easily enough to get published. My general objection to much of what is published is that Western authors seem compelled to provide a buffer for their adolescent readers; while they provide happy endings for the protagonists, they displace the more gruesome realities of fleeing for your life onto secondary characters whose stories are submerged. Dan Thuy's story, for example, is upbeat, barely mentioning her family's troubles in Vietnam, focusing instead on her new life in America. Well, after all, that is the title of the book. In Gloria Whelan's 1992 *Goodbye, Vietnam*,[18] Mai's family of Boat People has an awful time in Hong Kong's refugee warehouses; nonetheless, in less than a year they emigrate to the United States, together. In a similar desperate escape from Vietnam, however, the secondary character Loi and the hundreds of people on his boat are attacked at sea by pirates. Loi is the sole survivor. Mai's boat saves him and they land in the same Hong Kong warehouse. But, having no relatives in the West—actually, having no relatives period—Loi is sent back alone to an uncertain future in Vietnam and that's the end of his story. The main plot continues with Mai's family excitedly on its way to California.

In Crew's *Children of the River*, the secondary character Moni is, like Sundara, a Cambodian refugee. Moni's stark story is more representative of Southeast Asian refugee experience as I hear it than is the Cinderella-like Sundara's. Crew's novel has been called "an above-average romance,"[19] for Sundara looks good, speaks English extremely well if with a charming accent, makes A's in all her subjects, and goes steady with Jonathan, the blond football-star son of a rich, open-minded doctor. The guilt and angst Sundara carries with her from Cambodia are resolved within the covers of the book, which ends with a refugee's ideal conclusion—a family reunion. Sundara is acceptable to the new society; Moni, a peasant, is not. Moni is neither charming nor pretty. Having given birth while fleeing from the Khmer Rouge, she is forced to leave her baby with relatives, sleeps in the jungle, eats scorpions, and spends years in refugee camps before arriving, alone, in the Pacific Northwest. An unaccompanied refugee, she has no support. Her attempt to make a new family is thwarted when the first wife of her Cambodian boyfriend is found to be alive in a refugee camp. Moni is again devastatingly and incurably alone. Her own sad future disclosed, and after serving her role as catalyst for Sundara's catharsis, Moni, like Loi, wanders out of the story like a ghost, like a displaced person.

The real value of *Children of the River* is the very Westernness of its authorship. Linda Crew is an American who first met Cambodians when they came to pick strawberries in her fields and who was never in Cambodia. Of necessity, Crew sets most of her book in the States, after Sundara's emigration; what one learns of Cambodia itself—the war, the camps—is sketchy. *Children of the River* is really the story in novel form of Crew's learning about Cambodians, as it is for many Western readers. Embarrassingly, reading Crew's book is the first realization many Western students have that Sundara and most refugees didn't choose to come here, would rather be back home; for them, Southeast Asian culture was rich and complete. Much about our culture as seen through the eyes of Crew's perceptive Sundara is shallow and crass; much about Cambodian culture as seen through the eyes of Sundara's boyfriend Jonathan is very appealing. Tactfully, the mother in *Dan Thuy's New Life in America* says: "I like living in the United States with my family, but I think if my country had not had the Communist regime, life would have been better there."[20]

I'll conclude by praising a book about Southeast Asian refugees but which takes place entirely there—Cambodia and Thailand. Thus it doesn't have the whole conventional ethnocentric overlay of that was then, this is now—How are the characters doing in the States? Minfong Ho's 1991 *The Clay Marble*[21] stands out for the details of her firsthand knowledge of the place, the confidence of her cadences, and her understanding of the politics of the time. For the reserved profundity of her emotions and her resourcefulness, Ho's narrator, Dara, reminds me of Karana in *Island of the Blue Dolphins*. In addition to her thorough knowledge of refugee life, Ho grew up in Thailand and speaks Southeast Asian languages. At the same time, she is a Western-educated Chinese who went to Cornell, who writes beautifully, and who interacts well with publishers (she has published several books). The one Westerner in Ho's novel is a minor character, an aid volunteer himself working in the Thai camps—like Ho herself worked, like my teammates at the Quaker Rehabilitation Center in Vietnam worked.

Speaking even as something of a Southeast Asia hand, I learned a lot from Ho's book, something I can't say about Crew's or Whelan's books. The very distinct individuals in *The Clay Marble* are fully realized; they all have faces. Through the barbed wire of Thai refugee camps, their faces are turned homeward to Cambodia, back toward the rice paddies of Siem Reap. That's where they want to be, not in the manicure salons of San Diego. Like the Southeast Asian students now in our classes, the individuals in Ho's book have important stories to tell about the long term effects of refugee status. Unfortunately, at the end of the century, with refugees all over the globe, we will clearly need that information for decades to come.

NOTES

1. This incident I saw fleetingly in a newspaper at the time it happened. I was struck by what I read, but unfortunately I cannot now document the source.

2. Reuben Rumbaut, "Southeast Asian Refugee Adolescents in San Diego." In *Refugee Children: Theory, Research, and Services*. Ed. Frederick Ahearn and Jean Athey. Baltimore: Johns Hopkins UP, 1991, p. 53.

3. Ibid., p. 53.

4. Ibid., p. 53.

5. Ibid., p. 61.

6. Ibid., p. 61.

7. Ibid., p. 58.

8. J. David Kinzie and William Sack, "Severely Traumatized Cambodian Children: Research Findings and Clinical Implications." In *Refugee Children*, p. 101.

9. Kenneth Wapner, *Teenage Refugees from Vietnam Speak Out*. New York: Rosen, 1995.

10. Gail Lando and Grace Sandness, eds., *Pearls of Great Price: Southeast Asian Writings*. Maple Grove, MN: Mini-World Publications, 1986.

11. Ibid., p. 8.

12. Rumbaut, *Refugee Children*, p. 61.

13. Linda Crew, *Children of the River*. New York: Dell, 1989.

14. Rumbaut, *Refugee Children*, p. 58.

15. Ahearn and Athey, *Refugee Children*, p. 4.

16. Kinzie and Sack, *Refugee Children*, p. 94.

17. Karen O'Connor, *Dan Thuy's New Life in America*. Minneapolis, MN: Lerner Publications, p. 14.

18. Gloria Whelan. *Goodbye, Vietnam*. New York: Knopf, 1992.

19. Ginny Moore Kruse and Kathleen Horning. *Multicultural Literature for Children and Young Adults*, Vol. 1, 3rd ed. Madison, WI: Cooperative Children's Book Center, 1988.

20. O'Connor, *Dan Thuy's New Life in America*, p. 24.

21. Minfong Ho, *The Clay Marble*. New York: Farrar, Straus and Giroux, 1991.

REFERENCES

Ahearn, Frederick and Jean Athey, eds. *Refugee Children: Theory, Research, and Services*. Baltimore: Johns Hopkins UP, 1991.

Crew, Linda. *Children of the River*. New York: Dell, 1989.

Ho, Minfong. *The Clay Marble*. New York: Farrar, Straus and Giroux, 1991.

Kinzie, J. David and William Sack. "Severely Traumatized Cambodian Children: Research Findings and Clinical Implications." In *Refugee Children*. Ed. Jean Athey and Frederich Ahearn. Baltimore: Johns Hopkins UP, 1991.

Kruse, Ginny Moore and Kathleen Horning. *Multicultural Literature for Children and Young Adults*, Vol. 1, 3rd ed. Madison, WI: Cooperative Children's Book Center, 1988.

Lando, Gail and Grace Sandness, eds. *Pearls of Great Price: Southeast Asian Writings*. Maple Grove, MN: Mini-World Publications, 1986.

O'Connor, Karen. *Dan Thuy's New Life in America*. Minneapolis, MN: Lerner Publications, 1992.

Rumbaut, Reuben. "Southeast Asian Refugee Adolescents in San Diego." In *Refugee Children*. Ed. Frederick Ahearn and Jean Athey Baltimore: Johns Hopkins UP, 1991.

Wapner, Kenneth. *Teenage Refugees from Vietnam Speak Out*. New York: Rosen, 1995.

Whelan, Gloria. *Goodbye, Vietnam*. New York: Knopf, 1992.

CHAPTER 12

The Sky Is Falling: Children as Environmental Subjects in Contemporary Picture Books

Clare Bradford

Most picture books, especially those intended for very young audiences, are shaped by metanarratives of progress or development, or the integration or reintegration of individuals into sociality. Thus, Max's foray into the land of the wild things, and his subversive appropriation of adult power, conclude with his reintegration into the world of home, family, and food; Rosie the hen skirts danger all unknowingly before her safe return to the henhouse "in time for dinner" in *Rosie's Walk*; and Eric Carle's caterpillar eats his way through the narrative of *The Very Hungry Caterpillar* to emerge as "a beautiful butterfly." But the metanarratives that circulate in Western culture around environmental topics rarely have happy endings; many, indeed, are apocalyptic in their depictions of ecological outcomes. My concern in this chapter, then, is to consider what happens when these two categories of metanarrative meet in contemporary picture books, which thematize environmental topics. There is, I think, a particular *fin de siècle* flavor about these books, because their stories of ecological disasters expose the errors of the past and the uncertainties of the future, and are projected into a global *fin de siècle* mentality marked by pessimism and unease as well as a sense of urgency.

Many environmental picture books wear their hearts on their sleeves, so to speak, by parading their intentions in their peritexts. Thus, the cover blurb of Peter Haswell's *It's Now or Never* (1992), an alphabet book on endangered animals, explains that "the birth of his grandson . . . prompted him to write and illustrate [the book] for baby Jack and his generation."[1] Similarly, an Australian picture book by Jill Morris and Lindsay Muir, *Green Air* (1996), which tells the story of Silus the Southern Platypus Frog, a species discovered in 1974 and extinct by 1981, is dedicated to "all the children who may one day rediscover Rheobatrachus silus."[2] These peritextual messages disclose a lively anxiety at the conjunction of a child audience and ecological narratives; for to explain to young children that pygmy hippos are under serious threat or that elephants are still being killed for their tusks or that wilderness areas are disappearing is to construct a dangerous and unstable world in which environmentalist values have largely failed to halt ecological problems. The actual children named in the dedications of these books, and the children implied as readers, are positioned as environmental subjects, but they also carry significances over and above those involved in narrative processes, because they represent various versions of an environmental future. Such an ideological load, projected onto child readers, manifests in a set of narrative and discursive features common to many environmental picture books: a tendency toward overtly-expressed ideologies; the deployment of exhortatory and even homiletic discourses; and a mix of narrative, didactic, factual, and emotive modes of address.

Environmental issues are located at the intersection of two highly complex systems: ecosystems and human social systems. It's therefore not surprising that there is a proliferation of environmental discourses—the shared assumptions, judgments, and contentions through which individuals and groups seek to make sense of and address environmental issues. John S. Dryzek distinguishes between reformist and radical discourses, as this table indicates:[3]

ENVIRONMENTAL DISCOURSES

Reformist	Radical
Problem Solving	Survivalism
Sustainability	Green Radicalism
Romanticism	Rationalism

Reformist discourses (problem solving and sustainability) typically treat ecological problems as manageable within the political economy of industrial society, whereas radical discourses (of survivalism and green radicalism) stress the idea that the Earth's natural resources are limited, and promote transformations of political-economic structures. Dryzek divides green radicalism into romantic and rationalist strands: green romanticism, he says, "rejects core Enlightenment principles,"[4] such as an emphasis on rationality and progress, and instead focuses on altering the consciousness of individuals, while green rationalism more often attends to the social and political dimensions of ecological issues.

Picture books of the last decade lean toward radical rather than reformist discourses; and they display many of the contradictions and tensions

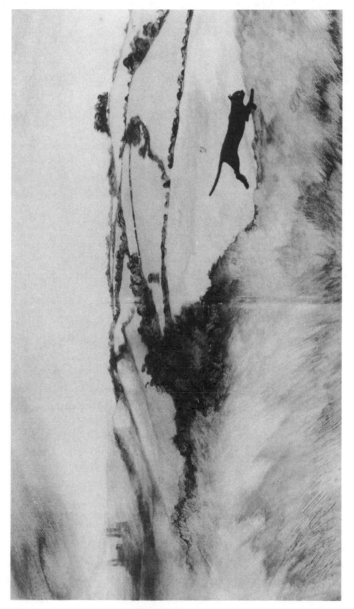

The World that Jack Built, by Ruth Brown. Courtesy of Andersen Press/Random House Australia.

that characterize them. For while green radicalism is the most significant environmental discourse at the end of the century, it's also the most fractured: it includes animal liberation, ecofeminisms, deep ecology, ecotheologies, ecoanarchism, and many other ideologies and movements; and it's riddled with uncertainty about how green politics should be practised in the face of an entrenched capitalist political economy. The picture books that I discuss, all published during the last decade, are linked by their critiques of industrialism and anthropocentrism, but they are anything but homogeneous in the ways they treat agency and relationships between humans and the nonhuman world.[5]

Many picture books range across discursive fields, sometimes in disconcerting ways. In Chris Van Allsburg's *Just a Dream*, the protagonist Walter starts off as a bad boy, environmentally speaking: he throws litter on the street, he doesn't value trees, and he fails to sort the rubbish. He gets his comeuppance when in his dream he travels to a dystopic future where houses are buried in rubbish, the motorway constitutes a giant traffic snarl and the Grand Canyon can't be seen for smog. These images of overshoot and imminent collapse evoke survivalist discourse, which calls for centralised and authoritarian remedies to curb the excesses of industrialism. And sure enough, when Walter goes back to sleep, he experiences a utopic dream of a future in which no one uses petrol-powered lawnmowers or tumble dryers.

But there's an incoherence at the heart of this narrative, and it relates to Walter's reaction when he awakes, safe in his room, after his terrible vision of the future. In a reversal of the beginning of the story, Walter runs outside, picks up the litter he has thrown down the day before, and sorts out the rubbish. These actions are, of course, perfectly commendable but in narrative terms they're incommensurate both with the nightmare visions that have preceded them and the semi-pastoral scene that constitutes the book's closure, so that Van Allsburg's insertion of a local and specific set of actions (straight out of a discourse of problem solving) and his evocation of a pre-industrial pastoral (common in green romanticism) clash with the survivalist metanarrative that informs *Just a Dream*. To put it another way, a metanarrative common in picture books (that involving an individual's self-realisation) fails to cohere with the environmental metanarrative in which the book is grounded.

The opening doublespread of *The World that Jack Built* shows a springtime scene that implies order and serenity, just as Ruth Brown's use of the traditional rhyme "The House that Jack Built" promises a cumulative pattern that begins and ends with a house—in this case, a particularly solid and stable—looking house, set squarely on green lawns and framed by a garden. The only unsettling element in this illustration is the black cat, framed in the sunlight and staring fixedly out of the picture. The cat's gaze constitutes a demand or challenge that positions the viewer to follow it from one scene to the next: from the house that Jack built, to the trees, the stream, the meadows, the woods, the hills, and the valley that encircle the house. But this sequence takes up only half the narrative space of the book, and in a transitional doublespread,[6] the cat's gaze, its pricked ears, and the directionality of the fence posts drive the reader's eye to the right, past wildflowers and grasses to a dystopic valley where every feature of the previous sequence is inverted in the form of defoliated trees, dying meadows and a polluted stream that "flows past the place where the trees used to grow—next to the factory that Jack built."

The insertion of past tense, and Brown's looming factory, color a reader's reaction to the final spread, which shows the two valleys side by side, so that the house that Jack built (at the far right of the picture) is now seen as subject to the creeping pollution that emanates from the factory. The black cat's escape from Jack's satanic mills models a reaction of horror and flight—but the house is no longer a place of safety and stability. Green romanticism in *The World that Jack Built* manifests in its representation of industrialism as unnatural, opposed to nature. Brown offers a negative example in order to change subjectivities, positioning readers to experience the world differently; and she relies not on argument but on evoking an emotional response.

A related move is more explicitly plotted in Jeannie Baker's *Window*, which locates the viewer inside a home observing the changing landscape seen through a window. Each doublespread advances two years in the life of Sam, seen as a baby in the first illustration and as a father in the last, which replicates the book's opening and looks out from another window in another house, to a scene already overtaken by urban development. The reader is separated from the scene outside the window by more than glass; the window frame, the depth of the windowsill, the positioning of participants in the room, and Baker's use of collage (which draws attention to the constructedness of the illustrations) create considerable distance between viewer and scene, inviting a style of reading that involves checking details from one picture to the next. The environmental narrative that Baker proposes is one of inexorable degradation: the kangaroos and native birds glimpsed in the first illustration are overtaken, by Sam's fourth birthday, by domestic animals, a rabbit, cat, and horse; the tree-covered hills in the distance are gradually filled with housing estates and the trees chopped down and sold as firewood. The boy Sam is, in effect, part of this book's ecological disaster story: in one illustration he is depicted shooting at pigeons with a slingshot; in another, he leaves McDonald's wrappers on the windowsill. Baker's illustrations are informed by a discourse located toward the misanthropic end of deep ecology, where urban development is treated as antithetical to the survival of wilderness. The inclusiveness of first-person plural address in the Author's Note at the end of the book is thus oddly disjunctive:

From the present rates of destruction, we can estimate that by the year 2020 no wilderness will remain on our planet, outside that protected in national parks and reserves. . . . However, by understanding and changing the way we personally affect the environment, we can make a difference.

The spectacle of degradation shown through the window implies that the best way that "we can make a difference" is not to exist; or not to live in urban settings. By narrativizing ecological decay through the character of Sam, Baker locates his journey from babyhood to manhood within a meta-narrative of destruction. Thus, despite the promise that "we can make a difference," the weight of the narrative argues against the possibility of human agency.

Nov·k's Birdman adopts a playful and parodic approach, identifying industrial society and consumerism with the figure of "the man" who was "always angry." "He blamed everyone, but most of all he blamed the bird. The bird dirtied all the monuments. It flew wherever it pleased, and it was always singing." The monument in question features "the man," in napoleonic mode; the bird that dirties it and that sings outside the man's window constitutes an affront to order and neatness, represented by the rows of houses and the spotless thoroughfare visible through the window. To get rid of the bird, the man invents an automobile, "which made poisonous black smoke," a factory that drives people to wear bird-like masks, and an airplane that chases the bird; but his *coup de grace* is a device called a "suctionkillerpluckingmachine," which finally destroys the bird.

However, industrialism as represented by the man is not an inexorable and unstoppable force, because his depiction, somewhere between a knave and a fool, allows for the possibility of his downfall. The man regrets the loss of the bird and invents a mechanical bird, which "flew and ate and walked and laughed and cried and even sang—but only at the man's command." But his invention does not please him, and just as another act of destruction seems imminent, Nov·k switches to "a forest not far from the city, the factory, the automobiles and the aeroplanes," and so the narrative concludes with a scene in which each tree in the forest holds a nest and an egg close to hatching. This closure mobilizes a common *fin de siècle* contrast, between creative and destructive forces, and depicts nature as alive with meaning and agency; but it also offers what I take to be an unintended implication, one evident in some interpretations of James Lovelock's Gaia hypothesis: that nature "may be . . . able to correct for any abuses that . . . humans can dream up";[7] taken further, this can produce an argument against the need for activism or even for environmentalist practices.

The romantic discourses that inform *The World that Jack Built, Window,* and *Birdman* are strong on articulating ecological crises, but weak on promoting political programs or collective action. A book that straddles

Window, by Jeannie Baker. By arrangement with the copyright owner, Jeannie Baker © Curtis Brown (Aust) Pty Ltd.

discourses of romanticism and rationalism is Janni Howker and Sarah Fox-Davies's *Walk with a Wolf*, which begins and ends with references to the hunting of wolves by humans. The washed-out blues and greys of Sarah Fox-Davies' illustrations take on a double meaning in the light of this framing: as a winter landscape or as a shadowy world populated by imagined wolves. Both text and illustration deploy direct address: the text works through a series of invitations or suggestions: "Walk with a wolf . . . Run with a wolf . . . Howl with a wolf," and so on, while the book's opening illustration is focused on the wolf's eye-level gaze out of the page. Here, the strategy of direct address promotes a reader position at once sympathetic to the wolf and conscious of its separateness from the wolf's world.

In many environmental picture books, like *Window*, the switch from one narrative mode to another discloses tensions within or between discourses. *Walk with a Wolf* integrates narrative modes, identifying them through the use of different fonts. Thus, the doublespread, which pursues a narrative based on the wolves' journey from winter to spring naturalizes the notion of the wolf as killer ("Hunt with a wolf on the trail of a bull moose") through the use of explanatory mode: "Wolves have to hunt as a pack if they are to kill large animals, such as moose and deer." Underlying this narrative is an insistence on the wolfness of wolves, rather than an anthropocentric projection onto them of human characteristics; and by framing the story of these particular wolves within a general account of the destruction of wolves by humans, *Walk with a Wolf* implies the more abstract principle that for humans to exploit and dominate nature is to disrupt its complex ecosystems.

The governing metanarrative of green rationalism is one in which social and ecological crises are resolved through radical political action and structural change. The promotion of activism in picture books is dogged by the dangers of explicit didacticism, readily visible in *One Child*, by Christopher Cheng and Steven Woolman. The book's narrative begins with a sequence in which a child grieves over scenarios of pollution and ecological destruction. Her development as an activist is plotted through a series of illustrations showing her first as a solitary figure cleaning her yard while around her the world is clogged with industrial and domestic waste, then in company with "the children of the world" through collective action. The hagiographical glow that surrounds the "one child" of the title is, I think, more likely to alienate readers than to offer a subject position that might empower them; moreover, the scenes in which children march, write, sing, speak, and so on, on behalf of the natural world, infer that environmental subjectivities are produced independently of individual and cultural identities. Thus, the book's depiction of a universal army of child activists elides distinctions, for example, between First-World and Third-World contexts.

John Burningham's *Oi! Get Off Our Train* promotes activism within a view of subjectivity far more subtle and dialogic than that implied in *One Child*. The boy at the center of the narrative dreams himself into a night-time train journey during which he and his pyjama-case dog take on board a series of endangered animals. While this narrative as a whole echoes the biblical story of Noah's Ark,[8] it comprises a number of smaller narrative moves encoding the boy's progress from solipsism to empathy. Thus, the elephant attempting to board the train is at first met by rejection, depicted in the gestures and stance of the boy and his dog, and in their words, "Oi! Get off our train." In the next illustration, the two attend to the words of the elephant, "Please let me come with you on your train. Someone is coming to cut off my tusks, and soon there will be none of us left," and their change of heart is enacted first through the nonchalant companion-ship of their journey, and then through Burningham's painterly repre-sentation of the three swimming together against the background of a sunny sky.

This pattern of interaction (rejection, communication, and acceptance) is sustained through a sequence involving four more animals, until the entourage returns to the mundane world of the boy's bedroom. Here his mother wakes him for school with the news that "there are lots of animals in the house. There's an elephant in the hall, a seal in the bath, a crane in the washing, a tiger on the stairs and a polar bear by the fridge. Is it anything to do with you?" This question works to position readers as active environmental subjects, for the book's narrative pattern affirms the answer "Yes." Burningham's representation of interactions in this text pro-motes an ecological democracy in which human subjects listen to what the nonhuman world has to say. Moreover, the child is constructed as an environmental subject open to reformulation and change through inter-action and empathy, rather than through the fixed and static models of subjectivity implied in *Just a Dream* and *One Child*. The boy's mother is, like most of Burningham's adult characters, oblivious to the child's inte-rior world, but in *Oi! Get Off Our Train* this lack of insight is broadened to an implied ignorance or apathy about ecological issues. In this secular Noah's Ark, then, the boy assumes the role of Noah, taking responsibility for a reordering of relations between the human and nonhuman world.

The end-of-century books I've discussed, and the many others I've sur-veyed, disclose a sharp consciousness of the immensity of ecological problems and of the shortness of time to address them. *Window* and *Oi! Get Off Our Train* exemplify two extremes of ideologies and narrative strategies; but the differences between them go far deeper than a contrast between pessimistic and optimistic outcomes. Rather, they represent con-trasting treatments of agency and subjectivity, which draw upon the en-vironmental discourses that inform them and that produce two very different versions of children as environmental subjects at the end of the millenium.

NOTES

1. Peter Haswell, *It's Now or Never*. London: Bodley Head, 1992.

2. Jill Morris and Lindsay Muir, *Green Air*. Maleny, Queensland, Australia: Arts Queensland, 1996.

3. This table is adapted from John S. Dryzek, *The Politics of the Earth: Environmental Discourses*. Oxford and New York: Oxford UP, 1997, p. 14.

4. Dryzek, *The Politics of the Earth*, p. 153.

5. Chris Van Allsburg, *Just a Dream*. London: Jonathan Cape, 1990, exemplifies a mix of environmental discourses. The "romantic" strand of green radicalism is represented by Jeannie Baker, *Window*. London: Julia MacRae Books, 1991, Ruth Brown, *The World that Jack Built*. London and Sydney: Random Century, 1991, and Jiři Tibor Nov·k, *Birdman*. Milson's Point, Sydney: Random House, 1994. The "rational" strand of green radicalism is represented by Christopher Cheng and Steven Woolman, *One Child*. Flinders Park, S.A.: Era Publications, 1997 and John Burningham, *Oi! Get Off Our Train*. London: Jonathan Cape, 1989, while Janni Howker and Sarah Fox-Davies, *Walk with a Wolf*. London: Walker Books, 1997, blends romantic and rationalist discourses.

6. Ruth Brown, *The World that Jack Built*, pp. 13–14.

7. Dryzek, *The Politics of the Earth*, p. 165.

8. See John Stephens and Robyn McCallum, *Retelling Stories, Framing Culture: Traditional Story and Metanarratives in Children's Literature*. New York: Garland, 1998, p. 56.

REFERENCES

Baker, Jeannie. *Window*. London: Julia MacRae Books, 1991.

Brown, Ruth. *The World that Jack Built*. London and Sydney: Random Century, 1991.

Burningham, John. *Oi! Get Off Our Train*. London: Jonathan Cape, 1989.

Cheng, Christopher and Steven Woolman. *One Child*. Flinders Park, S.A.: Era Publications, 1997.

Dryzek, John S. *The Politics of the Earth: Environmental Discourses*. Oxford: Oxford UP, 1997.

Haswell, Peter. *It's Now or Never*. London: Bodley Head, 1992.

Howker, Janni and Sarah Fox-Davies. *Walk with a Wolf*. London: Walker Books, 1997.

Morris, Jill and Lindsay Muir. *Green Air*. Maleny, Queensland, Australia: Arts Queensland, 1996.

Nov·k, Jiři Tibor. *Birdman*. Milson's Point, Sydney: Random House, 1994.

Stephens, John and Robyn McCallum. *Retelling Stories, Framing Culture: Traditional Story and Metanarratives in Children's Literature*. New York: Garland, 1998.

Van Allsburg, Chris. *Just a Dream*. London: Jonathan Cape, 1990.

CHAPTER 13

Playing with Frames: Spatial Images in Children's Fiction

Cheryl McMillan

In 1980, Michel Foucault tentatively characterized the twentieth century as predominantly "an epoch of space,"[1] despite the traditional historicist perspectives still very much in evidence. Drawing on the postmodern perspective, Edward Soja has argued that Foucault's epoch of space has gained momentum as the century draws to an end. He explains: "The material and intellectual contents of modern critical social theory have begun to shift dramatically. In the 1980s the hoary traditions of a space-blinkered historicism are being challenged with unprecedented explicitness by convergent calls for a far-reaching spatialiation of the critical imagination. A distinctively postmodern and critical human geography is taking shape, brashly reasserting the interpretative significance of space in the historically privileged confines of contemporary critical thought."[2]

One of the ways in which children's literature has launched an attack on what, in the light of changing cultural expectations, might now be viewed as "hoary" traditions, is in the postmodern boundary-breaking concepts that bear on the treatment of spatiality in children's fiction. The concept of spatiality encompasses a wide disciplinary culture in theoretical studies. It includes real and imagined geographies[3] and the location of new radical geographies,[4] as critical thinking examines the significance of space and spatial metaphor in a variety of social and cultural discourses. In a literary text spatiality refers broadly to the description of setting and place in relation to characters. Spatiality includes choices of spatial composition, which affect ways in which the text might be read, and these choices may involve the manipulation of the text's physical features for metafictive purposes.[5] Spatial images are constructed within the spatial framework and really reflect an arrangement of textual selections that incorporates a point of view and positions readers in some relationship to it.

Postmodernist children's texts noticeably concern themselves with variation of perspective, not so much to offer multiple subjective versions of truth, as also do some modernist texts, but to position readers where they might critique society. If this postmodernist concern seems a little ambitious when we consider that children are the readers in question, we might consider how successfully Chris Van Allsburg and John Burningham have used the picture book's spatial framework as a means of combining fantasy and realist discourses to distance the reading audience from single world versions and to challenge reality assumptions.

Setting may be considered as a particular component of a text's spatio-temporality, and is clearly subject to change and substitution, according to story purposes. Both realist and fantasy settings represent imagined worlds, while the real but rather intangible worlds, which lie behind them and expose the world of ideas, are at least partially accessible through linguistic and stylistic analysis.[6] The rather traditional site of textual analysis has perhaps yet to be matched in sophistication and amplitude by critical readings of visual codes in children's books. A visual grammar is evolving,[7] which the children of our focus may practise quite competently, given that they are reared with and versed in a reading process made more complex by the "greater number of representational forms than at any time in the past."[8] After all, the ideology operating in postmodernist picture books is accessible through the composite text. And postmodernist picture books, with their polyphonic discourse via the dual codes, meta-fictions, wide use of allusion, and maximization of compositional features to reinforce themes, invite a particularly active and competent reading audience.

In this chapter I apply some of this visual grammar to examine aspects of the shifting use of spatiality in the construction of the fictional frame. The exercise may reveal how the positioning of spatial images in relation to the frames constructed by the text impinges on the thematic signification of the narrative. If playing with frames builds new thematic contexts, it might imply that re-encoding images by maximizing the spatial features of the text encodes shifting cultural comment. A postmodernist use of space, as witnessed in the picture books of Anthony Browne, Chris Van Allsburg, David Wiesner, David McKee, David Macauley, John Burningham, and Tohby Riddle, generally asserts that cultural shift. The late twentieth-century works of these author/illustrators also attest to a primary audience with lately and keenly developed textual skills.

The fictional frame works to create the representation, which in children's fiction then offers a view encoded in story form of the child and childhood, positions readers and suggests how the events and existents of the text are to be read. The idea of the "frame" in picture books has multiple reference points, since it has particular application in visual as well as verbal art. In pictorial art "the frame . . . functions either as the immediate designation of the limits of the painting (as the actual frame), or as a special compositional form which structures the representation and invests it with symbolic meaning."[9] When authors/illustrators play with the fictional frame to layer the discourse, spatial images tend to be repositioned and reassessed, and a weighting of authorial attitudes and values in relation to the representation is effected.

While postmodernist children's books, with few exceptions, preserve traditional story shapes, they tend to utilize strategies that challenge the notion of spatial images as fixed and concrete representations. Basically, these postmodernist works are concerned with reality assumptions, because they insistently use metafictive and self-reflexive techniques to expose the fictionality of text and destabilize unitary views of the world. In the picture book postmodernist motifs, such as fragmentation, multiple viewpoints, decentering, and metafiction, may be represented visually, verbally, compositionally, or in the tension enacted by dual semiotic codes.

We can draw on particular works of Anthony Browne as representing a postmodernist ethos and many of postmodernism's formal aspects. *Voices in the Park* (1998), a re-encoding of Browne's earlier work *A Walk in the Park* (1977), shows how an evolving postmodernist use of space has gained momentum and exposed some *fin de siècle* motifs. Speaking of Browne's *Zoo*, Jane Doonan suggests that

principally through his use of perspective, frames and the recurring image of barrier of one kind or another, Anthony Browne's illustrations are constructed to support the meanings to be made from the (mother's) words. . . . Perspective (the deliberate control of space in a picture) and frames are two of the graphic systems available to an artist/illustrator in that aspect of visual communication that functions to influence and affect the viewer.[10]

Doonan's observations seem just as relevant to *Voices in the Park* (she notes the parallel constructional aspects of the two texts), which she contrasts with *A Walk in the Park* in the same article, particularly in regard to density of meaning and intertextuality.

Though the "bones" of *A Walk in the Park* and *Voices in the Park* are more or less the same, and many of the textual references overlap, the linguistic and visual aspects of the later work are more complex and seem representative of shifting social and textual emphases. *Voices in the Park* is focalized by its four main characters who narrate in textual sequence a version of their walk in the park. The individualized versions are, however, undercut by the visual code that works to destabilize the "truth" of each version, not to overturn each one's truth, though the discourse does favor a particular "truth," but to make each truth more complex than the verbal code signifies. Each version, in fact, inscribes many hidden truths, and the overlapping yet contrastive worlds of child and adult are called into play.

In both picture books, Browne examines class division and makes this division completely binary in the adult world. He suggests that children label difference less in terms of class, and more in terms of friendliness and shared interests. In *Voices in the Park* labelers of class operate in the verbal code, with four distinct shifts in register, though only two classes are represented. The difference in register is not just a question of the register change between a child and adult voice for each class, but in a postmodernist way the difference of linguistic register between the children suggests that language and language acquisition encode difference and differences, even where social attitudes would not ratify them (as in the case of the child characters). The typeface used for each version also represents shifts in register, as a visual stamp of difference.

This framing and ordering of the four voices evoke a complex dynamic of spatiality, since the discourse suggests that the arrangement of voices may be grouped in a number of ways: four separate versions (the individual's view); two adult versions and two children's versions (a contrasting adult and child view); two middle-class versions and two working-class versions (a classist view). To an extent the composition of *Voices in the Park* achieves this multiple signification, as does the verbal code, through the central focus of each character in each narrative frame and in its use of phrases and signifiers that denote class differences in language, behavior and attitudes ("pedigree Labrador," "scruffy mongrel," "frightful types"; "me and Smudge," "got to have a bit of hope"; "a funny name"; "silly twit," "a bit of a wimp"). Actually, to isolate such phrases and signifiers reflects the inadequacy of this type of process. Each voice has its own context that forms a schema for its interests. However, the cliches, like the use of space in the visual code, do connote the divisive prejudices that are entrenched in our culture and that language perpetuates. The visual code designates space in classist terms (physical and emotional spaces are allotted differently between classes) and works to value the contrasts and comparisons created by the intersecting codes.

Browne actually structures *Voices in the Park* after the symbolism of seasonal growth created in the visual code of *A Walk in the Park*. However, in *A Walk in the Park* he emphasizes the differences between adult and child in terms of behavior and attitudes that do not refer to class; he does not encode class difference between the children. Doonan's semiotic analysis shows how the seasonal depictions for each voice comprise settings that "function as a symbolic reflection of the attitudes of each character,"[11] although I suggest that the use of seasonal associations in *Voices* not only helps to shape readers' response to each character, but also effectively weights the truth value of each version. As a *fin de siècle* representation, the visual code's use of seasons casts a bittersweet mood on the social concerns of the text, though this mood is also reinforced by the visual contrasts of night and day, and light and shade. In particular, the encoded difference between the positions of freedom exhibited by the children drives the contrastive mood of the narrative.

The four voices of Mrs. Smythe, Mr. Smith, Charlie Smythe, and Smudge Smith (all the names gleaned from the earlier work) in sequence move from position of lowest truth status to fullest truth status. This structuring may be derived from the symbolism of the seasons in *A Walk in the Park* in the doublespread, which depicts the four trees and their seasonal development from the first hint of spring to full summer. Here the visual code appears to negate its own suggestion of the increasing distance (adult characters) and closeness (child characters) by physically barring the literal, in favour of the symbolic. The literal is visually represented by the positioning of the characters at the bottom of the page and verbally represented at the top of the page. The trees are depicted with increasing modality and the horizontal lines of the park bench, the horizon, and the chasing dogs lead viewers to focus on the spatial image of the tree in full summer leaf on the far right. Thus the strong linear and temporal framework culminates in a spatial image that preempts the symbolic flower (Charlie's parting gift to Smudge). Together these images realize the main signification of the discourse.

Although the four versions could be read in any order, as Doonan has pointed out, a dynamics of spatial form underlies their temporal sequencing. That the parents speak first allows both children a right of reply, which may act as corrected versions, especially given the end position of the children's stories. Kress and van Leeuwin have argued that the left-right structure in a layout represents a horizontal account of "space of the 'Given'" on the left and "space of the 'New'" on the right. The side of new information realizes higher salience than the "Given" and generally indicates "what the reader must pay particular attention to" and where established values might be challenged.[12] Since the formal structure of *Voices* helps to create a narrative and attitudinal split between adult and child versions and positions readers accordingly, the binary principle offered by Kress and van Leeuwin may be applied to Browne's arrangement of versions. To achieve its purposes, the text effectively commands a particular way of reading, even if actual readers choose to ignore this directive.

Modality in language or in images is an expressive means of judging the truth or "credibility" of the representation.[13] That is, it is a means of encoding or framing a particular worldview. Of the four voices, the highest modality, by the standard of children's illustration, is realized in the visual code for the last voice, so as to privilege Smudge's version, and to position the child audience more closely to the ideology represented in her version than to the lingering sadness of Charlie's version. The general use of strong primary colors to accord with a child's view is picked up in the yellow border, which frames the final symbolic image of the flower as a token of friendship. As in *A Walk in the Park*, this framed image is used to formalise and verify a prior, highly symbolic image, that of the two children exchanging the flower on the left-hand page of the last double-spread.

The use of hyperreal color in both the illustrations has the effect of overriding the realist verbal code in favor of the text's symbolic meaning. The single-point perspective is emphasized by the inward shape of the path and the corresponding shadows of the trees. The yellow light surrounding the children somewhat idealizes their distant figures, and the vertical tree trunks that echo the lines of the figures confirm that this image of the children is the focal point of the narrative. Thematically, the narrative climaxes with this illustration, which concludes a series of recurring spatial images in the text. The image first appears in the cover illustration, which is almost mirrored by the frame depicted above the words in Mrs Smythe's version, "Then I saw him talking." Then Browne encodes a similar spatial realization of the image, though what is represented appears quite different.

Take a look at how closely the arrangement of spatial images in the illustration of the children on the slide (in Charlie's version) reflects and becomes part of the recurring pattern. It is most closely related to the last of the set; the angle of the poles supporting the slide and the shadows of the boy's shoes parallel the long shadows cast by the trees. Like the path, the slide converges to a point where the children are located. In this way, although four voices, four versions are represented, the series of images highlights the child characters as the central focus of the story. The discourse seems to say that children have the right values, and as a *fin de siècle* motif, invests hope and rebirth for the new century in the young. On a more pessimistic note, the discourse also points to the narrow vision found in adult power structures that can inhibit progressive and liberating thought. In *Voices*, some children are freer than others to express their innate sensitivities.

To a far greater degree than in *A Walk in the Park*, *Voices* takes up the possibilities offered by physical frames. Browne makes strong use of lines and angles and the composition to create frames that play with notions of freedom and inhibition. He relates these concepts to the theme of class division, in the containment of classes within established (and somewhat stereotyped) parameters. However, the positioning of spatial images in relation to the edges and boundaries created by the lines, and the pictorial definition of the images, subtly imply a particular authorial weighting of the social freedoms and restraints attributable to the two represented classes. By contrast, *A Walk in the Park* is much less concerned to value the differences between classes and directs its focus on the difference between child and adult. In *Voices in the Park* these two themes overlap and by the end of the last version are fully integrated.

To take just a couple of examples in *Voices*, let's examine the representations on the double page in Charlie's voice: "The two dogs raced around like old friends" and "The girl took off her coat and swung on the climbing frame, so I did the same." To this point in the text, the various depictions of the dogs have encoded the most active movement and concomitant notions of freedom. On the left hand page the dogs are flanked by two plinths on which rest two rather comical statues. Their poses suggest that the two figures represent Browne's satirical comment on the stance taken or not taken by the adults. Straight lines and uniformity often denote formality and tend to demarcate space, and the quite formal design of the park, its trees and architectural features, mock and contradict the ridiculous informality of the statues. Nevertheless, the spatial arrangement of the plinths encloses the racing dogs, at least temporarily. The horizontal lines of the fence, the path, sections of the plinths and of the dogs, and their visually implied movement in a direction beyond this enclosure lead the viewers' glance to the next page illustration. Here the horizontal line is continued with the grassy strip, which completes the frame created by the climbing frame on three sides. The dogs, already associated most closely in the text with notions of freedom, come to a halt directly beneath Smudge. Their tails form a visual pun and are conceptually related to the children's outstretched limbs. The action denoted by Smudge's swinging legs seems an extension of the dogs' suggested freedom of play and movement and thus the text loads its established signals of freedom onto character. Although Charlie is part of this child-oriented scene, the vertical lines of his figure conform to the suggestions of formality and enclosure created in the two illustrations.

So the text yields evidence of its preferred ideology. Browne's use of frames works to foreground particular spatial images that in his later work carry his thematic interests with bolder emphases. These spatial images compound an image of a real world whose complexity, fragmentation, and social divisiveness impinge on a child's view. The discourse in the two texts favors and gives credence to the child's world, suggests adult exclusion from its insights, and ironizes adult constraint. *Voices*, particularly, evokes a postmodernist use of space and spatiality in its exploration of the compositional framework as a means of re-examining the historically shifting parameters of story and its processes.

NOTES

1. Cited in Edward Soja, "History: Geography: Modernity." In *The Cultural Studies Reader*. Ed. Simon During. London: Routledge, 1989.

2. Ibid., p. 137.

3. Ibid., discussing Foucault's heterotopias.

4. See the concluding chapter in Michael Keith and Steve Pile, *Place and the Politics of Identity*, London and New York: Routledge, 1993.

5. Brian McHale, *Postmodernist Fiction*. London and New York: Methuen, 1987.

6. See, in particular, John Stephens, *Language and Ideology in Children's Fiction*. London and New York: Longman, 1992.

7. See Perry Nodelman, *Words About Pictures: The Narrative Art of Children's Books*. Athens, GA: U of Georgia P, 1988; Gunther Kress and Theo van Leeuwin, *Reading Images*. London and New York: Routledge, 1996; and Jane Doonan, *Looking at Pictures in Picture Books*. South Woodchester, UK: Thimble Press, 1993.

8. Margaret Meek, "Introduction." In *International Encyclopedia of Children's Literature*. Ed. Peter Hunt. London and New York: Routledge, 1996, p. 4.

9. Boris Uspensky, *A Poetics of Composition*, trans. Valentina Zavarin and Susan Wittig. Berkeley: U of California P, 1973, p. 140.

10. Jane Doonan, "Drawing Out Ideas: A Second Decade of the Work of Anthony Browne." *The Lion and the Unicorn*, 23 (1999): 30–56.

11. Ibid.

12. Kress and van Leeuwin, *Reading Images*, p. 104.

13. Ibid., pp. 49–51.

REFERENCES

Browne, Anthony. *Voices in the Park*. London: Doubleday, 1998.

———. *A Walk in the Park*. London: Julia MacRae, 1977.

———. *Zoo*. London: Julia Macrae, 1992.

Doonan, Jane. *Looking at Pictures in Picture Books*. South Woodchester, UK: Thimble Press, 1993.

———. "Drawing Out Ideas: A Second Decade of the Work of Anthony Browne," *The Lion and the Unicorn*. 23 (1999): 30–56.

Keith, Michael and Steve Pile. *Place and the Politics of Identity*. London and New York: Routledge, 1993.

Kress, Gunther and Theo van Leeuwin. *Reading Images*. London and New York: Routledge, 1996.

McHale, Brian. *Postmodernist Fiction*. London and New York: Methuen, 1987.

Meek, Margaret. "Introduction." In *International Companion Encyclopedia of Children's Literature*. Ed. Peter Hunt. London and New York: Routledge, 1996.

Nodelman, Perry. *Words About Pictures: The Narrative Art of Children's Books*. Athens, GA: U of Georgia P, 1988.

Soja, Edward. "History: Geography: Modernity." In *The Cultural Studies Reader*. Ed. Simon During. London: Routledge, 1989.

Stephens, John. *Language and Ideology in Children's Fiction*. London and New York: Longman, 1992.

Uspensky, Boris. *A Poetics of Composition*. Trans. Valentina Zavarin and Susan Wittig. Berkeley: U of California P, 1973.

CHAPTER 14

We Are All in the Dumps with Bakhtin: Humor and the Holocaust

Lydia Williams

8,000 Jews were executed by the Security Service.[1]

The above quotation is a single line in a report of the local military headquarters in Mariupol, dated 29 October 1941. Visualizing 8,000 individuals is beyond my imaginative capacity, and six million is totally beyond my comprehension. Fiction offers a means of putting a face on these figures. Walt Whitman described literature as a "means of morally influencing the world," and in the discussion of Holocaust fiction for children, his comment seems particularly pertinent. Writing about the Holocaust for children immediately presents authors with a complex set of problems. The etiquette of writing about the Holocaust and that of writing for children dictate unusual requirements. On the one hand, writing about the Holocaust is subject to similar sets of concerns as any other historical material. On the other hand, the Holocaust is unique in terms of its enormity and implications. Certain expectations have been created, although these are usually left implicit.

My introductory comments rest upon a number of implicit conventions I would now like to make explicit:

1. The Holocaust should be represented, in its totality, as a unique event in history.
2. Representations of the Holocaust should be as accurate and faithful as possible. No changes, even for artistic reasons, are acceptable.
3. The Holocaust should be treated as a solemn, even sacred, event, with a seriousness admitting no response that might obscure its enormity or dishonor its dead.

4. All writing about the Holocaust should adopt an ethical position that fosters resistance.

5. We must not forget.[2]

These conventions are not all-powerful and there are many texts that do not bow to the restrictions they would impose. Nevertheless, as a guiding set of principles, they touch the core of what writing about the Holocaust entails.

These five principles need to be combined with an equally ill-defined, but nevertheless powerful, set of principles for writing for children. This is no easy task. Holocaust stories immediately break some of the generally accepted norms of children's fiction. They introduce the child to a world in which parents are not in control, where evil is truly present and where survival does not depend upon one's wits, but upon luck. Despite these complications, the subject cannot simply be avoided. The "rule" that we must not forget places a moral obligation upon adults to tell children what happened.

Despite the emergence of so-called "problem" novels (YA books), which focus on politically correct issues and problems, the tendencies to protect the child, to seek out happy endings, and to "promise happiness"[3] have remained common aspects of children's fiction. Even texts that ignore these conventions tend to provide a sense of resolution, which is not as easy when the subject matter is genocide. A further element in the etiquette of writing is based on the belief that young readers are more likely to empathize deeply or identify with fictional characters. Whether children identify with the aggressors or with the victims, they are placed in an agonizing situation. Thus readers either need to be discouraged from identifying or the protagonist must be suitable.

I'll briefly summarize: writing about the Holocaust for children requires authors to engage with conventions for writing for children and conventions that relate specifically to the Shoah as a subject. This presents authors with a challenging set of limitations. In my forthcoming book,[4] I examine a range of strategies used to combine these two sets of etiquette. Some authors' attempts are so rigid their texts are static and, frankly, soulless. Some fall into the trap of writing adventure stories. Other authors, however, respond imaginatively to this challenge. Those that walk closest to the borders of breaking the rules of decorum or etiquettes of writing are often the most successful.

Blending humorous elements with Holocaust fiction has proved effective, although not all critics approve. Such humor is subversive: it challenges the requirement that the Holocaust be treated seriously, allowing no room for responses that might obscure its enormity or dishonor its dead. When it is successful, humor opens up new ways of seeing history. Consequently, there are a number of quality books about the Holocaust

for children that employ humor to combine the two etiquettes of Holocaust fiction for children. In this chapter, I examine one such work: Maurice Sendak's *We Are All in the Dumps with Jack and Guy*, hereafter referred
to as *In the Dumps*.⁵ *In the Dumps* is a richly layered illustrative interpretation of the two well-known nursery rhymes: "We are all in the dumps"
and "Jack and Gye."⁶

Sendak's illustrations make interpictorial references to such things as
the homeless in modern America, the Vietnam War, the coming of the
Messiah, as well as the Holocaust. None of these subjects is directly referred to in the rhymes (they predate the Shoah by almost two centuries).
The mood is humorous, despite the sombre tones and diluted colors. The
protagonists are Sendak's familiar "little greenhorns just off the boat. They
. . . look as if the burdens of the world were on their shoulders."⁷ The
other characters include a Christ-figure, whom some critics think of as a
Somalian refugee and others regard as Ghandi, and some anthropomorphic kittens and rats respectively representing Jews and Nazis. The use of
animal figures is one of the main elements of humor. It has been successfully used in Holocaust fiction before. Art Spiegelman's ground-breaking
Maus books use comic-strip techniques to create a highly original novel.⁸
The Nazis are depicted as cats, the Jews as mice, the Poles as pigs, and
the Americans as dogs. Sendak's decision to reverse the natural roles and
depict the Jews as kittens and the Nazis as rats can be read as a commentary on Spiegelman's books. Spiegelman portrays his father as a penny-
pinching, bitter, warped man. Vladek Spiegelman is so cantankerous, no
one enjoys his company, not even his wife. In the second *Maus* book,
Spiegelman tells his therapist how difficult he finds it to create an anti-
Semitic view of his father as a miser. Sendak, it would seem from his
inversion of the logical order, is even more displeased.

The idea of combining humor with the Holocaust seems deeply dis-
tasteful, if not offensive or vulgar. It also seems not to take the Holocaust
seriously. The cat and mouse iconography appears to bring the events of
the Holocaust down to a grossly oversimplified level. But Bakhtin's notion
of the carnivalesque provides a useful framework for understanding
comic elements in Holocaust fiction. Carnival attacks the rules, regula-
tions, and hierarchies that it addresses. Actuality is acknowledged, and
even celebrated, but it is not accepted as final. Carnival requires the deliberate suspension of actual order in favour of an imagined order. The
new order faithfully reproduces the old order, while at the same time
parodying specific elements within the old order. While the festival spirit
reigns, the logic of the community is preserved even though the "real"
world has been turned upside down.

Carnival humor is subversive. In attacking the rules, especially the rules
of decorum, carnival allows the community to temporarily step outside
itself in order to gain the necessary distance for self-examination. The

same holds true for fiction. All fiction attempts to displace the real world and impose an imaginary world in its stead; humorous fiction merely does so to a greater extent. Rather than getting bogged down and depressed, authors like Sendak use humor to hold their material at a distance and pass a sharp, analytical eye over the scenes. By attacking the rule of etiquette that suggests laughter should not be placed in tandem with genocide, Sendak creates a new position from which to view history. Sendak's reference to homelessness and the power of corporate America creates a particular viewpoint that is held together by comedy.

One of the few critics to examine Holocaust comedy, Terrence Des Pres,[9] argues that ironic humor is often the best attitude to adopt. Since verisimilitude is impossible, realistic fiction often seems bland. A comically ironic stance allows authors freedom from having to describe. As a result, they are better equipped for analytical commentary. This position has also been more generally argued about humorous genres as a whole by Mikhail Bakhtin.[10] His views are particularly appropriate for examining humorous elements in Holocaust fiction for children.

John Stephens has applied Bakhtinian theory to the study of children's literature and identified three types of carnivalesque texts: time out, inverted ideology, and endemically subversive.[11] "Time Out" texts provide the child protagonist with the means to step outside the socialisation process temporarily. During the time out, the protagonist experiences the possibility to take on a new role, but returns to the established order, usually with greater self-knowledge. "Inverted Ideology" refers to texts that gently mock socially received ideas by replacing them with their opposite. Weakness is valued over strength, female values over male ones, and so on. "Endemically Subversive" texts challenge the existing order by transgressing received paradigms of authority. *In the Dumps* can be read in terms of a "time out" text, although the process of "socialization" is, in part, what is being interrogated. In the fantasy world of *In the Dumps*, the protagonists are temporarily transported from their lives in modern day New York and transported to Auschwitz. During this excursion, they take on adult responsibilities, which they maintain upon their return. I will return to the specific issue of role changing after I consider some of the other, more obvious, elements of carnival in *In the Dumps*.

The first, and arguably most dominant, expression of carnivalesque in *In the Dumps* is the unorthodox manner in which Sendak plays with the genre of nursery rhyme. Nursery rhymes form an unexpected medium for addressing the Holocaust. This genre-confusion reduces the possibility of a clichéd response. The alienation effect enables the onlooker (in this case, the reader) to listen to information afresh. On one level, we adults have become used to images of emaciated bodies lying in bunks in concentration camps. We have seen pictures of the piles of corpses and the smoke rising from the stacks. On one level we "know" about the Holocaust. On another level, how can we ever "know" all the stories of the millions of individuals who were murdered? Sendak's use of an alienating format allows sophisticated readers to reexamine what they "know."

The alienation effect is also valuable for unsophisticated readers because it prevents them from knowing more than they want to know. The picture of the kittens in their bunks is only frightening if one has already seen photographs of victims in their bunks. The kittens are drawn in a stylized manner that links the shape of their heads with the Star of David. Whether or not this is picked up depends of the reader's prior experience and background knowledge. Some of the images Sendak employs are only accessible to the most mature of readers. Neumeyer[12] picks up an inter-pictorial association with van der Weyden's painting of the deposition, which leads to an interpretation of *In the Dumps* as recounting the coming of the Messiah. Neumeyer's association is well beyond the reach of most child readers (and, I suspect, a great many adult readers). Nevertheless, the image has been planted. If the reader has no prior knowledge of the Holocaust, the smoke belching out of the "bakery" chimneys will hold no sinister implications. Nevertheless, the oppressive mood of this illustration encourages a particular set of attitudes to be reawakened when the image is reencountered at a later date. Thus, even when readers lack background knowledge, the iconotext can inspire the spirit of resistance.

The distancing or alienation afforded by the use of humor also helps authors overcome one of the problems of writing about the Holocaust I mentioned earlier: identification. Stephens notes that characters in carnivalesque texts invite sympathy, not empathy. He describes a "splitting of attitude between the character and the action. . . . The effect is to discourage identification with the character as subject."[13] Humorous fiction about the Holocaust operates in a similar manner. By discouraging identification between child-readers and protagonists, the author is able to get closer to the horror.

Jack and Guy, the heroes of *In the Dumps*, are two of a very limited number of characters in children's literature to actually enter a death camp. In sending them, Sendak satisfies many of the unspoken rules of etiquette governing both Holocaust fiction and writing for children. He treats the Holocaust seriously, not shying from the enormity of the events as he lays open the most frightening aspect for the reader's perusal. Despite the obvious importance of mentioning the "eerie, silent world of gas, ashes, and flame"[14] if the Holocaust is to be represented "in its totality," they are generally considered too frightening to mention. In my research on Holocaust fiction for children, I have come across a considerable number of texts dealing with exile, hiding, partisans, and ghetto life, but relatively few camp stories. The crematoria, the focal point of the Holocaust, need to be addressed in Shoah fiction for children. Yet, in keeping with the basic etiquette of writing for children, that they should not be frightened, the key elements of the gas chambers and ovens are often missing.[15] Humor enables Sendak to approach the camps, literally sending his protagonists crawling through the smoke belching out of the crematoria into the heart of the killing fields. At the same time, he uses humor as a means of distancing the child-reader from identifying with the young protagonists.

Let us examine the sequence of nine pictures in which Jack and Guy enter Auschwitz, since it contains many elements of carnival. The moon "in a fit" unceremoniously dumps the protagonists in a rye field. Up until this point, Jack and Guy have been parts of a single collective personality; however, their encounter with the poor little kid in the rye field causes them to split into two distinct characters. Jack stumbles over the little kid, while Guy cheerfully recognizes one of the missing kittens. The innocence of the little kid is emphasised in the naive way in which he first plays with and then kisses the rough, street-wise Jack. Jack's dandling has a distinctly awkward element, but he nevertheless lifts the baby boy into his arms in an embrace. The kiss of the little child, the Christfigure, is so confusing and threatening to Jack that he fails to notice Auschwitz. Guy, on the other hand, has seen the crematoria chimneys and can hear what the kitten is explaining. Thus when Jack expresses the regressive desire to knock the little kid on the head, Guy chooses to adopt the socialized adult role and care for both the little kid and the kittens. The adoption of the socialized position is rewarded by the arrival of the moon/Cheshire cat figure who takes the dominant role in the final destruction of the rats and the returning of the victims home. However, this physical return does not mean a return to childhood. Jack and Guy become parent figures to the little kid, although they are not alone in this task; the community steps in to help. This, again, signals the use of carnival as a means of communicating horror within the confines of the two sets of etiquette.

Community is another key element of carnival. Even though carnival humor degrades that which has been held reverent or solemn, it celebrates the regenerative powers of human community, usually by indulging in food and sex. Rejoicing in food is particularly prevalent in the context of Holocaust literature for children, which is hardly surprising given its centrality in children's fiction generally.[16] The search for food and its discovery take on exaggerated importance at the plot level as survival literally comes to depend on a loaf of bread. Food, as we are aware, is often symbolic of love. Unconditional amounts of food are equated with unconditional love. *In the Dumps* is built around a rhyme that celebrates community spirit in the providing of bread. Guy's adoption of the role of parent is tied to his proposal that they buy the little boy some bread. With this act, Jack and Guy display their love for the socially "undesirable" elements of their community. The final scene, depicting Jack and Guy raising the little kid "as other folk do," is simultaneously a celebration of community spirit in a ghetto and a critical attack that such "sterling products" have been left outside in the cold, separated from their mainstream community.

Stephens states that carnivalesque texts take the world "less seriously,"[17] and this is precisely what enables them to step outside and critically evaluate what is happening. This would imply that carnival instantly breaks one of the requirements of Holocaust writing. However, I argue that carnivalesque in the hands of a skilled craftsman like Sendak takes power structures very seriously. *In the Dumps* examines the implicit assumptions on which power is based; it pays attention to how power operates and, in doing so, it makes links between current policies and history. Although the tone of this examination is humorous, Sendak is clearly very serious and concerned. Humor enables Sendak to go deeper into the subject than most realistic fiction. Realistic texts tend to edit out elements such as the gas chambers, leaving children with a distorted view of the events. By an odd quirk of human sensibility, humor enables the child-reader to get closer, to bear witness, and to escape unscathed, but wiser.

NOTES

1. Raul Hilberg, "I Was Not There." In *Writing and the Holocaust*. Ed. Berel Lang. New York and London: Holmes & Meier, 1988, p. 18.

2. Points 1–3 are paraphrased from Terrence Des Pres, "Holocaust Laughter?" In *Writing and the Holocaust*, p. 217.

3. Fred Inglis, *The Promise of Happiness: Value and Meaning in Children's Fiction*. Cambridge: Cambridge UP, 1981.

4. Lydia Williams, *Representations of the Holocaust in Children's and Young Adult Fiction*. New York and London: Garland, forthcoming.

5. Maurice Sendak, *We are all in the Dumps with Jack and Guy: Two Nursery Rhymes with Pictures by Maurice Sendak*. New York: HarperCollins, 1993.

6. See Iona and Peter Opie, *The Oxford Nursery Rhyme Book*. Oxford: Clarendon Press, 1955, pp. 95, 143.

7. Maurice Sendak in Selma Lanes, *The Art of Maurice Sendak*. New York: Harry N. Abrams, 1980, p. 26.

8. Art Spiegelman, *Maus: A Survivor's Tale*. New York: Penguin, 1987–1990.

9. Des Pres, "Holocaust Laughter?", pp. 216–233.

10. Mikhail Bakhtin, *Rabelais and His World*. Bloomington: Indiana UP, 1984.

11. John Stephens, *Language and Ideology in Children's Fiction*. London and New York: Longman, pp. 121ff.

12. Peter Neumeyer, "We Are All in the Dumps with Jack and Guy: Two Nursery Rhymes with Pictures by Maurice Sendak," *Children's Literature in Education*, 25 (1994): 38.

13. Stephens, *Language and Ideology*, p. 125.

14. Eric A. Kimmel, "Confronting the Ovens: The Holocaust and Juvenile Fiction." *The Horn Book*, LIII (1977): 90.

15. Ibid., pp. 84–91.

16. Ulla Bergstrand and Maria Nikolajeva, *Lockergommarnas Kungarike Om matens roll i barnlitteraturen*. Stockholm: Centrum fur barnkulturforskning vid Stockholms universitet, 1999.

17. Stephens, *Language and Ideology*, p. 156.

REFERENCES

Bakhtin, Mikhail. *Rabelais and His World*. Bloomington: Indiana UP, 1984.

Bergstrand, Ulla and Nikolajeva, Maria. *Lockergommarnas Kungarike Om matens roll i barnlitteraturen* [*The Realm of Gourmands: The Role of Food in Children's Literature*] Stockholm: Centrum fur barnkulturforskning vid Stockholms universitet, 1999.

Des Pres, Terrence. 1988. "Holocaust Laughter?" In Lang, *Writing and the Holocaust*. Ed. Berel Lang. New York and London: Holmes and Meier, 1988, pp. 216–233.

Hilberg, Raul. 1988. "I Was Not There." In *Writing and the Holocaust*, pp. 17–25.

Inglis, Fred. *The Promise of Happiness: Value and Meaning in Children's Fiction*. Cambridge: Cambridge UP, 1981.

Kimmel, Eric A. "Confronting the Ovens: The Holocaust and Juvenile Fiction." *The Horn Book*, LIII (1977): 84–91.

Lanes, Selma G. *The Art of Maurice Sendak*. New York: Harry N. Abrams, 1980.

Neumeyer, Peter. "We Are All in the Dumps with Jack and Guy: Two Nursery Rhymes with Pictures by Maurice Sendak." *Children's Literature in Education*, 25 (1994): 29–40.

Sendak, Maurice. *We are all in the Dumps with Jack and Guy: Two Nursery Rhymes with Pictures by Maurice Sendak*. New York: HarperCollins, 1993.

Spiegelman, Art. *Maus: A Survivor's Tale*. New York: Penguin, 1987–1990.

Stephens, John. *Language and Ideology in Childrenís Fiction*. London and New York: Longman, 1992.

Williams, Lydia. *Representations of the Holocaust in Children's and Young Adult Fiction*. New York and London: Garland, forthcoming.

PART IV

Science Fiction and Fantasy

Shifting Shapes of Fear in Contemporary Children's Fantasy: Philip Pullman's *The Golden Compass* and *The Subtle Knife*

Millicent Lenz

WHY SO MANY HAIR-RAISING PHANTOMS?

At the beginning of the twenty-first century, a striking number of contemporary books of fantasy for young people portray children or teenagers caught in dramatic interplay with phantom-like shape-shifters, specters, and daemons. Why, one wonders, such a proliferation of such characters at this time? Is it a phenomenon born of the dark side of our *fin de siècle* collective unconscious, fraught with apocalyptic fears? Are such stories a way of engaging some deep-seated anxieties and, perhaps, putting our spectral enemies to rest by battling them in our imaginations—calling at the same time on friendly spirits to help us triumph?

These are weighty questions, and satisfying answers elude us. Those who write the history of our era may put the chaos and anxieties of our times in perspective; in the meantime, it may be fruitful to examine a particular fantasist's work as representative of the contemporary shapes of fear in children's books, hoping to come to a few understandings about the imaginative worlds presently available to young readers.

KINDS OF SPECTRAL BEINGS

In *The Golden Compass* and *The Subtle Knife*, volumes one and two respectively of his trilogy, "His Dark Materials," Philip Pullman creates a universe of uncountable billions of parallel worlds. In these worlds, spectral beings are broadly speaking of two types: the first are friendly allies, helpers in the struggle for survival; the second are embodiments of dangerous and destructive alien forces. Pullman has portrayed his worlds in shimmering, metaphorical language equal to his epic theme.[1] His daemons are souls in animal form, each twinned for life with a human being, "a thinking, talking, feeling, animal-shaped being [usually] of the opposite sex" (Bethune 58). Until a person attains the age of puberty, his or her daemon can shift shape freely; with puberty, daemons become "fixed" in shapes that represent their respective human's established soul states. Thus Pullman artfully conveys the fluidity of the child's nature versus the rigidity of the adult's, and at the same time communicates an immediate impression of a character's essence or, in the case of the child, the current state of soul. Thus in *The Golden Compass*, eleven-year-old Lyra's daemon, Pantalaimon, can be a mouse or a wildcat or whatever the two of them wish.

In contrast, Pullman's Specters are soul-eaters, phantoms who snatch and devour the daemons of any hapless adults who fall into their clutches (for unexplained reasons, they are oblivious to the daemons of children). Children's daemons, however, have equally terrible predators—adults such as Lyra's mother, the coldly beautiful but wholly evil Mrs. Coulter—who prey upon them for the purposes of separating them from their child, thus foully perpetrating soulmurder, leaving the child soul-dead. Mrs. Coulter heads the hated G.O.B., General Oblation Board, aptly termed "the Gobblers," whose practice is to kidnap children, spirit them away to a station in the far North, and mercilessly sever them from their daemons, all in the interest of a misguided desire to control the destiny of the world.

OBJECTS OF FEAR, LITERARY DEPICTION OF FEAR, AND CHILDREN'S REACTIONS, AND RESOLUTIONS

I survey these two novels in terms of the three major fears they depict, the figurative means of representing these fears, and the child protagonists' responses to fear. The chapter will close with some speculations on how figures of fear might be understood in terms of millennial, apocalyptic, or *fin de siècle* considerations.

THE FIRST FEAR: SOUL LOSS

Lyra's first fear in *The Golden Compass* is fear of the loss of her daemon, Pantalaimon, for she hears rumors of the terrible Gobblers. Fortunately, countering the predatory adults there are others who seek to protect the children from enemy assaults, notably Iorek Byrnison, the armored bear, and Lee Scoresby, the balloonist, both of whom befriend Lyra. There are also the sympathetic witches, such as Serafina Pekkala. In *The Subtle Knife*, Will's daemon is invisible, internalized as a voice of conscience, thus not so obviously in peril, but he must combat the evil forces arraigned against the Bearer of the Knife. Both Will and Lyra are destined to be in greater jeopardy when they reach puberty, when the Specters will seek to devour them.

THE SECOND FEAR: FEAR OF ABANDONMENT

A second, closely related fear central to both books is the fear of abandonment. Lyra and Will are, for all practical purposes, orphaned, for they are separated from their biological parents by physical absence and emotional distance. Their parents are either incapable of nurturing them because of psychological illness (Will's mother), absence (Will's father), or worse, prove to be their mortal enemies (Lyra's mother), or are otherwise preoccupied (Lyra's father, obsessed with his seemingly mad quest to topple the Authority). Becoming aware of her mother's complicity in the intercision of children at the euphemistically named "Station," called more accurately by others "Bolvanger, the fields of evil" (*Golden Compass* 187), Lyra fears her more than anyone else. Will finds loyalty and emotional support from Lyra. Will's role, like Lyra's, is predestined: he is to be a warrior in an epic struggle; Lyra's destiny is, as Serafina Pekkala notes, to "bring about the end of destiny" (*Golden Compass* 310).[2] In *The Subtle Knife*, however, Lyra gives priority to a personal relationship; she must help Will find his father. Both Will and Lyra counter their fears of abandonment in part through action and through mutual support.

As Lyra fears her mother, she grows to feel revulsion for her father. First introduced as her uncle but then revealed to have fathered her in an adulterous relationship with Mrs. Coulter, Lord Asriel is the hubris-intoxicated scientist whose grandiose scheme, revealed in *The Golden Compass*, is to find a way to travel to a world beyond the Northern Lights to solve the mystery of the origin of Dust. Dust, he is convinced, is the source of "all the death, the sin, the misery, the destructiveness in the world." Eradicating Dust would mean eradicating original sin, the inherent defect of human nature: "Human beings can't see anything without wanting to destroy it," he asserts; then he vows, "Death is going to die" (*Golden Compass* 377). The one way to tear a hole in the barriers between worlds, however, is to harness the colossal energy released by severing a child from his daemon. Late in *The Golden Compass* Lord Asriel cold-bloodedly sacrifices Roger, Lyra's friend, in order to pierce the vault of heaven and open a pathway to a new world. Earlier, Lyra herself has barely been spared being severed from Pantalaimon: she is rescued from the blade of the Silver Guillotine by Mrs. Coulter just in the nick of time. In *The Subtle*

Knife, however, Mrs. Coulter vows to destroy her daughter, when she learns Lyra's true destiny: to be a new Eve. The second great fear for children thus involves betrayal by the adults who ought to be their protectors.

Like Lyra, Will has been virtually alone in the world since the mysterious disappearance of his father on a research project in the Arctic when Will was too young to have any memory of him. His mother is physically present but emotionally remote; she regales him with tales of his father's adventures and tells him he will assume his father's mantle, but she sadly suffers from a depression Will later suspects may be Spectre-induced. Will must protect her, rather than the other way around: for Will, "Home was the place he kept safe for his mother, not the place others kept safe for him" (*Subtle Knife* 307). Both children are sexually innocent, standing on the verge of puberty.[3] Their situation differs from that of most adolescents, for instead of needing to loosen familial ties and assert individual selfhood, Lyra and Will, already isolated, must rather seek connection, from their own virtual "family," to find their individual destinies.

THE THIRD FEAR: LOSS OF ONE'S WORLD AND EMBROILMENT IN A COSMIC STRUGGLE

The third fear is related to the fear of abandonment, but it has an existential and cosmic dimension. In an entire world grown treacherous, mere parental treachery seems minor. The third fear concerns the loss of one's accustomed world, one's familiar environs, governed by reliable, unswerving natural laws and protective adults: all is in flux, and to borrow Yeats's phrase, the center cannot hold. Universes are crumbling, for the boundaries between worlds, hitherto known only by witches to be permeable, have been breached by Lord Asriel. The two child heroes are swept into a cosmic struggle against a mysterious adversary: it has some link to "Dust," newly discovered charged particles, also termed elementary particles, which stream through the Aurora Borealis to Earth. Visible through the Northern Lights of the mystical, magical Arctic is an image of a Celestial City, but Pullman's City is a far cry from John Bunyan's, just as his universe stands Bunyan's on its head. The exact nature of the threat posed by Dust is ambiguous, but it promises to bring chaos and alter everything in some sinister way. It is Dust that motivates Lord Asriel's obsessive quest for power. Pullman's narrative challenges Milton's *Paradise Lost* and "the conventional Miltonic version of good and evil" (Craig 66), portraying the metaphysical value struggle between two forces that have warred against each other since the beginning of time. The struggle is described for Will Parry by the mysterious Dr. Grumman (aka "Jopari," John Parry, and not yet revealed to Will as his father) after Will has unwittingly become the bearer of the Knife:

There are two great powers. . . . And they've been fighting since time began. Every advance in human life, every scrap of knowledge and wisdom and decency we have has been torn by one side from the teeth of the other. Every little increase in human freedom has been fought over ferociously between those who want us to know more and be wiser and stronger, and those who want us to obey and be humble and submit. (320)

The two great powers, he continues, are now lined up for battle, and each desires the knife desperately: it is the only weapon that can cut windows between the parallel worlds of the universe and, even more terrifying, the only weapon that can destroy the Authority, Pullman's name for God. In this subversive reimagining of the events leading up to the War in Heaven between God and the rebel angels, the child characters will fight on the side of the fallen rebels, who are aligned on the "right" side in a monumental struggle for truth, joy, and freedom, against the forces of repression and dulling of consciousness.

DEFENSES

These two children are armed in their struggles against the fearful realities of their worlds by two magical objects, an alethiometer, presented to Lyra by the Master of Jordan College, a truth-telling symbol-reader that looks like a golden compass, and by the magical Subtle Knife, won by Will with Lyra's help in the adventures of Book Two. A parallel is drawn in Book Two between Lyra's alethiometer and the computer of Dr. Mary Malone of the Dark Matter Research Unit at Oxford, who has christened the computer "The Cave," because, as she says, "Shadows on the wall of the Cave, you see, from Plato" (*Subtle Knife* 88).

Will's subtle knife can cut through dimensions of time and space, making windows between worlds, and (some believe) has the power to win in a contest in Heaven against the Authority. A historical contrast is revealing: where the spiritual questers in Milton's literary world, as in that of John Bunyan, had Biblical faith and humility as the mainstays of their strength, the worlds of Lyra and Will require not faith and humility but rather intellect, competence beyond their years, mutual support (from one another and from their daemons), sexual innocence, and a possession of magical objects that comprehends an intuitive knowledge of the iconography of symbols.

Yet another defense against fear, one common to many children's stories, is demonstrated by Lyra when, having discovered the astonishing truth of her parentage, she begins to make up stories to help her cope with it. Thus she invents a history for herself, in her own voice, finding temporary safety in fantasizing.

A FEW SPECULATIONS

I believe that the population explosion of daemonic figures will continue in the twenty-first century because they allow the fantasy-writer to explore new and different ways of being human in an increasingly complex and highly technological world. Examples of related figures and instances of humans "morphing" into animal form can be seen over a range of reading levels, as for instance Janet Anderson's *Going Through the Gate*, where the candidates for graduation from sixth grade undergo an initiation that involves becoming, briefly, an animal of their choice, so they may gain empathy with living creatures. For purposes of social satire in a cautionary ecological tale, Peter Dickinson's *Eva* shows a girl's essence embodied in a chimpanzee. Patrice Kindl's *Owl in Love* depicts a girl with shape-shifting powers who copes with her adolescent anxieties by carrying on a double life as an owl. The "Animorphs" series features gross shape-shifting episodes, and some of the "Goosebumps" books similarly bridge and blur the boundaries between human and nonhuman natures.

Finally, what are some implications of these phenomena? One psychology-based interpretation is that these fear-evoking demonic and daemonic beings signal a profound confusion over the boundaries of the self and how to distinguish between "self" and "Other." They may also serve as players in ecological parables reminding us of the need to honor the biological basis and interdependence of all life, a truth important to the survival of all species in a time of untold threats to the natural environment. The proliferation of fantasy creatures who close the gap between the human and animal worlds also signifies a reaction to an overly mechanized, drearily technological world and a keen desire to reintegrate the sensual and soulful aspects of life, to return to the pastoral "green world," a desire now exacerbated by the shrinking of natural resources. Furthermore, there may be the desire to plumb the depths of a mythic consciousness, to enrich individual identity through a connection to a "totem animal" emblematic of an essential tie to the natural world. Shape-shifters define our era as one when human identities are in flux, when in the words of the title of Robert J. Lifton's book, The Protean Self is in ascendance.

The portrayal of human-animal ties and shifting human-animal forms signals a contemporary crisis in human identity, marking the need for a shift of consciousness to another level that can comprehend and heal the "split" so many thinkers of the past have mistakenly perpetuated between our animal and our so-called "higher" consciousness. It may be, as some believe, that we are evolving toward "cosmological" consciousness, manifesting as a "meta-mind"—a conscious awareness of consciousness.

What can be said, in closing, of Pullman's recently completed trilogy? Is the trilogy a *fin de siècle* "pilgrim's progress," an opening on the sun of another world, as Lord Asriel rapturously declares to Mrs. Coulter at the close of *The Golden Compass*? In an echo of the German poet Stefan George ("EntrFckung," or "Transport") he further rejoices in "A wind from another world!" (*Golden Compass* 395). Does the trilogy herald a truly luminous, enlightened new world? Or is Pullman's story a perilous drama of darkness at the close of an unimaginably dark and destructive century, opening on yet greater horrors? Are we witnessing breakdown, or breakthrough? Or both?

NOTES

1. An example of Pullman's ability to convey a sense of the epic and the sublime occurs in his description of the result of Lord Asriel's terrible deed of piercing the vault of heaven by using the energy of Roger's separated daemon: "At the moment he [Roger] fell still, the vault of heaven, star-studded, profound, was pierced as if by a spear. A jet of light, a jet of pure energy released like an arrow from a great bow, shot upward from the spot where Lord Asriel had joined the wire to Roger's daemon. The sheets of light and color that were the Aurora tore apart; a great rending, grinding, crunching sound reached from one end of the universe to the other; there was dry land in the sky—sunlight" (*Golden Compass* 393).

2. Twice in *The Golden Compass* there is mention of prophecies of Lyra's destiny, first by Dr. Lanselius, who recognizes her as the child the witches "have talked about. For centuries past" (176), for they live close to the spot where the veil between the worlds is thin, and "hear the whispers of the immortals." Lyra is under a prohibition, however, for she must fulfill her destiny in ignorance of what she is doing. Lanselius adds, "Without this child, we shall all die" (176). Later in the book Serafina Pekkala alludes to the "curious prophecy" already mentioned, to bring about "the end of destiny," but she too cautions that Lyra must not be told what she must do, or all will fail, and then "Death will sweep through all the worlds; it will be the triumph of despair, forever. The universes will all become nothing more than interlocking machines, blind and empty of though, feeling, life" (310).

3. Pullman artfully portrays adult sexual passion through the behavior of the adults' daemons, as in the scene where Lyra uncomprehendingly witnesses her father's snow leopard and her mother's golden monkey ecstatically caressing one another, though to Lyra it seems "more like cruelty than love" (*Golden Compass* 395).

REFERENCES

Bethune, Brian. "Daemons and Dust: A Fantasy Writer Creates a Haunting World" [Review of *The Golden Compass* by Philip Pullman]. *Maclean's*, 109.30.58 (1996).

Craig, Amanda. "Window Into Souls" [Review of *The Subtle Knife* by Philip Pullman]. *New Statesman* 126.4353.7 (1997).

Lifton, Robert J. *The Protean Self: Human Resilience in an Age of Fragmentation*. New York: Basic Books, 1993.

Pullman, Philip. *The Golden Compass*. "His Dark Materials," Book 1. New York: Knopf, 1995. (Original title: *Northern Lights*)

———. *The Subtle Knife*. "His Dark Materials," Book 2. New York: Knopf, 1997.

CHAPTER 16

The Ethical Dimension of Children's Literature: A Study of *Drejcek in Trije Marsovcki (Drejcek and the Three Martians)*

Metka Kordigel

Any detailed analysis of literary works for children shows that their ethical messages function on several levels. The nature of these levels appears in the example of the science-fiction novel for children, *Drejcek in Trije Marsovcki (Drejcek and the Three Martians)* by Slovene author Vid Pecjak. Below is a short summary of the story.

One night, three children from Mars visit Drejcek, an eight-year-old boy. They tell him that they came to Earth against their father's orders. Martian laws strictly forbid such visits, because people on Earth still fight wars and are very backward. Everything on Mars is arranged in a far better way than on Earth: wars are forbidden, there is a law according to which children are to be happy (meaning that nobody forces them to learn mathematics or to go to bed at night). Martians also solved all ecological problems (by moving their industries to one of their moons, and building a huge playground similar to Disneyland on another one) as well as the food problem—food is produced from rocks and eaten in the shape of pills.

The Martian children open Drejcek's eyes; he now sees the shortcomings of the way parents on Earth arrange life and the lack of purpose in such order. He becomes aware of the war and peace issue, of the violence of parents toward their children. In short, he begins to observe the world around him from a critical distance and, in the process, he begins to grow up.

Even such a sketchy summary shows that the novel's objective is (among other things) to draw children's attention to important problems in the contemporary world and to mobilize them to do something about it.

A more detailed analysis of the ethical component in *Drejcek in Trije Marsovcki* shows that the problem of ideology/ethics in children's literature cannot be simplified, as it regularly occurs on several levels. In *Drejcek in Trije Marsovcki*, the moral and ethical principles occur on three levels:

1. Moral and ethical principles that the author intentionally conveys to the young reader. These principles are salient ideological markers in the literary work and represent the ideals of the adults. Children are supposed to adopt these ideals.

2. Moral and ethical principles that the author chooses to make salient through a special narrative perspective—the world of adults and their errors.

3. Moral and ethical principles that are included in the text but not on purpose. Rather, they become visible because of the specific narrative perspective in children's literature-ethical principles presented on the first two levels are being eroded on the third level!

THE FIRST LEVEL

The basic ideological message in *Drejcek in Trije Marsovcki* is clear: conflicts should not be resolved by violence. Both the macro- and micro-dimension of this principle are presented in the story. The macro-dimension involves the problem of war and peace. The message is contained in the following passage:

> Then they spoke about war and peace. Drejcek was trying to persuade (the doctor) that wars are damaging, that they may destroy the world and that it is not enough to love peace.
> We have to do something for peace. (126)

The micro-dimension involves aggressiveness at solving interpersonal conflicts, where the stronger (adults) usually impose their will on the weaker (children):

> "Do all parents on Earth beat their children?" asked Miö.
> "Other parents only beat them every now and then," replied Drejcek.
> "Why?" asked Miö.
> "So that they would be good," explained Drejcek. "Children are punished when they are naughty, when they don't want to go to school, when they refuse to wash themselves and in similar cases."
> Miö, Maö and Saö looked at each other, bewildered. (51)

In addition to the theme of violence, two other ethical messages occur on the first level. The first should be interpreted as a kind of indoctrination of ideological principles on which the country's dominant political elite of the time was based. Mars (which the story presents as an utopian country where everything is best and meaningful) has a social order that, when compared to the situation on Earth, comes closest to the communist social order, where everybody is rich.

> "There are no poor on Mars," said (the Martian father).
> "Everybody is rich. Everbody gets what he or she wants."
> "Are goods in your shops free?" asked the surprised Drejcek.
> "Free," confirmed the Martian father.
> "Then you can get everything that you want. Even a hundred robots."
> "Why should we want a hundred robots?" replied the surprised Martian father.
> "Nobody needs as many. We have five, which is more than enough." (107)

The author portrays a society where each takes only as much as he or she needs. Such an ideal was foreseen in the socialist-communist vision of Marx and Engels.

Such ideas could easily lead us into a faulty interpretation, that is, that *Drejcek in Trije Marsovcki* belongs to the first type of children's literature (the one that is written with the purpose of indoctrinating the reader with political principles). The fact that the story did not lose its appeal with the political changes that took place in Slovenia best proves that the indoctrination claim would be wrong. The story remains in school textbooks and children read it equally enthusiastically as they did in the time when one school subject was the fundamentals of social morale.

The reason for such acceptance in the post-Soviet era lies in the fact that *Drejcek in Trije Marsovcki* is a novel where the cognitive and aesthetic components are not dominated by the ethical one. It remains a literary work of art and should be distinguished from the kind of literary production that was offered to children as ideology in aesthetic packaging (to be more appealing) for forty years after World War II.

The fourth message that is found on the first level of the ethical in *Drejcek in Trije Marsovcki* is the educational preaching about homework.

> "Robots are smart machines," replied Miö.
> "They can cook, wash the dishes, dust the furniture."
> "They can calculate, too," added Maö.
> "Does he ever write the maths homework instead of you?" asked Drejcek.
> "No," answered Maö. "I do my homework myself and if I don't know something, then I don't write it."
> "Isn't the teacher angry then?"
> "Why?," asked a surprised Maö. "If I don't know something it is better that I don't write it. If the robot were to do my homework, it would no longer be mine. (106)

In a word, homework should be done by children. Copying from others doesn't make any sense, as one would never grow wise and learned in this way.

The first level of the ethical component of *Drejcek in Trije Marsovcki* thus allows Vid Pecjak to present three topics: the topic of aggressiveness and violence in interpersonal conflicts, the topic of ideal interpersonal relations, and the topic of sincerity and honesty (writing math homework). All three topics are presented from a narrative position of the adult that knows what is best (for the child and the world) and who thinks that this knowledge is so important that children, too, should possess it (and act accordingly). We are faced with a classic adult (the author)-child relation, typical of the older Slovene children's literature. Here, however, it is used in the modern story of *Drejcek in Trije Marsovcki*.

THE SECOND LEVEL

The second ethical level of *Drejcek in Trije Marsovcki* includes those ethical principles that are made visible through a special narrative perspective. Duplicity, insincerity, and compromise have become so commonplace that adults don't even notice them any more. It is different with children. For them the world is black and white. Things are either good or bad; there is nothing in between. The uncompromising childlike perspective detects when adults lie (but think that their lies are acceptable), when they are aggressive (but find justification for their aggression)—in a word, when adults say one thing, but do the opposite and yet always manage to find an (adult) excuse for their actions.

It is not a coincidence that Martians, the representatives of the ideal (perfectly white) world, choose to communicate with a child, Drejcek.

"The teacher told us that we should not trust people from Earth," warned Maö.
"But Drejcek can be trusted," said Maö. "He is not like people from Earth. If his arms did not grow out of his body he would be no different from Martian children." (24)

The message is clear: People from Earth (adults) are not to be trusted. Those who represent the good and the pure can communicate only with those who have equal confidence in the good and who are capable of distinguishing very accurately the good from the bad. The world of adults as seen from such (childlike) perspective is of course very different from the world the adults would like to present to the children through their preaching.

The figure who represents the ethical on the second level is Drejcek's father. In principle he should be counted among the positive characters. Our first impression is that he is a tolerant father who understands how Drejcek could eat the marmalade and even destroy his toys (on purpose). In addition, he claims that he loves peace and that he is against war. Also, he doesn't beat his children as does Mihec's father next door. But as soon as we begin to examine his behavior more closely, from a stricter, childlike perspective (as does the author together with his readers), his facade of blamelessness starts to crumble. When Drejcek asks him why people don't simply forbid wars on Earth, the father explains that this cannot be done and that he (Drejcek) will understand why only when he is grown up and wise (like his father).

The continuation of the same conversation also reveals his rather questionable democratic attitudes.

> "Father, why don't we wear socks instead of shoes?"
> "Now, I've had enough of your never-ending whys!" was the angry father's reply.
> "Have you done your homework yet?" (27)

It is typical of a tolerant, democratic dialogue that we listen to the interlocutor's arguments or his questions, respond to them and present arguments during the discussion. If the interlocutor's arguments carry greater weight than ours, we admit that he is right; if we run out of arguments, we admit that we do not know the answer.

The reaction of Drejcek's father completely contradicts the rules of a democratic dialogue. As soon as the speech situation becomes uncontrollable, that is, when he runs short of arguments and when he no longer can produce answers, he looks for the other person's weakest point and hits him where he is certain to force a retreat. Drejcek's weak point is mathematics—as we know from the story—and the question about his math assignment is sure to end the discussion. The father will get his way; he will be able to read the newspaper in peace and quiet.

The father's behavior becomes even more reprehensible when his son travels to Mars together with Miö, Maö, and Saö and stays there the entire next day. We can understand that the father was worried to death for his son (we even learn that he had called the police to find him). Nevertheless, it is precisely during this suspension of logical thinking that his real self is revealed.

> "He's back!" shouted the mother when Drejcek showed up on the doorstep.
> The father pushed her away and stepped in front of Drejcek. He looked at him angrily, pointed to the stick in the corner and said: "Do you see it? You'd better tell me where you were and fast!" (121)

In a word, whenever the principles of the adults are challenged, they waver; adults always act contrary to their declared positions. From the child's viewpoint, the viewpoint that knows no nuances between right and wrong, such things are very obvious and deserve to be condemned.

All of this is observed by the author. Like children, he condemns compromising, hypocrisy, and inconsistency, which is why the communication situation on this ethical level differs from that on the first level (where he is an adult who knows what is right and wants to teach). On the second level we no longer deal with an adult who is patronizing a child. As far as ethics are concerned, the author and the child speak the same language. They think the same thoughts, feel the same feelings, and experience the same wonderment. The story and its experience originate in the author's own childlike mind, that is, his poetic orientation manifested in his wondering at things and phenomena (cf. Grafenauer). Discovering one's own childlike impulse in contemporary poetry implies the poet's ability to be fascinated by things, his ability to transform reality through play, and at the same time his ability to observe the world from the black-and-white perspective, unburdened by circumstances, goals, unwritten rules and so on. In short, the poet is free of everything that determines adults as adults.

On the second level of the ethical, the author, together with the reader, reveals those ethical elements in the world around us that are visible and accessible only when placed in a different perspective, under the spotlight of the childlike that allows for no compromise.

THE THIRD LEVEL

The third level of the ethical in Pecjak's story *Drejcek in Trije Marsovcki* includes those ethical principles that seem to be interwoven into the text without the author's conscious intention. These are the principles that represent the erosion of those ideological values on which the author had been building on the first two levels.

In Pecjak's science-fiction story Mars and Martian society are used as an example, an illustration through which the author attempts to explain hard-to-comprehend abstract principles. Following this logic, we would expect interpersonal relations on Mars to be ideal, and, indeed, it seems that the author tried to show them as such. On Mars there is a law that prohibits wars, nobody there is greedy, children go to bed because they realize that they are sleepy, and they write their math homework because they know that this is the only way to learn calculus. They even have a law requiring that children be happy.

The spacemen in science-fiction literature (and *Drejcek in Trije Marsovcki* undoubtedly is a science-fiction story) assume the role of a mirror. It is because of their whiteness and flawlessness that our mistakes are so visible. That Pecjak himself planned such roles for them is evident from the following passage:

Drejcek had expected that the mysterious guests would come again during the night and burden him with a new sin. He thus took a battery and a toy gun and hid them under his pillow so as to be able to surprise them at the slightest noise. (12)

As a child Drejcek adheres to positive ethical principles. Still, when he comes into contact with the unknown and unexplainable, he, too, reacts instinctively; the first solution that comes to his mind is the use of force. This is very clear from his conversation with space children:

> "Strange?" repeated Drejcek. "You don't think that we are strange, do you?"
> "You are strange," replied the Martian, "because your arms grow out of your bodies and even more so because you fight wars."
> Drejcek glanced at the toy gun that he still held in his hand and felt ashamed. (12)

Even though the author planned for Martians to be a test that should make the characteristics of people from Earth more salient (which is why he painted the Martian world as an ideal), we cannot overlook the fact that even in that supreme world where everybody strives to be equal and maximally honest, fair, and democratic there still exists the law of the stronger. The weak have to obey the strong.

When Drejcek discusses with his Martian friends the possibility of visiting their planet, his friends from space begin to have serious doubts about the law that requires that children be happy. When they return to Earth after asking their father if Drejcek can visit them in their house, we learn what happened:

> "It was within a hair's breadth and you would have never seen us again!" cried Miö and began to tell the story. When they told their father that they had visited Earth, he was enraged. Their mother fainted. The father was trying to impress on them that they had broken the Martian rule no. 2 and exposed the entire Mars to a horrible danger. Only after they had cried night and day, did their father's heart soften . . . When Saö fell to his knees and held up his his hands, he gave his permission for Drejcek to spend one day in their house. (87)

The ethical message is unmistakable: despite everything the strong and the big will always have the power to force the weaker and the smaller into submission. It depends on the degree of their tolerance whether they will resort to this power or not. The decision remains exclusively in their hands!

This last principle completely contradicts those that we find on the first and the second levels. It seems almost as if it had found its way into the text against the author's will. The moral and ethical principles that we encounter on the third level have not been included in the text on purpose. This third-level ethical dimension erodes the ethical principles that Pecjak had built in "intentionally" on the first two levels. The third level becomes salient through the realization that democracy and equality are only temporary values even in the most ideal of worlds. The strong are the ones who decide when these values no longer correspond to their interests and may therefore suspend them and reintroduce the rights and arguments of force.

NOTE

All translations are the author's.

REFERENCES

Avajncer, M. "Etika in mladinska knjiñevnost." *Otrok in knjiga* 32. Maribor, 1991.

Grafenauer, N. "Sodobna slovenska poezija za otroke." *Otrok in knjiga* 31. Maribor, 1991.

Kobe, M. *Pogledi na mladinsko knjiñevnost*. Ljubljana, 1987.

Kordigel, M. "Nastanek in razvoj termina znanstvena fantastika na Slovenskem." *Slavisticna revija*, 41 (1993): 4; str. 571–580.

———. *Znanstvena fantastika*. Ljubljana, 1994.

Kos, J. *Ocrt literarne teorije*. Ljubljana, 1983.

Novak, B. A. "Igre otrok-igre za otroke." *Otrok in knjiga* 32. Maribor, 1991.

Pecjak, V. *Drejcek in Trije Marsovcki*. Ljubljana, 1961.

PART V

Masculinities

CHAPTER 17

Uneasy Men in the Land of Oz

Yoshido Junko

L. Frank Baum's *The Wonderful Wizard of Oz*, which was later published under the new title of *The Wizard of Oz*, has been widely read since its first publication in 1900; the book's success prompted the culture industry to produce its various adaptations, including the MGM film of 1939; *The Wizard of Oz* TV series in the 1950s; both the Broadway musical version and the film version of *The Wiz* in the 1970s; Philip Farmer's novel *Barnstormer in Oz*, published in 1982; and Jeff Ryman's novel *Was*, published in 1992. Neil Earle, in his study of *The Wizard of Oz* as popular culture, says, "[T]he decades of the 1930s and 1970s, both periods when the nation's economic arrangements were out of joint, were periods when Baum's optimistic egalitarianism was reworked and represented."[1] It is indeed interesting that notable adaptations appeared not only during periods of economic recession but also during periods of cultural and social change. Jack Zipes maintains, "Both film and book formed a utopian constellation, a reference point, one that fortunately has not gone away and compels us to return time and again to determine our national character and identity."[2] In other words, the land of Oz in each adaptation reflected authors' and artists' hopes and despair as well as those of the audience who accepted these adaptations. My concern in this chapter, therefore, is to place Baum's *The Wizard of Oz* in the social and cultural context of America, and read it as a "reference point" of American culture and society.

Although *The Wizard of Oz* has been variously interpreted by critics, most interpretations have focused on Dorothy's struggle to find her way home. They tend to see her as an American female-hero, and her journey as a representative quest for national identity. For example, Henry Little-field, reading *The Wizard of Oz* as a symbolic allegory, says, "Dorothy is Baum's Miss Everyman. She is one of us, levelheaded and human, and she has a real problem."[3] Brian Attebery compares Dorothy with Lewis Carroll's Alice and with Irving's Rip Van Winkle and concludes that "Dorothy is aggressively, triumphantly American." Dorothy is the "explorer, the wanderer, who penetrates ever wilder regions of the world."[4] Madonna Kolbenschlag, in her feminist reading of the story, regards Dorothy as "the classic archetype of the spiritual orphan,"[5] the orphan who "is a metaphor for our deepest, most fundamental reality: experiences of attachment and abandonment, of expectation and deprivation, of loss and failure and of loneliness. . . . Dorothy is a classic New World hero."[6] Lastly, focusing on the psychological trajectory of Dorothy and reading it in a psychohistorical fashion, Jerry Griswold says, "The Land of Oz is the Kingdom Without: an imaginative and extravagant version of America. But it is also and simultaneously the Kingdom Within: Dorothy's own circumstances reimagined at large, an extrapolation of her own Oedipal or family problems."[7]

Such interpretations focus on Dorothy's journey, not on the journey of the male characters: the Scarecrow, the Tin Woodman, and the Cowardly Lion. Unlike Dorothy's journey, which was accidentally started by a tornado, the males' journey is self-motivated. The male characters think they lack essential elements in their personalities, and this lack makes them less than whole. They have compulsive desires to become whole and think they have to meet the Wizard of Oz to ask him for a brain, a heart, and courage, respectively. Later, these qualities eventually help them become rulers. Meanwhile, Dorothy's quest is closely related to the notion of female sphere, home. Thus, the motivations for their journeys are obviously based on gender. Although Kolbenschlag says that the three male companions embody aspects of Dorothy's own autonomy that she must develop,[8] their desires to seek these aspects should not be mixed up with Dorothy's desire for home.

What I have said so far indicates that there are two types of journey in the story. Dorothy's journey starts at the farmhouse in Kansas and ends at the same place, whereas the males' journey starts at the time each of them encounters Dorothy, and ends when each of them successfully becomes a ruler in Oz. Although the two different types are often confusingly treated as though they were the same journey, we should discuss them separately. It would be worthwhile to explore this misunderstanding that the book only contains a single journey.

In studies of Baum's *The Wizard of Oz*, most critics refer to the film version of *The Wizard of Oz* produced in 1939. Therefore, Dorothy's motivation to leave Kansas in the film is worth examination. In part, Dorothy "escapes" from Kansas in search of the dream land "over the rainbow."

Dorothy is threatened by Miss Gulch, a wealthy woman in the neighbor-
hood, who is trying to kill Dorothy's pet dog, Toto. When Dorothy appeals
to Aunt Em about her dog, the aunt replies, "You always get yourself into
a fret about nothing. . . . Find yourself a place where you won't get in any
trouble."[9] Then Dorothy says to herself, "Some place where there isn't any
trouble. Do you suppose there is such a place, Toto? There must be. It's
not a place you can get to by a boat or a train. It's far, far away. Behind
the moon . . . Beyond the rain . . . " And then she begins to sing that
famous song, "Over the Rainbow."

Salman Rushdie, in his interpretation of this scene, says, "What she
expresses here, what she embodies with the purity of an archetype, is the
human dream of leaving, a dream at least as powerful as its countervailing
dream of roots."[10] This song eloquently explains her motivation to escape
from her Kansas home. It is no wonder that the tornado which has affinity
with her surname, Gale, helps her dream of leaving come true. Furthermore, the latest technology of Technicolor used in the film heightens the
effect of exodus from the greyness of Kansas and entering into the col-
orfulness of Oz. Through this combination of action, song, and color, the
film represents many critics' assumption that Dorothy "escapes" from
Kansas. However, a careful reading of Baum's book will show that there
is no inevitability for Dorothy to escape from her home in Kansas.

The opening two pages of Baum's book contain descriptions of the greyness of the Kansas prairies, and ten repetitions of "grey" occur. Eight of
these depict the dry and bleak environment on the prairie and the exhausted and desolate expression of Dorothy's aunt and uncle. Only twice
is the word "grey" used in relation to Dorothy and Toto, but in a context
that reverses its significance. Toto makes Dorothy laugh, and saves her
from growing grey like her surroundings. Toto is not grey; he is a little
black dog, with long, silky hair and small black eyes that twinkled merrily
on either side of his funny, wee nose.[11]

It is her aunt and uncle who are exhausted with the greyness and the
hardships of pioneer life. There is no mention of Dorothy being actually
overwhelmed by the greyness. On the contrary, Dorothy is portrayed as
a pleasant and innocent girl whose cheerfulness is protected by Toto. She
represents the happiness, innocence, and hope that Aunt Em and Uncle
Henry have lost in the course of their pioneer lives.

After hearing Dorothy's story about Kansas, the Scarecrow wonders
why she wishes to leave the beautiful land of Oz and go back to a dry,
grey place like Kansas. Dorothy answers, "No matter how dreary and grey
our homes are, we people of flesh and blood would rather live there than
in any other country, be it ever so beautiful. There is no place like home."[12]
Here it is obvious that she did not "escape" from Kansas.

In addition, Dorothy's journey does not have the motivation of the universal hero's journey as defined by Joseph Campbell. He says, "The usual

hero adventure begins with someone from whom something has been taken, or who feels there's something lacking in the normal experiences available or permitted to the members of his society."[13] And this is exactly the case with the Scarecrow, the Tin Woodman, and the Cowardly Lion. They feel they must become whole.

In the case of Dorothy, however, her discretion and practical way of thinking are distinctive, and her unique personality is clearly portrayed in the scene where she and the house are blown away by the cyclone.

> Dorothy sat quite still on the floor and waited to see what would happen. . . . but as the hours passed and nothing terrible happened, she stopped worrying and resolved to wait calmly and see what the future would bring. . . . In spite of the swaying of the house and the wailing of the wind, Dorothy soon closed her eyes and fell fast asleep.[14]

Thus, even in the beginning of her journey Dorothy has enough discretion to control her emotions and behavior.

Then we should wonder why Dorothy, who is innocent "like a baby in a cradle,"[15] and fearless, joyful, and thoughtful as well, has to be dispatched to the land of Oz. Most critics suggest that Dorothy has to travel all the way to find her own potential represented in the Silver Shoes which she takes from the Wicked Witch. At the end of Dorothy's journey, Glinda, the Good Witch of the South, says to her, "Your Silver Shoes will carry you over the desert. . . . If you had known their power you could have gone back to your Aunt Em the very first day you came to this country."[16] Griswold, responding to this passage, says, "Glinda points out that the girl has had the ability to return all along. . . . Dorothy comes into her own and recognizes her own power."[17]

However, is it possible to call some stuff stolen from the Wicked Witch "her own power," whereas males are given elements of their personalities? Moreover, the Silver Shoes are not something Dorothy brought with her from Kansas, that is, something that originally belonged to her. In addition, she cannot bring them back home because she loses them on her way, as we see in the following quotation: "Dorothy stood up and found she was in her stocking-feet. For the Silver Shoes had fallen off in her flight through the air, and were lost for ever in the desert."[18]

All these things suggest that Dorothy's mission is to meet the Scarecrow, the Tin Woodman, the Cowardly Lion, and the Wizard of Oz. Dorothy was transported to the Land of Oz in order to encounter these males and help them solve their problems. In this sense, the central characters are male figures who make journeys in quest of their masculine identity.

Now, let us look more closely at each of their "problems." The Scarecrow is the first male companion Dorothy meets after starting to follow the yellow brick road. When she meets him, the Scarecrow is in a cornfield with his back stuck to a pole. As soon as Dorothy rescues him from this situation, he laments his lack of brain. However, she does not think he has a real problem; rather, she thinks he is a sensible person. Therefore, Dorothy's reaction to his lament is not compassionate; she remains unruffled:

"Do you think," [the Scarecrow] asked, "if I go to the Emerald City with you, that Oz would give me any brains?"

"I cannot tell," [Dorothy] returned; "but you may come with me, if you like. If Oz will not give you any brains you will be no worse off than you are now."[19]

The Scarecrow's thinking that he has no brain comes from his lack of self-confidence, which in turn is caused by his traumatic experience in the cornfield. That is, an old crow exposed his identity as a stuffed man, and then led a great flock of crows to plunder the corn, all the while making a fool of the Scarecrow. He lost his confidence in himself because he thought he did not have enough brains to assume his full responsibility as a "man" to guard the cornfield against the enemies. In short, he felt his manhood diminished. Critics have pointed out that the Scarecrow's experience represents that of American farmers at the turn of the century.

Pioneer farmers toward the end of the century were experiencing many and drastic changes. Although the increase of homestead farmers in the Great Plains had been moderate in the antebellum years, the extension of the railroads across the continent, especially between 1870 and 1880, stimulated the rapid increase in population of new settlers on the frontier. Especially with the booming speculative business of buying farmland in 1880, an increasing number of people rushed to the frontier. But the Homestead Act did not take effect, and as Hamlin Garland wrote in the preface to his novel *Jason Edward* (1891), "The last acre of available farmland has now passed into private or corporate hands."[20] Kansas, in particular, saw excessive cultivation of farmland. Then the draught in 1887 caused serious damages to the agricultural products in west Kansas. Furthermore, the deflation after the booming land speculation gave an additional blow to the struggling farmers. The historian Samuel Morison writes about the economy of America at the turn of the century: "Virgin prairie land, and peak prices of wheat and corn in 1881, had induced excessive railway construction . . . and oversettlement of the arid western part of [Kansas]."[21] During four years after 1887, half of the pioneer farmers left Kansas.[22]

Baum was in a position to be well-informed about practical problems of pioneer farmers. In 1888 he and his family moved into a frontier town, Aberdeen, in South Dakota Territory just before it was granted statehood. For more than a year Baum edited a weekly journal, *The Aberdeen Saturday Pioneer*, and wrote a column under the title of "Our Land Lady." It was the paper's most popular feature, in which Mrs. Bilkins, an imaginary character, discusses current events with the residents of her boarding-house. They pick up various topics including the drought, the Sioux tribe, railroads, and the woman's suffrage movement.

The next companion on Dorothy's journey is the Tin Woodman, who has been standing motionless in the woods. He has been tasting the fear of rust, isolated from the rest of the world for more than a year. Here's their first conversation:

> "Did you groan?" asked Dorothy.
> "Yes," answered the tin man, "I did. I've been groaning for more than a year, and no one has ever heard me before or come to help me."[23]

The tin man was originally a human being, but the enchanted axe given to him by the Wicked Witch of the East caused him to lose one part of his body every time he wielded it. The lost part of his body was replaced by a tinsmith each time. His whole body has now become metallic; he is, in effect, a machine. Fearing that joints of his body might rust, he always has to bring an oilcan with him. Strangely enough, however, rather than re-gretting of the loss of his human body, he feels proud of his metallic body, saying, "My body shone so brightly in the sun that I felt very proud of it and did not matter now if my axe slipped, for it could not cut me."[24] And he thinks his real problem is the loss of his heart. It is indeed ironic that he can be emotional enough to shed tears and still is obsessed with the loss of his heart, lamenting that he cannot love his sweetheart anymore.

His personal history, in fact, testifies to the changing image of men in the history of pioneers. Mark Gerzon says, "All kinds of men moved west: farmers and trappers, adventurers and misfits, ministers and schoolteach-ers, soldiers and miners. But only one type of man became a national hero, only one became a cultural archetype that would embed itself in the mas-culine mind . . . the Frontiersmen-Daniel Boone, Kit Carson, Wild Bill Hickock, and of course Davy Crockett-are the stuff of boyhood dreams."[25] The Frontiersmen represent the ideal image of men who are self-reliant and courageous subjugators of the "virgin land." However, in white so-ciety at the turn of the century, this ideal manhood was no longer easily accepted because the rapid industrialization and urbanization caused a change in the conception of ideal masculinity. The fact that the woodman loses parts of his body one after another because of the enchantment of the Wicked Witch reminds us that the manhood of self-reliant Frontiers-men is gradually replaced by that of "breadwinners" who, domesticated by the industrial capitalists of the East, work mechanically in order to earn their living. During this period of industrialization when workplaces were separated from home, men were forced to identify with a different manhood that could separate their emotions from themselves in order for them to survive the competitive society, or the battlefield. They could successfully survive only by hiding their human hearts behind the tin mask and pretending to be a labor machine in the "battlefield" of men. It is significant that the Tin Woodman's mutilation occurs whenever he works with his axe. In this sense, his workplace, the woods, actually has turned into a battlefield.

The third companion of Dorothy's journey is the Cowardly Lion, who worries that he does not have enough courage to meet other animals' expectations.

"What makes you a coward?" asked Dorothy.
"It's a mystery," replied the Lion. "I suppose I was born that way. All the other animals in the forest naturally expect me to be brave, for the Lion is everywhere thought to be the King of Beasts."[26]

His worry also comes from his low self-esteem. Ironically, he proves his bravery by fighting one hardship after another in the course of his journey. The Lion's worry seems to represent one aspect of white men's masculinity at the turn of the century.

According to Anthony Rotundo, owing to industrialization, the number of white-collar workers multiplied eight times between 1870 and 1910. In big cities where the number of corporations increased, a bureaucratic new order was born. Within the new order, every businessman had to submit himself to his boss. Rotundo writes, "In the nineteenth century, middle-class men had believed that a true man was a self-reliant being who would never bow to unjust authority or mere position. The new structures of work and opportunity in the marketplace did not support such a concept of manhood."[27] Moreover, with the increase of women in the workplace, previously men's domain, Rotundo maintains "[men's] sense of prerogative was threatened. Women's presence made a symbolic statement to men that the world of middle-class work was no longer a male club . . . the subjective reality for men was that their workplace was not masculine in the same sense that it had been."[28]

In addition to the changes of atmosphere in their workplace, the cultural phenomenon of what is called "feminization" of masculinity in the late nineteenth century should not be overlooked. Boys were educated and civilized by female caretakers based on the ideology of separate spheres, which eventually caused them to imprint female values on some boys. Rotundo argues, "The fear of womanly men became a significant cultural issue in the late nineteenth century . . . Men . . . began to sort themselves out into hardy, masculine types and gentle feminine types."[29] In other words, the masculine type and the feminine type existed even in an individual male's psychology as conflicting cultural values.

We can readily assume that Baum himself underwent a similar psychological conflict, if we pay attention to his personal history of growing up in an educated white family in the East. Baum, as a sickly and delicate boy, was not allowed to attend school, but was educated at home by private tutors. He enjoyed reading books by himself in a secret place, acting out fantasies, and playing with imaginary friends. At the age of twelve, Baum enrolled in Peekskill Academy, whose "goal was to develop 'true manly character,' gentlemanly conduct, and instant obedience."[30] He never agreed with the military way of thinking in training male students, and left Peekskill after two years.

The last man Dorothy meets is the Wizard of Oz himself. As Dorothy approaches the Emerald City, she obtains information concerning Oz from the people she meets on the way. First, Oz is great and terrible, and can grant anyone's request. Second, "Oz can take on any form he wishes. . . . But who the real Oz is, when he is in his own form, no living person can tell";[31] his identity is shrouded in mystery. The residents in the land of Oz whom Dorothy meets unanimously say, "You must see Oz." When she finally visits the Wizard, she is tantalizingly granted an audience. However, when Dorothy visits him again in order to have her request granted, she discovers that he is far from Oz the Great and Terrible, but "a common man," and "a humbug" as well. She also learns that this man has been obliged to confine himself within the palace and lead a solitary life for fear that his identity of impostor might be revealed. Oz says:

I am tired of being such a humbug. If I should go out of this Palace my people would soon discover I am not a Wizard, and then they would be vexed with me for having deceived them. So I have to stay shut up in these rooms all day, and its gets tiresome.[32]

Dorothy's disclosure does, in fact, save Oz. After this incident, Oz ends his impostor's life, and goes back home to Omaha in a balloon. In a sense, Oz's imposture closely connects with the nature of the Emerald City itself. He has been pretending to be the Great and Terrible Wizard, a figure larger than life, and he displayed an infinite power that is not his own so that he could maintain the illusion of the city as a "green utopia." The mandatory wearing of green glasses by the city dwellers is one strategy he uses to maintain the fiction of a green city. However, this does not mean that Oz is completely a humbug. The city gate is actually "all studded with emeralds that glittered so in the sun that even the painted eyes of the Scarecrow [are] dazzled by their brilliancy."[33] Also it is true that "[e]veryone seemed happy and contented and prosperous."[34] Oz's self-portrait, therefore, is contradictory: "I am Oz, the Great and Terrible."[35] "I am a humbug."[36] "I'm really a very good man, but I'm a very bad Wizard."[37] Then we should ask what element of the Emerald City causes him to have such a contradictory picture of himself.

As many critics have pointed out, the Emerald City is associated with "the White City," a nickname of the fair of 1893, the World Columbian Exposition, held in Chicago. Baum moved to Chicago in 1891, and eventually became a reporter for *The Evening Post*. In those days Chicago was the next largest city to New York in population, and the symbol of economic and industrial development in the Midwest. Historian Emily Rosenberg maintains that the Columbian Exposition was held in the first period of the promotion of the American Dream. As is awesomely demonstrated in the Edison Tower of Light erected by General Electric in the midst of the fairground, the exhibition emphasized "technological wizardry," and the fair was filled with "a strong international spirit and a faith in American-led progress."[38]

As the various glittering exhibitions in the urban wonderland showed, this world fair was a testament to the spreading American Dream. We should note that during the same period America was pursuing an expansionist policy on the international front because the American frontier had closed at home. In other words, the expansion of American territory and the country's economy heavily depended on the exploitation of ethnic, social, and cultural "others" both inside and outside the country. In the same year, 1893, American farmers and laborers were hit by a serious economic depression. And three years before the fair the gruesome massacre of Native Americans of the Sioux tribe at Wounded Knee occured. Five years after the fair, America expanded its territories by defeating the Spanish in the Spanish-American War.

Samuel Morison maintains, "In the experiment of much disdained 'colonialism' and 'imperialism,' none had succeeded in achieving more brilliant results than America's governance over the Philippines."[39] Reflecting the national consensus of anticolonialism, the Philippines became a protectorate, not America's territory. As a result the customs law was applied to the Philippines, which means "Although the residents in the protectorate were supposed to possess American nationality, they were not admitted as American citizens unless they were specially granted American citizenship."[40] This was the "open door" policy, which historian Howard Zinn says, "was a more sophisticated approach to imperialism than the traditional empire-building of Europe."[41]

It is interesting to note that, during the same period when *The Wizard of Oz* was written, both inside and outside the country, America was assuming an exploitative and expansionist attitude toward "others" on the pretext of "civilization," just as the Wizard of Oz was exercising "deceptive and illusionary" magic over the people of the Emerald City.[42] As the manhood of the Wizard of Oz is closely connected to his domination over the Emerald City, the "manhood"of the American empire was on display in the sparkling exhibitions of the Columbian Exposition. How Baum felt about American civilization can be easily imagined from the words of the Wizard of Oz when he is finally identified as a humbug. The Wizard apologetically says, "I am a good man, though I am a bad wizard."[43] Baum as a liberal Easterner still believed, or tried to believe, in the manifest destiny of America, but he must have been beginning to feel uneasy about America's masculine identity.

NOTES

1. Neil Earle, *The Wonderful Wizard of Oz in American Popular Culture: Uneasy in Eden*. Dyfed, Wales, UK: The Edwin Mellen Press, 1993, p. xiv.

2. Jack Zipes, *Fairy Tales as Myth, Myth as Fairy Tale*. Lexington: Kentucky UP, 1994, p. 122.

3. Henry Littlefield, "The Wizard of Oz: Parable on Populism," *American Quarterly* 16 (Spring 1964): 52.

4. Brian Attebery, *The Fantasy Tradition in American Literature: From Irving to Le Guin*. Bloomington: Indiana UP, 1980, pp. 96–97.

5. Madonna Kolbenschlag, *Lost in the Land of Oz: Befriending Your Inner Orphan and Heading for Home*. New York: Crossroad, 1988, p. 18.

6. Ibid., p. 9.

7. Jerry Griswold, *The Audacious Kids: Coming of Age in America's Classic Children's Literature*. New York: Oxford UP, 1992, p. 41.

8. Kolbenschlag, p. 19.

9. Noel Langley et al., *The Wizard of Oz: The Screenplay*. New York: Delta, 1989, p. 39.

10. Salman Rushdie, *The Wizard of Oz*. London: BFI Publishing, 1993, p. 23.

11. L. Frank Baum, *The Wizard of Oz*. 1900. London: Penguin, 1982, p. 10.

12. Ibid., p. 32.

13. Joseph Campbell, *The Power of Myth*. New York: Doubleday, 1988, p. 152.

14. Baum, *The Wizard of Oz*, p. 13.

15. Ibid., p. 13.

16. Ibid., p. 168.

17. Griswold, p. 39.

18. Baum, *The Wizard of Oz*, p. 171.

19. Ibid., p. 28.

20. Hamlin Garland, quoted in Howard Zinn, *People's History of the United States: 1492 to Present*. Rev. and Updated ed. New York: HarperCollins, 1995, p. 276.

21. Samuel Morison. *The Oxford History of the American People*. New York: Oxford UP, 1965, p. 789.

22. Ibid., pp. 789–790.

23. Baum, *The Wizard of Oz*, p. 38.

24. Ibid., p. 43.

25. Mark Gerzon, *A Choice of Heroes: The Changing Faces of American Manhood*. Boston: Houghton Mifflin Company, 1982, p. 19.

26. Baum, *The Wizard of Oz*. p. 48.

27. Anthony Rotundo, *American Manhood*. New York: Basic Books, 1993, pp. 249–250.

28. Ibid., p. 250.
29. Ibid., p. 265.
30. Angela Shirley Carpenter and Jean Shirley, *L. Frank Baum: Royal Historian of Oz*. Minneapolis: Lerner Publications, 1991, p. 16.
31. Baum, *The Wizard of Oz*, p. 75.
32. Ibid., p. 137.
33. Ibid., pp. 76–77.
34. Ibid., p. 81.
35. Ibid., p. 124.
36. Ibid., p. 126.
37. Ibid., p. 129.
38. Emily Rosenberg, *Spreading the American Dream*. New York: Hill & Wang, 1982, p. 9.
39. Morison, *The Oxford History of the American People*, p. 806.
40. Ibid., p. 806.
41. Zinn, *People's History of the United States*, p. 294.
42. L. Frank Baum, *Our Land Lady*. Lincoln: Nebraska UP, 1996, p. 147.
43. Baum, *The Wizard of Oz*, p. 129.

REFERENCES

Attebery, Brian. *The Fantasy Tradition in American Literature: From Irving to Le Guin*. Bloomington: Indiana UP, 1980.

Baum, L. Frank. *Our Land Lady*. Ed. & annoted Nancy Tystad Koupal. Lincoln: Nebraska UP, 1996.

———. *The Wizard of Oz*. 1900. London: Penguin, 1982.

Campbell, Joseph. *The Power of Myth*. New York: Doubleday, 1988.

Carpenter, Shirley Angelica and Jean Shirley. *L. Frank Baum: Royal Historian of Oz*. Minneapolis: Lerner Publications, 1991.

Earle, Neil. *The Wonderful Wizard of Oz in American Popular Culture: Uneasy in Eden*. Dyfed, Wales, UK: The Edwin Mellen Press, 1993.

Gerzon, Mark. *A Choice of Heroes*. Boston: Houghton Mifflin, 1982.

Griswold, Jerry. *Audacious Kids: Coming of Age in America's Classic Children's Literature*. New York: Oxford UP, 1992.

Kolbenschlag, Madonna. *Lost in the Land of Oz: Befriending Your Inner Orphan and Heading for Home*. New York: Crossroad, 1988.

Langley, Noel, Florence Ryerson, and Edgar Allan Woolf. *The Wizard of Oz: The Screenplay*. New York: Delta, 1989.

Littlefield, Henry. "*The Wizard of Oz*: Parable on Populism," *American Quarterly* 16 (Spring 1964): 47–58.

Morison, Samuel Eliot. *The Oxford History of the American People*. New York: Oxford UP, 1965.

Rosenberg, Emily S. *Spreading the American Dream*. New York: Hill & Wang, 1982.

Rotundo, E. Anthony. *American Manhood*. New York: Basic Books, 1993.
Rushdie, Salman. *The Wizard of Oz*. London: BFI Publishing, 1992.
The Wizard of Oz. Dir. Victor Fleming. Metro-Goldwyn-Mayer, 1939.
Zinn, Howard. *People's History of the United States: 1492 to Present*. Rev. and
     updated ed. New York: HarperCollins, 1995.
Zipes, Jack. *Fairy Tale as Myth, Myth as Fairy Tale*. Lexington: Kentucky UP,
     1994.

CHAPTER 18

Representations of Masculinity in Australian Young Adult Fiction

Kerry Mallan

One issue which has been discussed among theorists of masculinity revolves around the terms "crisis" and "change."[1]

INTRODUCTION

One could be forgiven for thinking that the "crisis in masculinity" rhetoric echoed in the popular press, in academic writing, and in popular cultural texts such as song lyrics and books for young people is symptomatic of some kind of end-of-millennium malady. However, masculinity has never been static or unitary and change is not the prerogative of the postmodern age. Integral to this rhetoric is the question of male identity. For some, there is the mourning of the loss of a masculine identity in the wake of the feminist and gay and lesbian movements. For others, the current debates, which can be seen as occurring within post-feminist times, give rise to the opportunity for problematising the notion of a gendered identity, thus opening the way for reexamining gender relations and perceived gender "norms."

In schools, the subject "English" has received particular attention, with commentators suggesting that we need alternative strategies and texts in order to redress the poor performance of boys and their apparent disinterest in reading.[2] Not only are teachers looking at ways of making English, and, in particular, literature a more relevant subject for many boys, but also many young adult writers have attempted to write novels that they consider reflect the changing realities and conditions of what it means to be a young man (and a young woman) in Australian society today. While these writers do not necessarily focus on the male protagonist exclusively, my interest in this chapter lies with those texts that place the male at the center of the fictional worlds these writers have constructed. One emergent feature arising from these texts and others by young adult writers consists of the strategies employed to valorize or reject traditional representations of masculinity in general, and the male hero in particular.

This chapter discusses the early stages of a research inquiry into the implications of changing representations of masculinity offered in young adult literature to adolescent, male readers. While my focus is on gender, I acknowledge the impact of other factors such as race, ethnicity, and class, which shape identity and influence the lived experiences and life trajectories of young people. The question that frames my research is: "To what extent is it possible to make distinctions between reactionary, and potentially, regressive constructions of masculinity and alternative constructions, which endeavor to valorize more liberating gender identities and relations?" In other words, do the young adult novels, by a selected group of writers, offer readers images of masculinity that react against current pro-feminist theorising of gender identity and relations by returning to a regressive model which embodies traditional notions of the male hero? Or, do they offer alternative models of what it means to be male in contemporary Australian society? While it may appear that there is a clear-cut response to this question, which is implied in its either-or construction, my inquiry to date has suggested that this is not the case.

Key components of the research project entail on-line chat sessions between four groups of 13- and 14-year-old boys and four popular Australian young adult writers (James Moloney, John Marsden, Margaret Clark, and Glyn Parry) and the boys' responses to questions posed after the on-line sessions in the form of a Web forum. In this chapter, I discuss only books and related on-line chat sessions with writers James Moloney and Margaret Clark. Short excerpts from *A Bridge to Wiseman's Cove* by James Moloney and *Famous for Five Minutes* by Margaret Clark were given to the boys as prompts for their on-line chats with the authors and the subsequent forums. While the chat sessions enabled a focused discussion on the selected excerpts, the questions posed in the forums were intended to explore the broader issues arising from the excerpts and the chat sessions.

THE "CRISIS" OF IDENTITY

My earlier reference to a current "crisis in masculinity" suggests that masculinity is becoming unsettled, destabilized and shattered. Perhaps more accurately, what is being experienced is a crisis or a turning point in the stereotypical portrayals and expectations of a particular kind of masculine subject, that is, "the hero." As Connell[3] has noted, masculinity has always been a fiercely contested construct, and struggles over establishing certain constructions of masculinity have often been played out through representations of men found in popular culture. Masculinity is also a performance,[4] and contemporary popular cultural texts such as film, video and books provide the contexts in which both traditional and new forms of masculine identity are performed. The traditional male hero is defined in terms of his morality, strength, and shrewdness (and often a good dose of physical attractiveness, though there were exceptions). While a considerable number of contemporary male heroes in literature and film exhibit these characteristics, others embody different characteristics, which are more in line with the image of the "New Age man"—a softer, more sensitive and caring individual. Either way the idea of a "true" masculinity that these images suggest centers on the body: a body that is strong, active, and impenetrable or one that is soft, passive, and vulnerable. As Connell suggests, "the first task of any social analysis is to arrive at an understanding of men's bodies and their relation to masculinity."[5] I want, therefore, to focus on the body in discussing the two novels and the writers' and readers' responses to them.

A HEROIC (NO)BODY

In *A Bridge to Wiseman's Cove*, Carl arrives at Wattle Beach with his 10-year-old brother, Harley, and his older sister, Sarah, after his mother has disappeared yet again from their lives. They are to stay with their aunt (who resents their coming) until their mother returns. However, she doesn't return and soon Sarah also decides to get on with her life and divests herself of the responsibility of being a surrogate mother to her brothers by leaving town. Moloney's main character is Carl, a most unlikely hero: fifteen years old, overweight, abandoned by his mother and older sister, sensitive, clumsy, lonely, and quiet. Despite his physical inadequacies, Carl's moral strength, age, gender, and underdog status are not at odds with traditional heroes who are invariably male adolescents who overcome great personal odds in order to survive and win approval.

Moloney commented in the on-line chat that he wanted to make Carl the outsider and thereby win readers' support for his plight: "I knew from the start I wanted Carl to feel he was different and unlikeable. Giving him a sack-like body shape seemed like a good way to do it. It isolated him from other kids effectively and affected his self-esteem . . . the more difficulties I loaded onto Carl, the more the reader would feel for him and want to see him come through. It is a question of empathy I suppose."[6] While Moloney's strategy was to make his protagonist inhabit a "sack-like body," the facade of the material body served to disguise the real man-in-the-making within. Moloney further subjects the visible body to subjugation and taunting when Carl is confronted by Nathan (the antithesis to Carl both physically and morally) at a party. In an effort to protect

Maddie from leaving the party with Nathan, Carl blocks the doorway. Nathan, confronted by Carl's immovable presence, taunts him:

"You, fat boy. You're going to stop us leaving, are you?"
The room was immediately tense and still.[7]

Moloney's stand-off between these opposites was a deliberate strategy for offering readers contrasting images of masculinity: peaceful-violent; moral-immoral; underdog-top dog. Such oppositional images serve to reinforce traditional accounts of male heroes and good-evil masculine stereotypes. Though the confrontation takes the form of a mini-battle of words, it has the potential for physical violence.

In commenting on this extract in the chat session, Moloney drew upon war imagery when he said: "Carl is a peaceful man. That is his nature. It is not in him to hurt others and when faced with violence, all he has [for] a shield is his moral authority."[8] It appears that Carl's inner resources surface and materialize in the form of a metaphorical shield to protect his outer body, a body that is variously described by Nathan as "fat" and a "tub of lard."[9] While Nathan is able to insult Carl's body and get away with it, when he attacks his moral integrity by asking the partygoers, "How can you respect this bloke here?"[10] he becomes the loser and Carl the clear and popular winner.

Hourihan comments that in the hero myths of the past, the "essence of the hero's masculinity is his assertion of control over himself, his environment and his world."[11] The hero's self-control is a struggle to suppress his emotions; to give into them would signal defeat to the enemy—both the enemy within and without. Carl, though inwardly fearful of being hurt ("Carl imagined the blow. . . . Wondered if the pain would knock him out."[12]), remains outwardly staunch and unmoveable. It is only in the final lines of the book when Carl learns of his mother's death, that he lets go of this self-imposed control and allows his emotions to surface:

And there on the deck of the red barge, Carl Matt opened up too, letting go and feeling a freedom flood into him. The tears he craved welled in his eyes. With them came the longed-for ache of his mother's death, and he knew at last that he was alive to feel it.[13]

At this point the author's strategy appears not to valorize conventional heroic masculinity, but to assert the importance of the inner life of emotion.

While Moloney sets up oppositional forms of masculinity, his intention, as evidenced through his on-line responses and his writing strategies, is to have the reader empathize with Carl and ultimately support his character. Such allegiance is not, however, so straightforward with the young male readers, as some ambivalence surfaced when they responded to one of the forum questions, which asked if they saw Carl's actions in the stand-off between him and Nathan as a sign of strength or weakness:

From what I can see this is probably a mixture of both. I mean, it's better to keep your mouth shut than to get yourself in bigger trouble than you already are. However, if you just keep it to yourself, this kid's gonna keep picking on you so it should probably be beneficial to give him a sore gut once, and have him leave you alone. You'd be surprised, most bullies are chickens at heart. Most boys would probably opt for the second option, and to be honest, so would I!

I think that the way Carl reacted or to be more correct didn't react could have been either a weakness or a strength depending on the size of Nathan compared to Carl, because if Nathan is a very large person then there would have been no point trying to resist but if Nathan is not so big and tough, Carl probably could have easily resisted Nathan and then at least restrained him.

I think that Carl is a bit of a fool for not standing up for himself. I mean, you should at least make a smart arse remark, so he can keep even a little dignity.[14]

These comments suggest that while moral strength might be admirable, asserting one's physical or linguistic dominance may be the most beneficial form of action, though the size of the opponent would clearly dictate which course to take: there is no point, it would seem, for a David-and-Goliath confrontation. The boys construct themselves as capable of physical aggression, yet tend to acknowledge Carl's self-discipline to control aggression only in terms of the size of his opponent and presumed physical superiority.

CROSS-DRESSING GUITARIST: HERO IN DRAG

In *Famous for Five Minutes*, Margaret Clark foregrounds gender relations and difference as the central issue. As part of the school's gender equity policy, an all-boy rock band must include a female member. Resisting such a directive, Peter decides to disguise himself as his female, guitar-playing cousin Peta and so lives the life of a girl for three weeks and experiences what it is like on the other side. Clark's strategy is not so much to problematize the issue of male-female dualism as it is to convince her (male) readers that only when one can literally step into the shoes of the other (female) can one truly appreciate the difficulties of being a woman in a man's world. As Clark commented during the chat session: "I was trying again to show how boys view things differently from girls, and it isn't til Peter becomes Peta that he gets a different perspective on gender in schools."[15] This device of the protagonist experiencing the plight of the marginalized other is not new nor is the technique of parodic inversion.

However, by using humor, the story serves to work both for and against its thesis.

This story foregrounds the performing body and the ways in which gender is a performance. Peter needs to transform the outward appearance of his body by putting on a dress, bra, blonde wig, stockings and shoes. He also needs to transform other parts of the body—his voice needs to be pitched higher and his walk needs to change. Consequently, Peter has to "discipline"[16] his body to perform like a woman, and his "femaleness" is established metonymically through his/her wig, clothes, voice, and movement. The problems of the male body coping with the cultural trappings of the female dress code are a source of humor (e.g., adjusting his wayward pantyhose and getting a rash from the socks stuffed in his bra). Clark's strategy of the cross-dresser offers a burlesque, which parodies the awkwardness of the male body inhabiting a female persona. It also highlights Judith Butler's point that gender, as an identity, is "instituted through a stylised repetition of acts" where "acts" refer to "bodily gestures, movements and enactments of various kinds."[17]

However, as Peter discovers, being a girl goes beyond the performing body and entails being positioned as a particular kind of person: "If you've got brains you get a real hard time; boys don't want you to be brainier than them so you get dumped before you start"[18]; "I'm finding that guys can get away with far more than girls"[19]; "If ya fight or swear or get with guys you're a slut, or a tart, or a slag, but if you're a guy . . . so what?"[20] The boys in the project were reluctant to answer the forum questions about this book. One boy (from a coeducational school), however, responded: "I'm a boy and I don't care if girls are smarter than me. I believe in equal opportunity." However, the boys felt that it "would be fun" to be a girl for a day, though a girl for three weeks was seen as taking the issue "too seriously."[21]

Despite the implausibility of the narrative and the all-too-convenient self-awareness of Peter regarding sexism and sexual inequality, Clark does offer readers a forum whereby characters and readers are presented with contexts for discussing gender (e.g., dis/advantages of being a girl). Peter struggles with his "natural" masculinity and his "unnatural" feminine disguise. While he comes to realize how boys' language and actions position girls as inferior, and objects of fun and scorn, he still finds that he can't help himself at times and old habits resurface. At one point he chastizes himself for being "a crude male again."[22] Yet by being in the company of girls and acting as a girl, Peter (Peta) finds that his masculine traits give way to feminine patterns of relating and behaving (e.g. he engages in "girly talk" and enjoys the friendship girls share). Clark has perhaps unwittingly used Peter as a New Age cape crusader, a hero whom women can look up to as he acts on their behalf to eliminate sexism and transforms his male friends' sexist attitudes and behavior. (Like the traditional hero,

Peter is surrounded by a small group of loyal, dim-witted companions.) Thus, under the wig and padded bra lurks the reformed male, the one who has seen the light.

CONCLUSION

The representations of masculinity discussed in this chapter offer male readers ambivalent male character types. On the one hand, the texts invite readers to desire and imitate the "approved" models of Carl and Peter while, on the other, they warn against the other possibilities, for example, Nathan and Peter's sexist friends. This intersection between representation and gender, therefore, serves a dual function—how to be and how not to be a male in society today. These texts, like all texts, not only function within an ideological framework, but also articulate and disseminate that ideology. As Gilbert and Gilbert have noted, "literary or text study has come to be associated with toeing an acceptable ideological line."[23] For many male readers, the profeminist approach taken in the two novels might be resisted, especially if it is seen as being antagonistic to the dominant school culture. The responses by the boys in this project indicate that "masculinity" in its various forms needs to be subjected to critical reassessment in much the same way that femininity has over recent years.[24]

Masculinity is constructed through various social practices and systems of representation; one context in which such practices and representations take place is reading of literature. While literature offers multiple messages about what it means to be growing up male in society today, some messages are more powerful than others and their impact will depend largely on the strategies used by the writers and readers' responses to them. For some boys, the influence of literature is quite marked on their lives, given its capacity to play with desire and to merge reality and fantasy. For others, the authority of these texts is limited or even nonexistent as other forms of popular cultural texts take precedence. The subjective effect of masculinity means that as boys live out their daily lives they are already interweaving the threads of their existence into a more complex web of social relations. As each thread intersects with various discourses of masculinity over time and space, the configuration changes.

While literature can open windows onto worlds, the representations of masculinity these worlds offer do not necessarily equate with young men's lives. Furthermore, the sense of these representations is made by the reader bringing particular references to the text: social reality is always mediated and so too is the reader's response to texts. Nevertheless, questions of representation are important in any social and textual analysis, as it is through their multiple meanings and interpretations that readers (and their teachers) can explore their own gendered subjectivities and the ways in which they are positioned within hegemonic and repressive discourses.

It is through critical reassessment of masculinity and its manifestation in various textual practices that the "crisis" rhetoric can be calmed and boys can move into the next millennium with a sense of direction and the confidence to construct different and positive ways of being male.

NOTES

1. Sara Willott and Christine Griffin, "Men, masculinity and the challenge of long term unemployment." In *Understanding Masculinities*. Ed. Mairtin Mac An Ghail. Buckingham, UK: Open UP, 1996, p. 89.

2. Wayne Martino, "Deconstructing masculinity in the English classroom: a site for reconstituting gendered subjectivity." *Gender and Education*, 7 (1995): 205–220.

3. R.W. Connell, *Masculinities*. St Leonards: Allen & Unwin, 1995.

4. Judith Butler, "Performative acts and gender constitution: an essay in phenomenology and feminist theory." In *Performing Feminisms: Feminist Critical Theory*. Ed. Sue-Ellen Case. Baltimore: Johns Hopkins UP, 1990, pp. 270–282.

5. Connell, p. 45.

6. James Moloney, on-line chat session, 6 May 1999.

7. James Moloney, *A Bridge to Wiseman's Cove*. St Lucia: U of Queensland P, 1996, p. 174.

8. Moloney, on-line chat session, 6 May 1999.

9. Moloney, *A Bridge to Wiseman's Cove*, p. 175.

10. Ibid., p. 176.

11. Margery Hourihan, *Deconstructing the Hero*. London: Routledge, 1997, p. 69.

12. Moloney, *A Bridge*, p. 175.

13. Ibid., p. 241.

14. Students' responses, Web forum, 7 May 1999.

15. Margaret Clark, on-line chat session, 14 May 1999.

16. Michel Foucault, *The Uses of Pleasure: The History of Sexuality*. Vol. 2. London: Penguin, 1989.

17. Butler, p. 270.

18. Margaret Clark, *Famous For Five Minutes*. Milsons Point: Random House, 1992, p. 114.

19. Ibid., p. 129.

20. Ibid., p. 130.

21. Students' responses, Web forum, 31 May 1999.

22. Clark, *Famous For Five Minutes*, p. 128.

23. Rob Gilbert and Pam Gilbert, *Masculinity Goes to School*. St. Leonards: Allen & Unwin, 1998, p. 212.

24. Ibid., p. 219.

REFERENCES

Butler, Judith. "Performative acts and gender constitution: an essay in phenomenology and feminist theory." In *Performing Feminisms:*

Feminist Criticial Theory. Ed. S. Case. Baltimore: Johns Hopkins UP, 1990, pp. 270–282.

Clark, Margaret. *Famous For Five Minutes.* Milsons Point: Random House, 1992.

Connell, R. W. *Masculinities.* St Leonards: Allen & Unwin, 1995.

Foucault, Michel. *The Uses of Pleasure: The History of Sexuality.* Vol. 2. London: Penguin, 1989.

Gilbert, Rob and Pam Gilbert. *Masculinity Goes to School.* St. Leonards: Allen & Unwin, 1998.

Hourihan, Margery. *Deconstructing the Hero.* London: Routledge, 1997.

Martino, Wayne. "Deconstructing masculinity in the English classroom: a site for reconstituting gendered subjectivity." *Gender and Education,* 7 (1995): 205–220.

Moloney, James. *A Bridge to Wiseman's Cove.* St Lucia: U of Queensland P, 1996.

Willott, Sara and Christine Griffin. "Men, masculinity and the challenge of long term unemployment." In *Understanding Masculinities.* Ed. Mairtin Mac An Ghail. Buckingham: Open University Press, 1996, pp. 77–92.

CHAPTER 19

Leaving the Men to Drown?
Fin de Siècle Reconfigurations
of Masculinity in
Children's Fiction

Beverley Pennell

The challenge of recomposing the dichotomized gender configurations of patriarchy, with its privileging of hegemonic masculinity and heterosexuality, remains a multifaceted problem that is very much unfinished business at the *fin de siècle*.[1] After all, the dissolution of gender dichotomies is not only difficult to envision; it is unthinkable in all cultures where this binarism is considered foundational.[2] In his groundbreaking study, *Masculinities* (1995), Bob Connell demonstrates very clearly why this is the case in Western society. He argues that hegemonic masculinity "is deeply entrenched in the history of institutions and of economic structures . . . it is also extended in the world, merged in organised social relations."[3] Given the complexity of the social, economic and institutional embeddedness of patriarchal power and privilege, it is hardly surprising that the literary project of reconfiguring the representations of masculine subjectivities proceeds slowly.

The discursive practices of literature also reflect the embeddedness of patriarchy and hegemonic masculinity when we consider the engendered nature of all metanarratives and genres. I have argued elsewhere with regard to picture books, and John Stephens with regard to children's fiction, that attempts to interrogate gendering in society by subverting storylines alone are not ultimately successful in undermining gender dichotomy. Stephens argues that texts can only be convincingly subversive with regard to gender when close attention is paid to genre and discourse as well as to storylines.[4] The first generation of feminist texts for children was not entirely satisfactory then, because it failed to take these literary considerations on board. Such texts clearly problematize the formerly positive attributes of hegemonic masculinity, arguing that it interpellates subjects whose relentless impetus to distinction means that competitiveness becomes the normative masculine experience. Winning and an imperative to distinction, consequently, become the predominant means of establishing self-worth.

Early feminist theorizing also effectively demonstrated the hierarchical nature of patriarchal social organization which used "difference," whether of embodiment, sexuality, race, religion, social class, or ethnicity, as a rationale for domination and as a legitimation of the use of violence as a means of social control. When these feminist insights were transferred into the field of children's literature there were negative consequences for representations of masculine subjectivities. Storylines often subverted patriarchal emplotments by representing fathers and men in traditional roles of authority as domineering, insensitive, silent, emotionally unavailable, and inarticulate. The actions of such characters are shown to have horrific effects on their partners and their children. The crisis in hegemonic masculinity was made visible by the removal of literature's traditional transgressive men—the cold-hearted villains—out of their dank, dirty alleyways and deep, dark caves and placing them inside the domestic household. Just consider the latest trend in such narratives where fathers who are in Witness Protection Programs are represented as devastating the lives of their families. David McRobbie's *See How They Run* (1996) and Alan Baillie's *Last Shot* (1997) exemplify recent powerful texts with such emplotments Addressing the implicit liberal feminist ideology construction in such representations of sociality, Connell writes:

If patriarchy is understood as a historical structure, rather than a timeless dichotomy of men abusing women, then it will be ended by historical process. The strategic problem is to generate pressures that will cumulate towards a transformation of the whole structure; the structural mutation is the end of the process, not the beginning. In earlier stages, any initiative that sets up pressure towards that historical change is worth having.[5]

I argue that early models of feminist intervention in the literature for children must be acknowledged as a worthwhile part of that "pressure for historical change" because these texts clearly undermine aspects of patriarchal mythology. However, they typically do not represent a degendered sociality and so tend implicitly to reinscribe gender as an oppositional dichotomy. Dismantling this oppositional gender configuration remains a challenge for progressive writers in this *fin de siècle* moment when postmodernist, postfeminist, and queer theory intersect to oppose all hegemonic discourses.

While my reading suggests that positive literary reconfigurations of the masculine in children's literature in English remain rare, there are some.

Two significant fictions in this regard are the Australian novel *Bruno and the Crumhorn* (1996) by Ursula Dubosarsky and *Covered Bridge* (1990) by Canadian writer Brian Doyle. Both texts attempt to represent a shift in focus away from the ideological and political need of patriarchy and hegemonic masculinity to pejorate and dominate the "other." These fictions support Connell's argument that literary constructions of masculinity are "inherently historical" rather than universal and "natural." Most importantly, they suggest that it is possible to envision change in gender configurations and to represent these in literary discourse for children. These fictions advocate reconfigurations of gendered social relations and offer the possibility of redemption of the masculine in the domestic scene and in relations of cathexis. *Bruno and the Crumhorn* and *Covered Bridge* are both highly amusing texts whose success in problematizing the masculine and feminine binarism depends largely upon the use of metafictive discoursal strategies: they are stories about writing and reading stories. In her comprehensive analysis of metafictions and experimental texts for children, Robyn McCallum states that metafictive texts employ

strategies which distance readers from a text and frequently frustrate conventional expectations about meaning and closure. Implied readers are thereby positioned in more active interpretive roles. By foregrounding the discursive and narrative structuring of texts, metafictions can show readers how texts mean, and by analogy, how meanings are ascribed to everyday reality.[6]

Both *Bruno and the Crumhorn* and *Covered Bridge* use metafictive strategies ironically to mark and parody conventional generic structuring of realist texts and the features of literary, and other, discourses. Self-reflexiveness is interestingly constructed as a part of the narrative framing of *Covered Bridge*. The first person narrator is the character "Young Hubbo" who appeared in Doyle's earlier novel *Easy Avenue* (1989). The narrator establishes the conventional "good faith" relationship with the implied reader. However, Hubbo's main intention is to record all that happens to him in a letter to his absent girlfriend, Fleurette Featherstone Fitchell, or F3.

And I tried to think of what to compare Mrs O'Driscoll's face to, to put in Fleurette's letter.

Her face was calm like the covered bridge. It was content like Mushrat Creek. It was clear like Dizzy Peak. It was funny like a gooseberry on a gooseberry bush. And it was full of love like the Gatineau Hills.

And it was wise, like the Gatineau River.

Fleurette would like the ways that I tried to say what Mrs O'Driscoll's face was like.

And I was writing how you get to like somebody's face. Like O'Driscoll's. At first I thought he was sort of funny-looking. Now I loved his face. What happened? It didn't look like the same face at all.

But mostly I was trying to explain how they were going to let the bridge get old and rotten. How you have to take care of things or they'll disappear.

Or maybe they would just let it get neglected until it got dangerous, and then they'd have to tear it down.

It didn't seem right.[7]

This narrative strategy instigates a discussion with the reader about the generic and discoursal choices that writers make. The strategy makes it clear to the reader that the intended audience of the text and the point of view adopted by the writer affect the tenor of a text and influence the selection of material for inclusion in the text. The reader is alerted to the ways that the combination of these narrative and discoursal choices alter the significances of a text. The shift in register from the heavy-handed metaphorical literary discourse describing Mrs. O'Driscoll's face to the confiding conversational register used to address the implied reader foregrounds the linguistic choices made by writers and speakers.

This distinction is drawn to the reader's attention regularly because each short chapter has a title that parodies the discourse used in newspaper headlines. This allusion to headlines comments ironically on both the fictive nature of the content of the chapter and the literary discourse in which it is constructed. The chapter title from which the extract above comes is a good example of this strategy: "Gooseberry has face of beautiful woman!"[8] This comically parodies headlines by the choice of a sensational angle to frame the text that follows and effectively foregrounds different discursive practices. A further level of irony exists in the contrast between the constructions of feminine beauty typically offered by the media and the beauty signified by Hubbo's poetic discourse when describing his adoptive mother's transformed appearance since her reunion with her husband and the move to Mushrat Creek.

The significance of the extract above, however, lies in the particular representation of a masculine subject. Hubbo is both sensitive to the emotional needs of others and able to articulate his own desires for positive intersubjective experiences. His desire for mutuality and reciprocity in peer and familial intersubjective relationships has made him aware of the range of views that can be found on any social issue. His awareness enables him to be considerate of the feelings of others within his social network. Hubbo is represented as very aware that negotiation and seeking of consensus are essential in order for all community members to be valued and to feel empowered. The need for hierarchical social relations is repudiated.

Bruno and the Crumhorn adopts a more common self-reflexive narrative strategy of the overly obtrusive third-person omniscient narrator. The narrator addresses the reader in the opening lines of the novel to foreground narratorial control of the choices made with regard to all aspects of textuality. By ironically highlighting the subjection of the characters to the narrator, the text marks the possibility of the reader's subjection to the ideology of the text in the act of reading. This turns out to be ironic because the text seeks to insist on active readers who negotiate their own decisions about the alternative worldviews and lifestyles represented in the text.

This book is called Bruno and the Crumhorn, but it's not just about Bruno. It's about Sybil. Sybil? And a thing, of course, the crumhorn. A crumhorn? Well, there is so much to be said about each of them, but someone has to go first. Perhaps seeing Bruno has the whole book named after him—quite unfairly really—it should be Sybil.[9]

This extract foregrounds numerous aspects of textuality and of fictions in particular. The reader's attention is drawn to the function and effects of conventions like book titles, story existents, to the linearity of texts and the disruptions to the spatio-temporal axis that are a feature of literary discourse. It is not till halfway through the novel that Sybil again appears in the story. Chapter 6 begins, "This is where Sybil comes in. You've guessed already, of course. Sybil found the crumhorn."[10] Here we see the narrator acknowledging the reader by referring to the reader's knowledge of how texts work, and to the fact that experienced readers of fictions will have expectations about how narratives develop, which lead them to predict story outcomes. These metafictive narrative strategies are used extensively and just as playfully in *Covered Bridge*:

Then the woman turned in the moonlight and hurtled through the space and disappeared into Mushrat Creek.
Then we heard a big splash.
That is I heard a big splash.
Nerves didn't hear a thing.
He was passed out.
That was the first night of my new job on the covered bridge.
The next day I was fired.
But we're going too fast.
I'd better go back a bit.[11]

Here the writer is constructing an oral narrative using the conventions of colloquial speech and the comic mode to overturn reader expectations about "normal" behaviors—dogs do not usually faint, people do. But more importantly, the reader is being alerted to the way material is selected and ordered in literary narratives. The high degree of narrative metalepsis in the extract foregrounds the artifice involved in the structure of a literary narrative.

It is clear from the openings of both novels that the formation of masculine subjectivities will be a central concern. Readers are asked to question the various representations of masculine characters and are constantly required by both texts to compare versions of the fictional masculine with those of their everyday experience. *Bruno and the Crumhorn* represents various contemporary schemas of masculinity dialectically and offers the reader a variety of subject positions to adopt with regard to engendered behaviors. *Covered Bridge* works very differently, creating a pseudo-historical 1950s spatio-temporal framework for the story. Here the writer mythologizes and valorizes rural and working-class versions of masculinity, which are represented as valuing collectivity, mutuality, and comradeship among men and women. Competitiveness and individual success are devalued in favor of promoting community welfare. Hierarchical patriarchal organization in the public sphere is symbolically overthrown by the rejection of inflexible religious authority represented by Foolish Father Foley from Farrelton. The institutionalized face of patriarchy is the enemy in this pastorale:

> The thing took more shape as it approached the wind space. The shape of a woman. And a voice saying words.
> "Please, father, let me in? Please let me in, father! May I please go in? Can't I please get in?"
> She wore a moonlight-coloured dress and a wide-brimmed dark hat.[12]

The patriarchal gender order is foregrounded immediately as it is in *Bruno and the Crumhorn*. This time, however, it is the position of a woman foregrounded by a male focalizer and the narrator is Hubbo. The ghostly apparition is in fact only a "pretend" ghost—a cross-dressed character in this episode—but later, in the climax of the story, it is just a goat wearing the hat and draped in washing from a clothesline that leads to Foolish Father Foley drowning in Mushrat Creek. His drowning parallels and avenges the death of Ophelia Brown, who was shown no compassion by patriarchal religious authority some decades in the past.

The predominant concern with masculinity in *Bruno and the Crumhorn* is made evident in the reader's introduction to twelve-year-old Sybil as she muses on some of the dominant masculine stereotypes with which she has become familiar from her own everyday experience and from constructions of the masculine in the media and films.

It was only men who lived on the street like this. Where were the women whose brains didn't work any more? Sybil wondered. Perhaps, if she'd been born a boy, she would have grown up into a man, and have had to join the army or go into parliament, or lie on the street with lots of other men. Although it may not have to be that way. There were three men who lived next door to them, who, when they went out to parties, put on make-up and shiny red dresses, and wore flowers in their hair, so they looked like air hostesses on advertisements for Philippine

Airlines. Perhaps you didn't have to be a man all the time, just because you were born one.[13]

The narrative convention of the defamiliarized gaze of the child works well to represent a parodic compilation of masculine stereotypes. Some are stereotypes that patriarchy judges to be powerful, while others are regarded as abject, veering from the heterosexist norm. The irony of Sybil inverting the normal patriarchal value system satirizes normative behaviors and effectively distances readers, challenging them to question what may formerly have seemed to be a "natural" gender order. Sybil pities the captain of the *Titanic* along with parliamentarians and military leaders, while the transvestites are represented as fortunate because they can escape being men for at least part of the time. Gender performativity is made clear by the reference to the airline poster.[14] Most significantly, Sybil's musings imply that the formerly singular and unitary masculine subject should be understood as the plural: masculinities are diverse, complex, and shifting. The problem of whether traditional patriarchy is in fact "leaving the men behind to drown" emotionally and socially becomes a central issue problematized by the novel.

The materialization of Bruno's subjectivity is fraught as he negotiates the various models of masculinity that he sees around him or that he imagines. There are, for instance, his imaginings about Great Aunt Ilma's four husbands, "all extant," as Aunt Ilma describes them. There are bus drivers, lost property officers, musicians, his father and his mother's reiteration of the desirable unitary form of masculinity exemplified by his brother Max. The wide representation of masculine subjectivities ensures that the reader is positioned to acknowledge the diversity of male subject positions, which operate in our social world. The fact that Max and Bruno are diametrically opposed in interests, educational achievements, and in "commonsense" negotiations of the world shows that resistance to rigid societal and parental expectations of patriarchal hegemonic masculine behavior is possible and often desirable.

Bruno and the Crumhorn and *Covered Bridge* succeed in making masculinities visible across a wide range of social contexts, but particularly in the domestic scene. The protagonists, Bruno and Hubbo, repudiate the heroic storylines of patriarchal narratives, yet they are not transgressive patriarchal figures. Both characters interpellate a range of subject positions, often valorizing qualities that have been traditionally devalued as defining the "feminine." In particular, both characters are represented as valuing cooperation in all work whether inside or outside the domestic household, being emotionally articulate and honest in their acknowledgment of their emotional vulnerability. Both characters resist normative masculine behaviors on occasion and both resist the imperative of distinction.

It is possible from our *fin de siècle* position to see why gender issues in the earlier feminist texts for children were inadequately addressed: replotting the feminine roles in narratives and the demonization of the masculine were not in fact a renegotiation of gender in literary discourse. An oppositional, dichotomized social order remained intact and was usually implicitly, if not explicitly, reinforced. As Stephens argues, to move beyond the early feminist interventions in literature for children it is necessary for writers to pay attention to genre and discoursal strategies as well as to the story constituents of patriarchal metanarratives. Redeeming the engendered masculine subject in children's literature requires, at the very least, the death of a unitary masculine hero and the birth of new plural signifier, masculinities, in order for further gender reconfiguration to proceed. Metafictions like *Bruno and the Crumhorn* and *Covered Bridge* have the potential to be positive steps toward envisioning a degendered social reality.

NOTES

1. See Mairtain Mac an Ghaill, ed., *Understanding Masculinities*. Buckingham and Bristol, UK: Open UP, 1996, pp. 10–11; and Annamarie Rustom Jagose, *Queer Theory*. Carlton South, Australia: Melbourne UP, 1996, pp. 133–136.

2. Nancy Jay, "Gender and Dichotomy." In *A Reader in Feminist Knowledge*, Sneja Gunew, ed. Sydney: Allen & Unwin, 1991, p. 106.

3. Bob Connell, *Masculinities*. St Leonards: Allen & Unwin, 1995, pp. 241–243.

4. These arguments are detailed in the papers published in 1996. See Beverley Pennell, "Ideological Drift in Children's Picture Books." *Papers: Explorations in Children's Literature* 6 (1996): 5–13, and John Stephens, "Gender, Genre and Children's Literature." *Signal* 79 (1996): 17–30.

5. Connell, pp. 71–86.

6. Robyn MacCallum, "Metafictions and Experimental Work." In *International Companion Encyclopedia of Children's Literature*, Peter Hunt, ed. London and New York: Routledge, 1996, p. 398.

7. Brian Doyle, *Covered Bridge*. Toronto/Vancouver: Douglas & McIntyre, 1990, pp. 27–28.

8. Ibid., p. 27.

9. Ursula Dubosarsky, *Bruno and the Crumhorn*. Ringwood, Victoria, Australia: Penguin, 1996, p. 28.

10. Ibid., p. 5.

11. Doyle, *Covered Bridge*, p. 10.

12. Ibid., pp. 9–10.

13. Dubosarsky, *Bruno and the Crumhorn*, pp. 8–9.

14. See Judith Butler, *Bodies That Matter: On the Discursive Limits of Sex*. London and New York: Routledge, 1993.

REFERENCES

Baillie, Allan. *The Last Shot*. Maryborough, Victoria, Australia: Omnibus Books, 1997.

Butler, Judith. *Bodies That Matter: On the Discursive Limits of Sex*. London and New York: Routledge, 1993.

Connell, R. W. *Masculinities*. St Leonards, Allen & Unwin, 1995.

Doyle, Brian. *Covered Bridge*. Toronto: Douglas & Macintyre, 1990.

———. *Easy Avenue*. Toronto: Douglas & Macintyre, 1988.

Dubosarsky, Ursula. *Bruno and the Crumhorn*. Ringwood, Victoria, Australia: Penguin Books, 1996.

Jagose, Annamarie Rustom. *Queer Theory*. Carlton South, Australia: Melbourne UP, 1996.

Jay, Nancy. "Gender and Dichotomy." In *A Reader in Feminist Knowledge*. Ed. Sneja Gunew. Sydney: Allen & Unwin, 1991, pp. 89–106.

McCallum, Robyn. "Metafiction and Experimental Fiction." In *International Companion Encyclopedia of Children's Literature*. Ed. Peter Hunt. London and New York: Routledge, 1996, pp. 397–409.

Mairtin Mac an Ghaill, ed. *Understanding Masculinities*. Buckingham and Bristol, UK: Open UP, 1996.

McRobbie, David. *See How They Run*. Ringwood, Victoria, Australia: Puffin, 1996.

Pennell, Beverley. "Ideological Drift in Children's Picture Books." *Papers: Explorations into Children's Literature*, 6 (1996): 5–13.

Stephens, John. "Gender, Genre and Children's Literature." *Signal* 79 (1996): 17–30.

PART VI

Cyberculture

CHAPTER 20

Welcome to the Game: Cyberspace in Young Adult Speculative Fiction

Elizabeth L. Pandolfo Briggs

Cyberspace has become the newest alien landscape appearing in young adult speculative fiction. And why not? Children growing up today are part of the computer culture, at ease manipulating and operating within technological creations. It's natural that they would want to read adventures that involve computers and cyberspace. And, naturally, authors want to explore and experiment with the thematic possibilities that technology in literature offers. Indeed, many themes related to technology are central to children's literature. Ironically, although many novels ostensibly portray cyberspace as exciting and full of possibilities, underneath a subtle current of unease and fear bleeds through, which reflects adults' concerns about cyberspace and computer technology. Books designed to appeal to technologically adept computer-age readers also carry the message that cyberspace is dangerous and to be feared.

Adults are used to asserting control over young people. Computer technology reverses the traditional adult/child paradigm; many adults sit bewildered trying to learn as young people zip around cyberspace teaching adults what to do. This reversal tends to make many adults rueful and uncomfortable. Popular media heightens the unease that stems from unfamiliarity with the medium, with stories of Internet harassment and abuse of innocent, unsuspecting young people. Adults tend to be uncomfortable with cyberspace being the best place (and/or medium) by which young people can escape direct adult control and be autonomous. Many adults also react strongly against how they see technology changing traditional lifestyles. At a children's literature conference I attended in the late 1990s, many attendees deplored that playgrounds were frequently battlefields rather than happy gathering places. Then they lamented that young people never seemed to go outside to play anymore, preferring solitary technological pursuits such as computer games and the Internet. The irony is striking, particularly since there was no mention of any positive communal interaction available to young people online; indeed, it is often difficult to find any mention of such positive aspects of the Internet. Young people today can find a variety of cyberspace communities in which to interact. Proximity no longer necessarily limits communal interactions. It is often less stressful (and certainly more natural) to criticize change than to find something positive in its, as Douglas Rushkoff points out in his intriguing, informally written book *Children of Chaos: Surviving the End of the World as We Know it.*

In many speculative fiction novels, the treatment of cyberspace subtly expresses these concerns about young prople and technology. Cyberspace frequently takes the form of a virtual reality game in texts. Typically the game takes over the setting, becoming not simply a tool or device within the plot but a narrative space in which protagonists operate. Sherry Turkle, a professor of the sociology of science at Massachusetts Instute of Technology, in *Life on the Screen: Identity in the Age of the Internet* (1995) notes: "in recent years, the designers of video games have been pushing the games further into realistic simulation through graphics, animation, sound, an interactivity . . . video games for most players carry ideas about a world one does not so much analyze as inhabit. In some games, rules have given way to branching narratives!"[1] Turkle uses the game Myst as her real-life example of such a phenomenon. Three texts that illustrate a similar principle (though not imitating the actual product) are *Skymaze* (1989) by Gillian Rubenstein, *New World* (1994) by Gillian Cross, and *The Web Sorceress* (1998) by Maggie Furey. All are good-to-excellent-quality speculative fiction novels, each centered on a virutual reality game. The game in each book quickly becomes the primary narrative setting, blurring the boundary between real and virtual, spilling over its edges into the physical world. The protagonists of each book become trapped within the game, and must puzzle their way out.

Doing so proves difficult, because these authors portray the game space as inherently negative, which reflects adult concerns about cyberspace and computer technology. Cyberspace has become, in fact, the most dangerous environment for young people. The games in *Skymaze* and *New World* are designed to terrify, though in *Skymaze* it is possible to go through the game without activating all the terrors. The situation in *The Web Sorceress* is slightly different; the game is an advanced type of adventure game that an evil character takes over and uses for her own ends. However, the book makes clear that the game was designed without proper safeguards in place, which might have prevented certain dangers from occurring. The physical world in all three books, on the other hand, is portrayed as far safer, brighter, and preferable, perhaps because it stays within its boundaries and is controllable. The concerns and sqabbles that characterize the protagonists' lives in these texts seem petty and inconsequential when compared to the real threats within the game space in each book.

Skymaze, by Gilliam Rubenstein is the story of four friends who have survived a previous dangerous computer game in the book *Space Demons*. Andrew, against the advice of his friend Ben, sends off for the next game by the same creator. When the game Skymaze arrives, Andrew begins playing it, only to find that the avatars in the game are tiny replicas of whoever is playing. Once players reach the end of Level 1 of the computer aspect of Skymaze, each may choose an ability to help him or her through the game. Force and weaponry are incorrect choices. Choosing those transforms one into an "evil" character, controlled by the game. Once a player chooses, the Skymaze (or the virtual reality aspect of the game) is then activated for that player. One enters the virtual reality Skymaze by physically running away from something deeply feared. Skymaze operates by honing in on players' secret fears and using them to keep players within the game and to prevent players from discovering the game's prize. Entering the game takes players out of the physical world. The virtual world of Skymaze is real enough though. After a player uses up his or her three lives, a player can be "killed," resulting in serious injury in the physical world. One protagonist, Mario, uses up his three lives in the virtual game and is "killed"; in the physical world he falls six stories from the roof of a car park and lies comatose in the hospital until his friends successfully finish playing Skymaze. The prize for successfully navigating Skymaze is a medallion representation of Earth and the accompanying knowledge that all living things are "part of the Earth, no part more important than the others, and that their interdependence was the Earth's life, their disunity its death."[2] Mario also comes out of his coma. If his friends had left Skymaze unfinished, he would have remained comatose. So, at the end of the text, the physical world is obviously prioritized.

In *New World*, by Gillian Cross, two young people, Miriam and Stuart, have been chosen to test a new virtual reality game called New World. The game is quite frightening at times, and it's this rush to which they become addicted. But the game has been programmed with their deepest fears in mind. New World soon becomes a threatening place, particularly after the designer's son, Will, is tricked into playing New World. Will sees two sprites he must annihilate, using whatever means within the game he can discover. The two sprites, Miriam and Stuart, on their side soon realize someone else is in the game, trying to hurt and terrify them. The situation comes about in the text because game experts are questioning virtual reality and its place in games because "real" aliens could be dangerously frightening. They could even cause "game trauma"—acute and damaging fear that leaves a child psychologically crippled. And the games companies could land up paying millions of pounds in damages. Unless they find a way to control fear itself.[3]

So that is what the game designer, Hesketh, is testing: his new system for controlling fear. Both Miriam and Stuart are children Hesketh indirectly knows, which is how he discovered their inner fears to program them into the game for his tests. The terror present in this book that *Skymaze* and *The Web Sorceress* lack is that Hesketh would exploit and physically endanger Miriam, Stuart, and Will to test the boundaries of fear, and use his own son to terrify other people. In the end, as in *Skymaze*, all protagonists' situations work out well, although not perfectly or ideally.

The Web Sorceress, by Maggie Furey, is part of a British publisher's line of cyberspace adventures by several authors, all texts loosely connected. In this series, the year is 2027 and the virtual-reality Web has truly transformed society. Almost all education, travel, entertainment, and recreation occur virtually in the Web. The protagonists are a group of young people from around the world, one of whom, Jack, lives temporarily with one of the most famous designers of Web games, Anna Lucas. Strange things start happening at the beginning of the story: part of the Web simply disappears; a friend of Jack's, Eleni, meets a menacing silver woman; and parts of the Web become inaccessible to people. Anna is unable to access her new prototype game. Another friend of Jack's, Cat, in the physical world meets Miss Aldanar, a recluse confined to a wheelchair. Miss Aldanar gives Cat a websuit of her very own to use, and traps Cat in the Web, inside Anna's new game. Miss Aldanar is the Web Sorceress, responsible for the disruptions to the Web, which are part of her plan to achieve health and youthfulness, and to control the Web. Jack, Eleni, and another friend, Rom, save Cat and trap Miss Aldanar inside the Web, in the rubble of Anna's destroyed game.

These three texts refashion several interesting thematic possibilities surrounding the choice to use cyberspace as a narrative space; these are issues virtual reality has made relevant again. First, Sherry Turkle makes the intriguing observation that

another way to look at the romantic reaction of the 1970s and early 1980s is to say that during that time the traditional boundaries between things and people softened. At the same time there was an attendant anxiety that demanded the assertion that these boundaries were sacred. In the years that followed, some of the anxiety about becoming involved with a machine began to abate and the blurred boundaries were exposed to view.[4]

These boundaries, between machine and human, between physical and virtual, fascinate me, particularly when considering the future and what may become possible through technological advances. It is also fascinating to question, as these texts do, what is real, what the notion of something being "real" means.

Turkle goes on to state that people she interviewed in the 1970s and 1980s about advances in artificial intelligence agreed "with the premise that human minds are some kind of computer but then found ways to think of themselves as something more than that. Their sense of personal identity often became focused on whatever they defined as 'not cognition' or 'beyond information'."[5] We see this attitude reflected in the texts as well. What saves each group of protagonists from the dangers of the games in which they're trapped are their efforts to work together as a united group and their collective sense that they have something more than the game does, even if it knows their fears. This belief reinforces notions of humanity in the face of rapid technological advances. In a young adult book, this belief provides reinforcement to maturing young people discovering their own abilities and individuality and how to live harmoniously in a community. In the end, in each book, focus returns to the physical world. Protagonists strengthen community ties among themselves, and even establish new, closer physical ties to one another. Even in *The Web Sorceress*, Cat physically moves from England to Ireland to live with Jack and Anna.

Another thematic possibility explored is that of technology challenging our traditional notions of community and self. Contemporary Western society is quite fragmented. As Turkle points out, "social beings that we are, we are trying . . . to retribalize. And the computer is playing a central role" through email, mailing lists, newsgroups, bulletin boards, chat rooms, MOOs, and so on.[6] This technology affects how we view the self. According to Turkle, "new images of multiplicity, heterogeneity, flexibility, and fragmentation dominate current thinking about human identity."[7] In cyberspace "people are able to build a self by cycling through many selves."[8] Turkle uses peoples' personas in chat rooms as an example. In chat rooms one constructs an identity. The dislocation of persona and person allows for experimentation in identity. People can play roles in cyberspace, whereas in the physical world such opportunities for identity experimentation are limited and carry stronger consequences. "Many more people [now] experience identity as a set of roles that can be mixed and matched, whose diverse demands need to be negotiated."[9]

Rubenstein, Cross, and Furey explore these ideas of community and self in their texts through utilizing cyberspace as a narrative space. A definite tension exists between the physical and virtual worlds. The protagonists all inhabit the same physical communities in *Skymaze* and *New World*. What is interesting is that in both books the groups of protagonists maintain close ties despite difficulties in getting together physically due to transportation problems and the physical distance across cities that separates them. These problems actually strain the ties somewhat. In contrast, the group of friends in *The Web Sorceress* live in Greece, England, Ireland, and the United States. Of course, the premise in this text is that the world operates largely as a virtual society. Differences in time zones, schedules, and so on don't hinder the protagonists from coming together in their own virtual community space. Their group friendship lacks some of the strain apparent in the friendships in the other two books. Gathering together is much easier in cyberspace.

Cyberspace also provides the protagonists with an environment conducive to self-exploration. *The Web Sorceress* opens with Eleni showing off her new avatar persona, a dragon. In the Web, physical appearance is completely fluid, as Eleni moves between her human avatar appearance and her new dragon avatar. Cat's customary avatar is a tabby cat. When Jack sees her in a human avatar persona, he wonders if that's really what she looks like in the physical world.

Appearance isn't the only experimentation. Some protagonists in *Skymaze* have noticeably different personas within the virtual environment than in the physical world. All three games in the texts challenge the protagonists playing them. The characters stretch their abilities to the limit, and discover new abilities and characteristics when tested. In cyberspace protagonists get to try out various roles: arctic explorer, dragon-rider, or gymnast. And they get to experiment with the personas they present in social interactions.

Cyberspace is an excellent medium for exploring power issues. Young people have a liberating power in cyberspace that they lack elsewhere. In cyberspace they have freedom from adults and from the rule-based tyranny of childhood. Cyberspace allows young people to accomplish things they couldn't necessarily do in the physical world, as the growing number of businesses on the Internet owned by people under the age of eighteen demonstrates. Nation 1, a nation created by people under the age of eighteen, has an international membership, corporate financial backing, and a virtual currency system. Its goal is to work on the problems adults are having such a difficult time solving: environmental issues, global community and peace objectives, and so on. The protagonists in these texts possess the ability in cyberspace to perform superhuman acts because of the enabling power and freedom of cyberspace and because of their own ability to manipulate their virtual environments.

There are other options for utilizing cyberspace within a text, other than as a narrative space, that don't reduce the thematic possibilities, as Monica Hughes illustrates with her book *Invitation to the Game* (1990). In this text, cyberspace also takes the form of a game, but it operates as an alternate setting within the text. This kind of utilization allows for a more positive treatment of cyberspace. In Hughes's futuristic world, most jobs are done by robots. Most young people graduate high school to find no opportunities for themselves. The government provides for the unemployed, restricting them to ghetto-like communities where gang violence is almost as common as the rampant boredom of the inhabitants. Lisse and her friends find themselves in this situation on graduating. After a few months Lisse and her friends receive an invitation to join the Game, a virtual reality game where the group together explores a foreign world. Later they discover that the Game is a means of preparing young people for what they'll find on the new planet to which they're transported. The Game is part of a government-operated plan to reduce overcrowding on Earth by shipping stable, cohesive groups of friends with varied skills to another planet.

In Hughes's novel cyberspace takes the form of a game, but it's not really a game. The virtual reality setting simply mirrors the new planet. There is an almost seamless flow between the Game and the physical world. There is no discernible goal or prize in the Game, no "bad guys" to evade. It is a benign setting, unlike the games in the other three texts. If a protagonist has an accident or sustains an injury in the Game, the entire group is automatically returned to the physical world before the trauma even completes itself. The entire purpose is exploration and discovery of the new landscape. In this sense, the Game is as different as the games in the other books as Myst is to conventional computer games.

What sets Hughes's text apart is that the Game is also an object functioning in the text, a training device within the text. This dual use of cyberspace expands its functional possibilities in the text. Because it doesn't fall into the typical pattern of cyberspace in a text, the range of what cyberespace in literature can accomplish is expanded, as are the possibilities within the narrative space created by the game. And this dual use heightens the dramatic tension of the text. Once Lisse and her friends are taken off Earth, for several days after arriving on the new planet they believe themselves to be in the Game back on Earth.

Invitation to the Game depicts cyberspace as a neutral space, and as a useful tool. Little of thte negative undertones from the other three books are present. Hughes does not glorify technology, just as Rubenstein, Cross, and Furey do not vilify technology. It seems that many authors enjoy writing exciting cyberspace adventures, yet depend on the technology to add the antagonistic angle; why this is so prevalent is a deeply layered question, I believe. Hughes, however, manages to open the range of possibilities cyberspace has in literature, without losing the ability to explore any of the related thematic possibilities. Although the negative aspect of virtual reality games provides an excellent venue for adventure, it is refreshing to see a book in which young people's involvement with technology has a positive outcome.

NOTES

1. Sherry Turkle, *Life on the Screen: Identity in the Age of the Internet*. New York: Simon & Schuster, 1995, p. 68.
2. Gillian Rubenstein, *Skymaze*. New York: Simon & Schuster, 1989, p. 215.
3. Gillian Cross, *New World*. New York: Penguin, 1994, p. 121.
4. Turkle, p. 110.
5. Ibid., p. 129.
6. Ibid., p. 178.
7. Ibid.
8. Ibid.
9. Ibid., p. 180.

REFERENCES

Cross, Gillian. *New World*. New York: Penguin, 1994.

Furey, Maggie. *The Web Sorceress*. London: Orion, 1998.

Hughes, Monica. *Invitation to the Game*. New York: Simon & Schuster, 1990.

Rubenstein, Gillian. *Skymaze*. New York: Simon & Schuster, 1989.

Rushkoff, Douglas. *Children of Chaos: Surviving the End of the World As We Know It*. London: HarperCollins, 1997.

Turkle, Sherry. *Life on the Screen: Identity in the Age of the Internet*. New York: Simon & Schuster, 1995.

CHAPTER 21

Competency and Resistance: A Double Perspective on Teaching Books to Children in the Next Millennium

Leona W. Fisher

BACKGROUND AND THE PROBLEM: INSTRUCTIONISM VERSUS CONSTRUCTIONISM

In the suburbs of Washington, D.C., one county's elementary schoolchildren recently passed their new Standard of Learning test at the rate of only 17 percent. As a result, the state has threatened to "take over" the schools and oversee the "learning" of those obviously underachieving pupils. Those of us who spend our time thinking about reading and writing do not believe that such centralization will lead to better-educated citizens or critical thinkers; we fear that "teaching to the test" will merely become the new, mechanized way to fill the "little vessels" with "Facts, Facts, Facts."

As a counter to this trend, I propose that we who work in the literary field actively take on the project of helping to define and disseminate new and daring ways to teach children's literature—working with both software designers and the teachers who are responsible for implementing those innovations.

PREMISES AND ASSUMPTIONS: CHILDREN (AND THEIR LEARNING), TEACHERS, AND PARENTS

My premises are the following: (1) children actually want to become competent readers and thinkers and are frustrated when their school systems do not know how to build these competencies; (2) children are "natural" resisters of rote learning and will flourish under a new dispensation that encourages both acquisition of new knowledges and questioning of received ideas; (3) children already possess incipient computer literacy, an ability to see new connections, and a creative imagination that cries out to be actively involved in the learning process; (4) parents need to (and can) be educated to learn along with their children, so that schools are not held in thrall to ignorance, prejudice, and a public discourse of failure; and (5) both the "classics" and the new postmodern innovations in children's literature(s) can be used productively to develop children's critical skills and desire to read.

THE PROPOSAL IN BRIEF: A COMBINATION OF LITERARY THEORY AND COMPUTER TECHNIQUES

In my project, both literary theory and computer skills would be integrated into the elementary classroom in a central and dynamic way. Specifically, from theory I propose to borrow the concepts of "defamiliarization" (the "making strange" of topics and themes so that children can see the world in fresh and startling ways) and "interpellation" (or "hailing"—that is, the call to unconscious identification of the child with the book's ideology), applying them to the presentation and reception of electronic texts. Ample evidence exists in the books themselves that the most engaging children's texts both shock and comfort through familiarity. Like Roderick McGillis, I believe that children are "nimble" enough to learn to negotiate these tensions; I do not see "focalization" as a dangerous and invisible practice that "hails" them into mindless acquiescence with hegemonic ideology. Indeed, even if ideology is invisible, the electronic text, with its potential for nonlinear "skipping" about and hypertext linkages, can actually "make visible" the hidden ideologies of traditional books; children can be encouraged to notice, interrogate, resist, and even change (interactively) the points of view of problematic "classics." Children are "natural" deconstructors.

To these literary theoretical concepts as informing principles, I suggest adding a combination of "hypertext" and multimedia interactive learning-specifically the construction of interactive CD-Roms, with easy "export" capacities and precise, printed teacher guidelines for using the CD-Roms to encourage student exploration, nonlinear learning, and deconstructionist activity. With the capacity to move back and forth within the text, to click on "links" that connect them to other relevant information both inside and outside the CD-Rom, and to export both collateral information and bits of text into their own Web sites and hypertext documents, children as young as age seven or eight should be capable of enhancing their understanding—even of controversial or censored texts and history.

THE STATE OF THE CASE

The debate between *instructionism* (the student's passive acquisition of facts and perspectives imparted by the teacher) and *constructionism*[1] (the child's active participation in his or her own intellectual development) has acquired new energy since the technological revolution. Will computers change learning styles or merely enhance the status quo? Related questions for debate are the "naturalness" of linear versus fragmented thought patterns in the human brain, as well as concerns about children's short attention spans and inability to retain information. Research is inconclusive, but the consensus seems to be that: (1) children learn best when they're actively engaged; (2) attention spans and long-term memory have in fact diminished in the post-television age; (3) interactive computer games actually do resupply some of the "action" and control that are lost in passive viewing;[2] (4) visual and oral proficiency exceed sophistication with print; and (5) a certain amount of linear order is required for memory retention.

The issue of order or schemata as necessary for reading competency is taken up by researchers in various ways, although most agree that reader understanding depends significantly on exposure to previous forms and genres—what we might call intertextual literacy. Davida Charney, for example, warns that random hypertext meandering may actually reduce students' understanding and that students who have been exposed to free-ranging hypertext do less well on tests of memory than those who have had no computer instruction at all.[3] Furthermore, the demands of memory indicate that readers actually impose linearity when they do not find it and, besides, for many readers, nonlinear processing is neither "natural" nor "intuitive."[4] It is important, therefore, to proceed with caution as we innovate, constructing what programmer Judah Schwartz calls "intermediate objects," which "allow users to raise their own questions and assess their own actions."[5]

Two recent essays on electronic learning help focus these issues: both offer case studies of existing CD-Rom fictional texts—available, incidentally, only in England. Maynard, McKnight, and Keady's "Children's Classics in the Electronic Medium" addresses the advantages of presenting the "classics" in CD-Rom format with the brief example of Europress Software's *Alice in Wonderland*.[6] Their central question, "How can children be encouraged to read the classics if they consider this to be an onerous task and do not like what they see in hard copy?"[7] is narrower than my own concern for critical literacy. But their conclusions are compelling, albeit conjectural: "If the electronic book can bridge the gap [through its introduction of 'animation, sounds, and a narrator,'[8]] it will introduce children to the classics in a form that is closer to the original text"[9] while appealing to the children's "visual literacy."[10] They do not, however, explore the possibilities of genuinely interactive, nonlinear, hypertextual CD-Roms with export capabilities.

Concerned more with the kinds of theoretical questions I have posed, Rebecca James's "Navigating CD-Roms: An Exploration of Children Reading Interactive Narratives" reports her findings when she tested two IMM (interactive multimedia) CD-Roms on four children.[11] The first, *Payuta and the Ice God* (London: UbiSoft Multimedia), she describes as conservative in both form and content. In the first option, "Clicking on . . . [the written text] activates the narrator's voice, nothing more."[12] In this traditional, home-away-home narrative, "Payuta sets off to rescue Opiak" from the Ice God Kiadnic and, of course, succeeds. Second, children may click on what James calls "hot-spots." which reveal secrets: "(hear page-by-page narration, followed by pause to allow interaction with the illustration)";[13] in the ice cave, "hot-spots made Kiadnic's face metamorphose menacingly out of the rock . . . accompanied by flesh-creeping music."[14] The third option is to play games "involving skills such as hand-eye coordination, shape-matching, and use of keyboard."[15] But *Payuta* also manipulates point of view and focalization, moving, for instance, between a bird's-eye view of "Payuta marooned on a ledge above a freezing river" and (through zoom techniques) "a first-person perspective . . . [that] empathiz[es] with how Payuta must have felt on the ledge."[16]

Since *Lulu's Enchanted Book* was created specifically as an IMM text, it differs from most CD-Roms in containing a verbal text with "as many hot-spots as its accompanying illustrations" (52), with "no 'right' or 'wrong' way of interacting" (53) with it.[17] Diversions from the story's linearity are allowed, including the ability to move back-and-forth in the text but not to change it; the idea is for the reader to experience multiple media, not self-creation-resulting in a vacillation between the reader's creative interruptions and the reassertion of the linear plot. Curiosity is satisfied, while order is maintained. James calls the format "metafictional" and "postmodern,"[18] and it definitely reveals self-reflexivity and interpretive indeterminacy.

Lulu's Enchanted Book thus seems to illustrate the productive tension I see as the central challenge: the need to keep a level of pedagogical control over narrative and comprehension, combined with the desirability of a high degree of interactivity. James concludes that both CD-Roms "encourage their users to become more active and reflexive, less passive readers."[19]

In contrast, two commercially marketed CD-Roms of Dr. Seuss stories, both by the Massachusetts-based The Learning Company, are markedly disappointing. *Green Eggs and Ham* offers at its set-up screen the options: Read to Me or Let Me Play, with the second offering links to supplemental activities.[20] The entire text appears in both, with only the original Dr. Seuss words appearing on the screen, highlighted as they are read by a narrator with an irritatingly high-pitched voice; additional phrases, in sometimes awkward approximations of Dr. Seuss rhythms, are merely aural; one of them, in frame 12, is downright anti-Seussian: "not smothered with raspberry jam." Perhaps the most irritating addition is the final phrase, spoken by the protagonist, "You know, Sam, this could be the beginning of a beautiful friendship," right after he has been offered "something blue."

The "Let Me Play" option contains the possibility for the child to click on both words and pictures: if on the words, the word is repeated; if on the icons, curious things happen. In frame six, for example, if one clicks on the mouse, he says, "Would you eat them with some cheese?"; if on Sam, he asks (as if he has not asked enough questions already): "Could you at the speed of light?" In frame eight, if one clicks on the girl passenger, she asks, "How much longer? Are we there?"; if on the train engine, the engineer puts a rose in his teeth and dances a fandango. In the one moment I found genuinely humorous, in the underwater scene of frame 13, when one clicks on the engineer, he submerges and resurfaces with a clam shell, which in turn opens and announces, "Clam I am!" And the process continues, with no apparent utility, except in frames 12 and 16, which present rhyming games: boat/goat, rain/train, box/fox. Finally, in frame eighteen if one clicks on the house, it plays "There's no place like home"; in frame nineteen (as all the characters are gathered), if one clicks on the woman, she states sappily, "I love happy endings, don't you?" while the boat captain cries "Hip, hip, hooray!" The frames change extremely slowly, there is no chance to move back and forth in the text, and the whole CD-Rom neither enhances the original nor produces an engaging independent product. It is obviously not interactive in any constructionist sense.

The second Dr. Seuss CD-Rom, produced by the same company, bills itself as *Reading Games*, and includes the complete texts of *The Cat in the Hat* and *Horton Hears a Who!*[21] Again, there is no genuine interaction nor instructional information included among the options. The edutainment focus is clearly on the entertainment and not on the education, though it is possible that the child will learn something incidentally.

A CASE STUDY: *THE STORY OF LITTLE BLACK SAMBO*[22]

I would like to propose the creation of an interactive, exportable CD-Rom of the suppressed 1899 "classic" by Helen Bannerman, *The Story of Little Black Sambo* (pp. 4–7). I have chosen it as a kind of "limit text" of controversy, but also because it embodies the home-away-home structure fundamental to children's stories—as well as historical specificity and a strong narrative with an "invisible" narrator who effaces her ideological perspective.

This text could be "linked" in several ways to African American and British colonial history: (1) to stereotyping of racial others at the turn of the century (in posters and artifacts, such as lawn jockeys or advertisements for Aunt Jemima pancakes); (2) to other texts (such as the Uncle Remus stories); (3) to the figure of the "trickster" in African American texts and folklore, and so on. Furthermore, Sambo himself is a self-deconstructing and richly contradictory character: he is victimized by the tigers, but he also devises a means to escape their violence, first by offering his beautiful new clothes, then by implicitly bringing them together in conflict so that he can reappropriate the clothes and retreat behind his umbrella; he is a child (producing identification), a "Black" from an exotic place and hence marginal, but he also exhibits the characteristics of the Superhero (producing emulation); the courageous facer-of-tigers who is rewarded with 169 pancakes; he is both identified with the animalism and ferocity of the tigers and radically separated from their uncollegial self-destruction, as he returns to the safety of his family. Sambo, therefore, embodies the culture's institutional and historical racism—as well as the possibilities of transgression and resistance.

Some words and phrases that would easily admit of hypertextual linkings and internal glosses include both "Black" and "Sambo." Sambo's deeply black skin and exaggerated full red lips, not to mention the loincloth-like garment and the open and vulnerable stance, could all be articulated and developed as semiotic signs of Sambo's stereotypical African-American identity. A gloss on Sambo's appearance might explore the racial implications, then tie the color to the predominance of colors in other parts of the text: the red coat (12), the blue trousers (13), the green umbrella, the purple shoes with crimson soles and crimson linings (16), the tigers' white teeth (43), and, of course, the yellow and brown pancakes that culminate the adventure (59) and ironically replicate the color of the extinguished tigers. Depending on the children's age, they could use these references to study color symbolism (political and aesthetic), the stereotyping of ex-slaves as preferring colorful costumes and exhibiting "cheerful" behavior, and so on.

The term "Sambo" itself has a dense history, reaching back to its appearance in many African languages and to the Middle Passage and establishing itself as a generic term for African male slaves as early as the late eighteenth century. Signifying the docile, cheerful, faithful slave, Sambo was considered both childlike and, necessarily, inferior—if romanticized. As part of the minstrel tradition, which evolved into the blackface vaudeville act by the mid-nineteenth century, this traditional depiction of the unthreatening "Uncle Tom" carried over into Reconstruction and beyond in the white cultural imagination. It would also be possible to move from that reference to a discussion of the problematics of African American names and naming.

The naming of Mother as Mumbo and Father as Jumbo also offers historical and cultural possibilities. Beyond the obvious near-assonance with Sambo, the names taken together implicitly suggest the "mumbo-jumbo" of voodoo, hoodoo, or conjuring. The illustrations of the parents suggest further stereotyping, of the "Mammy" (overweight, with her head rag) and the "Trickster" figure dressed nattily, smoking a pipe and carrying an umbrella as a parasol, but with bare feet and a comic stance, despite his being headed to work.

But perhaps the most interesting "hot-spots" are the explicit ethnic and geographic references to India, in both the text and pictures. For example, the narrative feels compelled to gloss "melted butter" with "(or 'ghi,' as it is called in India)" and on page 57 the "Tiger Ghi" is depicted as contained in the brass pot (another reference to Indian culture) which Father Jumbo has brought home. The exploratory possibilities here include: the disjunction between the racial stereotyping of the illustrations and the specific cultural reference to a continent that is clearly not Africa or America; the history of British colonialism and racism in comparison to the U.S. version; and the ideological implications of Bannerman's conflation.

I can imagine self-contained CD-Roms of texts like *Little Black Sambo* that would contain an array of cultural, historical, and ideological information and topics for discussion, including intertextual material that would send students to other sources.[23] Such a product would contain easily exportable chunks, which could be transferred to the students' own Web sites, where they could in turn construct links to other sites on the Web.[24] Set in such a rich context, *Little Black Sambo* would, potentially, no longer offend. Furthermore, parents who objected to politically sensitive material for young children could see exactly what is going on in the classroom and would themselves be drawn into the "domain" of learning.

I can see similar applications of this process to texts like Burgess's *Goops and How to Be Them* (1900),[25] with its delightfully comic exposition of bad manners at the turn of the last century; this text could offer readers an opportunity to explore changing conventions of child behavior, as well as the aesthetics of children's verse. Postmodern, indeterminate texts like David McKee's *I Hate My Teddy Bear*[26] and, for slightly older children, Anthony Browne's *King Kong*[27] could easily be converted into CD-Roms, since their visual defamiliarization and complex contradictory surfaces already invite the type of deconstruction I am describing.

THE BENEFITS?

My broad theoretical project thus proposes the breakdown of a set of binaries: defamiliarization versus identification or interpellation; destabilization versus comfort; and computer versus print media. Practically speaking, this would mean reading the sexist and bourgeois "Snow

White" alongside postmodern experiments like Art Spiegelman's *Open Me
. . . I'm a Dog*, classics alongside R. L. Stine or Sweet Valley High. Understanding a multiple and multiracial culture, both its history and its current
practice, requires acknowledgment that critical literacy skills are not built
on ignorance or suppression. Since, unlike mathematics or the sciences,
literature and history are acknowledged by new-technologies theorists to
be "ill-structured domains" (that is, areas of inquiry that do not yield to
reductionist, simplistic conclusions),[28] it is crucial that we replicate the
messiness of these areas of inquiry into the classroom—as early as possible
in the intellectual cycle. I believe that children, like adults, will experience
Freud's "return of the repressed" if they are not exposed to the range of
cultural ideologies and technological practices that actually exist—both in
the past and in their complex and un-innocent futures.

NOTES

1. Yasmin Kafai and Mitchel Resnick, eds. *Constructionism in Practice: Designing, Thinking, and Learning in a Digital World*. Mahway, NJ: Erlbaum, 1996. "Constructionism is both a theory of learning and a strategy for education. It builds on
the 'constructivist' theories of Jean Piaget, asserting that knowledge is not simply
transmitted from teacher to student, but actively constructed by the mind of the
learner. Children don't get ideas; they make ideas." Introduction, p. 1.

2. See, for example, Sandra L. Calvert, "The Social Impact of Virtual Reality."
In *Handbook of Virtual Environment Technology*, K. Stanney, ed. Hillsdale, NJ: Erlbaum, 1999, passim.

3. Davida Charney, "The Effect of Hypertext on Processes of Reading and Writing." In *Literacy and Computers: The Complications of Teaching and Learning with
Technology*, Cynthia L. Selfe and Susan Hilligloss, eds. New York: Modern Language Association, 1994, p. 251.

4. Ibid., p. 242.

5. Judah L. Schwartz, "The Right Size Byte: Reflections of an Educational Software Designer." In *Software Goes to School: Teaching for Understanding with New
Technologies*, David N. Perkins, Judah L. Schwartz, Mary Maxwell West, and Martha Stone Wiske, eds. Oxford and New York: Oxford UP, 1995, p. 175.

6. Sally Maynard, Cliff McKnight, and Melanie Keady, "Children's Classics in
the Electronic Medium." *The Lion and the Unicorn*, 23 (1999): 184–201.

7. Maynard, McKnight, and Keady, p. 191.

8. Ibid., p. 193.

9. Ibid., p. 198.

10. Ibid., p. 192.

11. Rebecca James, "Navigating CD-Roms: An Exploration of Children Reading
Interactive Narratives." *Children's Literature in Education*, 30 (1999): 47–63.

12. Ibid., p. 48.

13. Ibid., p. 49.

14. Ibid., pp. 50–51.

15. Ibid., p. 49.

16. Ibid., p. 51.

17. Ibid., pp. 52, 53.

18. Ibid., p. 56.

19. Ibid., p. 62.

20. Dr. Seuss, *Green Eggs and Ham*, CD-Rom. Cambridge, MA: The Learning Company, 1996.

21. Dr. Seuss, *Reading Games*, CD-Rom. Cambridge, MA: The Learning Company, 1999.

22. Helen Bannerman, *The Story of Little Black Sambo*. London: Chatto and Windus, 1899.

23. It is also important to remember that children can be counted upon to draw on their previous knowledge; teachers can help them to connect their earlier, experiential learning to the new challenges. For a discussion of this point, see, for example, Raymond S. Nickerson, "Can Technology Help Teach for Understanding?" In Perkins et al. "An overarching idea that emerges from these discussions is the idea of the importance of connections: connections between old concepts and new ones, connections among the concepts that define a field of inquiry, connections between what is being studied in the classroom and what one has learned without formal instruction in everyday life," p. 17.

24. For example, a CD-Rom for adults is about to be released, entitled "The Valley of the Shadow": its subject is the Civil War and it will constitute a subset of what is already on the Valley of the Shadow Web site; the CD-Rom will provide "gateway buttons" to that site and allow the user to move fluidly between the environments.

25. Gelett Burgess, *Goops and How to Be Them: A Manual of Manners for Polite Infants Inculcating many Juvenile Virtues Both by Precept and Example, with Ninety Drawings*. 1900. New York: Dover Publications, 1968.

26. David McKee, *I Hate My Teddy Bear*. 1982. London: Red Fox, 1990.

27. Anthony Browne. *King Kong, from the story conceived by Edgar Wallace and Merian C. Cooper*. Atlanta, GA: Turner Publishing, 1994.

28. For a thorough discussion of the difference between "ill-structured" and "well-structured domains," see, for example, Amanda C. Meehan, "Hypermedia and Constructive Learning" (unpublished M.A. thesis, Communication, Culture, and Technology Program, Georgetown University, 1999), Chapter 3 passim.

REFERENCES

Bannerman, Helen. *The Story of Little Black Sambo*. London: Chatto & Windus, 1899.

Browne, Anthony. *King Kong. From the story conceived by Edgar Wallace & Merian C. Cooper*. Atlanta, GA: Turner Publishing, 1994.

Burgess, Gelett. *Goops and How to Be Them: A Manual of Manners for Polite Infants Inculcating many Juvenile Virtues Both by Precept and Example, with Ninety Drawings*. 1900. New York: Dover Publications, 1968.

Calvert, Sandra. "The Social Impact of Virtual Reality," In *Handbook of Virtual Environment Technology*. Ed. K. Stanney. Hillsdale, NJ: Erlbaum, 1999.

————. *Children's Journeys Through the Information Age*. Boston: McGraw-Hill, 1999.

Charney, Davida. "The Effect of Hypertext on Processes of Reading and Writing." In *Literacy and Computers: The Complications of Teaching and Learning with Technology*. Ed. Cynthia L. Selfe and Susan Hilligloss. New York: Modern Language Association, 1994, pp. 238–378.

Dr. Seuss. *Green Eggs and Ham*. CD-Rom. Cambridge, MA: The Learning Company, 1996.

————. *Reading Games: [including The Cat in the Hat and Horton Hears a Who]*. Cambridge, MA: The Learning Company, 1999.

James, Rebecca. "Navigating CD-Roms: An Exploration of Children Reading Interactive Narratives." *Children's Literature in Education*. 30 (1999): 47–63.

Kafai, Yasmin, and Mitchel Resnick, eds. *Constructionism in Practice: Designing, Thinking, and Learning in a Digital World*. Mahwah, NJ: Erlbaum, 1996.

Maynard, Sally, Cliff McKnight, and Melanie Keady. "Children's Classics in the Electronic Medium." *The Lion and the Unicorn*. 23 (1999): 184–201.

McGillis, Roderick. *The Nimble Reader: Literary Theory and Children's Literature*. New York: Twayne, 1996.

McKee, David. *I Hate My Teddy Bear*. 1982. London: Red Fox, 1990.

Meehan, Amanda C. "Hypermedia and Constructive Learning." M.A. thesis, Communication, Culture, and Technology Program, Georgetown University, 1999.

Nickerson, Raymond S. "Can Technology Help Teach for Understanding?" In Perkins et al., eds. pp. 7–22.

Perkins, David N., Judah L. Schwartz, Mary Maxwell West, and Martha Stone Wiske, eds. *Software Goes to School: Teaching for Understanding with New Technologies*. Oxford and New York: Oxford UP, 1995.

Schwartz, Judah L. "The Right Size Byte: Reflections of an Educational Software Designer." In Perkins et al., eds. pp. 172–181.

Selected Bibliography

Althusser, Louis. *Lenin and Philosophy*. London: New Left Books, 1971.

Appleyard, J.A., and S.J. Appleyard. *Becoming a Reader: The Experience of Fiction from Childhood to Adulthood*. Cambridge: Cambridge UP, 1990.

Attebery, Brian. *The Fantasy Tradition in American Literature: From Irving to Le Guin*. Bloomington: Indiana U P, 1980.

Bal, Mieke. *Narratology: Introduction to the Theory of Narrative*. 2nd ed. Toronto: Univ. of Toronto P, 1997.

Beckett, Sandra, ed. *Reflections of Change: Children's Literature Since 1945*. Westport and London: Greenwood, 1997.

———, ed. *Transcending Boundaries: Writing for a Dual Audience of Children and Adults*. New York: Garland, 1999.

Bergstrand, Ulla and Maria Nikolajeva. *Lockergommarnas Kungarike Om matens roll i barnlitteraturen* [*The Realm of Gourmands: The Role of Food in Children's Literature*] Stockholm: Centrum für barnkulturforskning vid Stockholms universitet, 1999.

Blink, Inge van den. "Als ik signeer komen er drie generaties voorbij." *Utrechts Nieuwsblad*, 12 October 1990.

Brooks, Ann. *Postfeminisms: Feminism, Cultural Theory and Cultural Forms*. London: Routledge, 1997.

Buckingham, David. *After the Death of Childhood: Growing Up in the Age of Electronic Media*. Cambridge: Polity Press, 2000.

Butler, Judith. *Bodies That Matter: On the Discursive Limits of Sex*. London and New York: Routledge, 1993.

Calvert, Sandra. *Children's Journeys Through the Information Age*. Boston: McGraw-Hill, 1999.

Connell, R.W. *Masculinities*. St Leonards: Allen & Unwin, 1995.

Deleuze, Gilles. *The Logic of Sense*. Trans. Mark Lester with Charles Stivale. Ed. Constantin V. Boundas. London: The Athlone Press (French version 1969), 1990.

Dijkstra, Bram. *Idols of Perversity: Fantasies of Feminine Evil in Fin-De-Siècle Culture*. New York and Oxford: Oxford UP, 1986.

Doonan, Jane. *Looking at Pictures in Picture Books*. South Woodchester, UK: Thimble Press, 1993.

———. "Drawing Out Ideas: A Second Decade of the Work of Anthony Browne." *The Lion and the Unicorn* 23.1 (1999): 30–56.

Dresang, Eliza T. *Radical Change: Books for Youth in a Digital Age*. New York and Dublin: H.W. Wilson, 1999.

Dryzek, John S. *The Politics of the Earth: Environmental Discourses*. Oxford: Oxford UP, 1997.

Eisenbud, Julie. *Love & Hate in the Nursery and Beyond*. Berkeley, CA: Frog, 1996.

Fortichiari, V. *Invito a conoscere il Decadentismo*. Milano: Mursia, 1987.

Gilbert, Rob and Pam Gilbert. *Masculinity Goes to School*. St Leonards: Allen & Unwin, 1998.

Grafenauer, N. "Sodobna slovenska poezija za otroke." *Otrok in knjiga* 31. Maribor, 1991.

Griswold, Jerry. *Audacious Kids: Coming of Age in America's Classic Children's Literature*. New York: Oxford UP, 1992.

Hourihan, Margery. *Deconstructing the Hero*. London: Routledge, 1997.

Hunt, Peter, ed. *International Companion Encyclopedia of Children's Literature*. London and New York: Routledge, 1996.

Inglis, Fred. *The Promise of Happiness: Value and Meaning in Children's Fiction*. Cambridge: Cambridge UP, 1981.

Inness, Sherrie A., ed. *Nancy Drew and Company: Culture, Gender, and Girls' Series*. Bowling Green, OH: Bowling Green State U Popular P, 1996.

James, Rebecca. "Navigating CD-Roms: An Exploration of Children Reading Interactive Narratives." *Children's Literature in Education* 30.1 (1999): 47–63.

Kafai, Yasmin, and Mitchel Resnick, eds. *Constructionism in Practice: Designing, Thinking, and Learning in a Digital World*. Mahwah, NJ: Erlbaum, 1996.

Kensinger, Faye Riter. *Children of the Series and How they Grew or A Century of Heroines and Heroes, Romantic, Comic, Moral*. Bowling Green, OH: Bowling Green State U Popular P, 1987.

Kimmel, Eric A. "Confronting the Ovens: The Holocaust and Juvenile Fiction." *The Horn Book* LIII, No. 1 (1977): 84–91.

Kobe, M. *Pogledi na mladinsko knjiñevost*. Ljubljana 1987.

Kordigel, M. "Nastanek in razvoj termina znanstvena fantastika na Slovenskem." *Slavisticna revija*, 41 (1993): 4; str. 571–580.

———. *Znanstvena fantastika*. Ljubljana, 1994.

Kos, J. *Ocrt literarne teorije*. Ljubljana, 1983.

Kusters, Wiel. *Salamanders vangen*. Amsterdam: Em. Querido, 1985.

Mairtin Mac an Ghaill, ed. *Understanding Masculinities*. Buckingham and Bristol: Open UP, 1996.

Malcolm, Noel. *The Origins of English Nonsense*. London: Fontana/HarperCollins, 1997.

Martino, Wayne. "Deconstructing Masculinity in the English Classroom: a Site for

Reconstituting Gendered Subjectivity." *Gender and Education*, 7, 2 (1995): 205–220.

Maynard, Sally, Cliff McKnight, and Melanie Keady. "Children's Classics in the Electronic Medium." *The Lion and the Unicorn* 23.2 (1999): 184–201.

McGillis, Roderick. *The Nimble Reader: Literary Theory and Children's Literature*. New York: Twayne, 1996.

———. "Ratten till en varld med oppna mojligheter: Postkolonialismen I Barnlitteraturen." *Halva Varldens Litteratur* 4 (1997): 21–25.

———, ed. *Voices of the Other: Colonialism, Postcolonialism, and Neocolonialism in Children's Books*. New York: Garland, 1999.

Meijer, Ischa. "Gegroet, ik zit onder de olijf," *Haagse Post*, 18 January, 1975.

Neubauer, John. *The Fin-de-Siècle Culture of Adolescence*. New Haven & London: Yale UP, 1992.

Neumeyer, Peter. *We Are All in the Dumps with Jack and Guy: Two Nursery Rhymes with Pictures by Maurice Sendak. Children's Literature in Education*, 25 (1994): 29–40.

Nikolajeva, Maria. *Children's Literature Comes of Age*. New York: Garland, 1996.

Nix, Don, and Rand Spiro, eds. *Cognition, Education, and Multimedia: Exploring Ideas in High Technology*. Mahwah, NJ: Lawrence Erlbaum, 1990.

Nodelman, Perry. *Words About Pictures: The Narrative Art of Children's Books*. Athens: U of Georgia P, 1988.

O'Harrow, Robert, Jr. "Beyond the Screen." *The Washington Post*, April 11, 1999.

Pennell, Beverley. "Ideological Drift in Children's Picture Books," *Papers: Explorations into Children's Literature* 6, No. 2 (1996): 5–13.

Perkins, David N., Judah L. Schwartz, Mary Maxwell West, and Martha Stone Wiske, eds. *Software Goes to School: Teaching for Understanding with New Technologies*. Oxford and New York: Oxford UP, 1995.

Perrot, Jean. *Art baroque, art d'enfance*. Nancy: Press Universitaires de Nancy, 1991.

———, ed. *Tomi Ungerer: Prix Hans Christian Andersen 1998*. Eaubonne: Intitut International Charles Perrault/Centre Tomi Ungerer, Musées de Strasbourg, 1998.

———, ed. *Tricentenaire Charles Perrault: Les grands contes du XVIIᵉ siècle et leur fortune littéraire*. Eaubonne: Institut Charles Perrault, 1998.

Petzold, Dieter. *Formen und Funktionen der englischen Nonsense-Dichtung im 19. Jahrhundert*. Nuerenberg: Verlag Hans Carl, 1972.

Platt, Charles. "Electronic Books." *The Washington Post*, May 9, 1999.

Reike, Alison. *The Senses of Nonsense*. Iowa City: U of Iowa P, 1992.

Reynolds, Kimberly. *Children's Literature in the 1890s and the 1990s*. Plymouth: Northcote House, 1994.

Rotundo, E. Anthony. *American Manhood*. New York: Basic Books, 1993.

Rushdie, Salman. *The Wizard of Oz*. London: BFI Publishing, 1992.

Sadler, Glenn Edward, ed. *Teaching Children's Literature: Issues, Pedagogy, Resources*. New York: Modern Language Association, 1992.

Schakel, Peter J. *Reading with Heart: The Way into Narnia*. Grand Rapids, MI: William B. Eerdmans, 1979.

Schmidt, Annie M. G. *De lapjeskat*. Amsterdam: De Arbeiderspers, 1954.

———. *Tot hier toe. Gedichten en liedjes voor toneel, radio en televisie; 1938–1985*. Amsterdam: Em. Querido, 1986.

Scutter, Heather. *Displaced Fictions: Contemporary Australian Fiction for Teenagers and Young Adults*. Melbourne: Melbourne UP, 1999.

Selfe, Cynthia L., and Susan Hilligloss, eds. *Literacy and Computers: The Complications of Teaching and Learning with Technology*. New York: Modern Language Association, 1994.

Sewell, Elizabeth. *The Field of Nonsense*. London: Chatto and Windus, 1952.

Stephens, John. "Gender, Genre and Children's Literature." *Signal* 79 (1996): 17–30.

———. *Language and Ideology in Children's Fiction*. London and New York: Longman, 1992.

Stephens, John and Robyn McCallum. *Retelling Stories, Framing Culture: Traditional Story and Metanarratives in Children's Literature*. New York: Garland Publishing, 1998.

Stewart, Suzanne R. *Male Masochism at the Fin-De-Siècle*. Ithaca & London: Cornell UP, 1998.

Stott, Jon. *Native Americans in Children's Literature*. Phoenix, AZ: Orynx, 1995.

Tigges, Wim. *An Anatomy of Literary Nonsense*. Amsterdam: Rodopi, 1988.

Turkle, Sherry. *Life on the Screen: Identity in the Age of the Internet*. New York: Simon & Schuster, 1995.

Verwey, Albert. *Verzamelde gedichten*. Amsterdam: W. Versluys, 1889.

Weinreich, Torben. *Children's Literature: Art or Pedagogy?* Denmark: Roskilde UP, 2000.

Williams, Lydia. *Images of the Holocaust in Children's and YA Fiction*. New York and London: Garland, forthcoming.

Wilson, Brent, ed. *Constructivist Learning Environments: Case Studies in Instructional Design*. Englewood Cliffs, NJ: Educational Technology Publications, 1996.

Zipes, Jack. *Fairy Tale as Myth, Myth as Fairy Tale*. Lexington: Kentucky UP, 1994.

———. *Sticks and Stones: The Troublesome Success of Children's Literature From Slovenly Peter to Harry Potter*. New York and London: Routledge, 2001.

Index

About the Contributors

ALIDA ALLISON is a Professor of English and Comparative Literature at San Diego State University, where she specializes in children's and young adults' literatures. Her most recent books are *Russell Hoban Forty Years: Essays on His Writings for Children* (editor) and *Isaac Bashevis Singer: Children's Stories and Childhood Memoirs*. For three years during the Vietnam War, Allison and her husband worked in Southeast Asia as members of the American Friends Service Committee's (Quaker Service) Vietnam Team.

CLARE BRADFORD is an Associate Professor at Deakin University in Melbourne, Australia, where she teaches literary studies and children's literature to undergraduate and postgraduate students. Her research interests focus on relations between children's texts and cultural and ideological formations. Bradford is the editor of the journal *Papers: Explorations into Children's Literature*. Her most recent book is *Reading Race: Aboriginality in Australian Children's Literature*.

ANNE DE VRIES is curator of the children's book collection at the Koninklijke Bibliotheek/Dutch National Library (The Hague) and Lecturer at the Free University (Amsterdam). His research concentrates on poetry for children and nursery rhymes. His most recent publication in this field is an anthology that gives a survey of poetry for children in the Dutch language, from the Netherlands and Flanders: *Van Alphen tot Zonderland; de Nederlandse kinderpozie van alle tijden* (*Poetry for Children from The Low Countries*, 2000).

SHEILA A. EGOFF is Professor Emerita of the School of Librarianship, the University of British Columbia. Among her many publications are *Worlds Within: Children's Fantasy from the Middle Ages to Today*, *Thursday's Child: Trends and Patterns of Contemporary Children's Literature*, and *The New Republic of Childhood* (with Judith Saltman). Egoff was the final Plenary Speaker at the 1999 conference, Children's Literature and the *Fin de Siècle*, effectively summing up the proceedings.

LEONA W. FISHER is Associate Professor and former Chair of the English Department at Georgetown University and cofounder and former director of the Women's Studies Program. She has published on Victorian theater, children's literature, and feminist topics and is currently working on two book-length projects: one on Nancy Drew, the Girl Scouts, and constructions of American girlhood from the 1930s to the 1980s; the other, a study of genre and narrative voice in English and American children's books of the last two centuries.

MICHAEL HEYMAN, a Lecturer at Boston University and an Assistant Professor at Berklee College of Music, has most recently published "A New Defense of Nonsense; or, 'Where then is his phallus?' and other questions not to ask" in the *Children's Literature Association Quarterly* (Winter 1999–2000).

MARGOT HILLEL is a Senior Lecturer in English at Australian Catholic University, in Melbourne, Australia. She is Past President of the Children's Book Council of Australia and has been a judge for a number of children's literature awards. She is the joint editor of three collections of short stories, joint compiler of a retrospective anthology published to celebrate 50 years of the CBCA Children's Book Awards, has cowritten several books on using literature with children, and is the author of a number of published conference papers. Hillel reviews regularly in a number of children's literature journals and on the radio. She is currently the Secretary/Treasurer of the Australasian Children's Literature Association for Research.

YOSHIDO JUNKO is a Professor of English at Hiroshima University in Japan, where she teaches adolescent literature and American culture. Her recent research interests focus on gender issues in adolescent novels. She has published several books in Japanese, including *Family Quest in American Children's Literature*. Junko is also a cotranslator of Jack Zipes's *The Trials and the Tribulations of Little Red Riding Hood*, *Fairy Tale as Myth, Myth as Fairy Tale*, and Jerry Griswold's *Audacious Kids*. Her articles in English have appeared in *Children's Literature* and *Bookbird*.

METKA KORDIGEL is an Associate Professor in the Faculty of Education, University of Maribor, Slovenija, where she teaches literature and literature education. Her publication, *Children's Literature: Children and Teachers*, aimed at elementary school teachers, defines theoretical and pedagogical implications for teaching children's and young adult literatures; it is a compulsory text in faculties of education at both Slovene universities. Kordigel also wrote a book, *Children's Literature in Kindergarden*, and a book on science fiction.

MILLICENT LENZ teaches courses in literature for young people at the University at Albany, State University of New York, where she has been a member of the faculty of the School of Information Science and Policy for fifteen years. Her doctorate is in English, with a specialty in *Beowulf*, and her background includes work as an English teacher and a librarian. Lenz's publications include *Nuclear Literature for Youth: The Quest for a Life-Affirming Ethic*, and the book, coauthored with Peter Hunt, *Alternative Worlds of Fantasy: Ursula K. LeGuin, Terry Pratchett, and Philip Pullman* (2001). She has published widely in journals (*Children's Literature Association Quarterly, The Lion and the Unicorn, Dragon Lode*). Special interests include fantasy, poetry, and the history of children's literature.

ROSE LOVELL-SMITH is a Senior Tutor in the English Department of the University of Auckland, where she convenes and lectures a first-year course in children's literature. Her interests include series and sequel reading and writing; the illustrated book for older children; fairy tales, especially as rewritten by women in the last two centuries; and Margaret Mahy.

ANN LAWSON LUCAS is a Lecturer in Italian Language and Literature at the University of Hull, in the UK. Besides standard courses in Italian, she teaches a module on nineteenth-century children's literature in Italy and, with colleagues, an interdisciplinary module on the fairy tale and the adventure story in European children's literature. Lucas's research is principally on Salgari and Collodi: her translation/edition of *The Adventures of Pinocchio* appeared in 1996 (Oxford World's Classics) and her monograph *La ricerca dellígnoto: i romanzi díavventura di Emilio Salgari* was published in 2000. She was also a member of the IRSCL Board from 1993 to 1997.

KERRY MALLAN is a Senior Lecturer in the School of Cultural and Language Studies at Queensland University of Technology, Australia. Her research and publishing are in the areas of youth literature, film, and new technologies with particular interests in gender, sexualities, and picture books. Mallan's most recent publication is "In the picture: perspectives on picture book art and artists" (Centre for Information Studies, CSU). She is currently co-editing (with Sharyn Pearce) a book on youth cultures.

RODERICK McGILLIS teaches in the Department of English, at the University of Calgary. He was, along with Claude Romney, coorganizer of the conference from which the essays in this volume derive.

CHERYL McMILLAN was a Ph.D. student at Macquarie University, where she researched postmodernist forms in children's fiction. She studied the uses of parody and the carnivalesque in works for the young. She was also a teacher of senior school English. Cheryl McMillan died in August 2001.

CLAUDIA NELSON is an Associate Professor of English at Southwest Texas State University. She is the author of *Boys Will Be Girls: The Feminine Ethic and British Children's Fiction, 1857–1917* and *Invisible Men: Fatherhood in Victorian Periodicals, 1850–1910*, and has recently completed a book on representations of adoption in American texts between 1850 and 1929.

ELIZABETH L. PANDOLFO BRIGGS is a Ph.D. candidate in children's literature at the University of Wales, Cardiff. The title of her thesis is "Dangerous Women of the Mabinogi? Women of The Mabinogi in Contemporary Young Adult Welsh Fantasy." Pandolfo Briggs is also editor of Alice's Academy, the refereed section of the online children's literature journal *The Looking Glass*.

BEVERLEY PENNELL spent many a delightful year as a secondary English teacher and Head of Department and now teaches English Curriculum Studies at the University of Western Sydney and Children's Literature at Macquarie University. She has published several papers in the field of Children's Literature and has coauthored numerous English curriculum books for use in Australian secondary schools. Pennell's research area is the changing representations of childhood in Australian children's fiction since about 1950, examined from the perspectives of historiography, gender studies, childhood studies, and postcolonial theory.

SUMANYU SATPATHY teaches in the Department of English at the University of Delhi (India). He is the author of *Re-viewing Reviewing: The Reception of Modernist Poetry in the Times Literary Supplement (1912–1932)*. He has published articles on Stevenson, Eliot, and Pound in Indian and international journals.

SUSAN TEBBUTT is Head of German and a Senior Lecturer at the University of Bradford, England. Publications include the monograph *Gudrun Pausewang in Context* (1994), the edited volume *Sinti and Roma: Gypsies in German-speaking Society and Literature* (1998), and numerous articles on socially critical German teenage fiction and on the Romanies. In 2000,

Tebbutt taught a module titled "War and Peace in Children's Literature" and is at present completing a volume on pacifist German children's literature.

JEAN WEBB is Senior Lecturer in English Studies and Director of the Primary English and Children's Literature Research Centre at University College Worcester. She is also Associate Head of the Graduate School.

LYDIA WILLIAMS, after working as a teacher of English in Finnish schools for a number of years, began to research the role children's literature could play in developing children's foreign language skills. Her main publication, *Young EFL Readers and Their Books* (1998), examined the texts used in immersion programs. Since completing that work, Williams has been working on a new project, Representations of the Holocaust in Fiction for Children and Young Adults, within the ChiLPA (Children's Literature: Pure and Applied) project at Akademi University, which was sponsored by the Finnish Ministry of Education. She is currently a lecturer at Turku University.